Advance Praise for *Most Likely to Secede*

"Imagination and hypothesis at once. Leavened by time and circumstance, an eclectic band of Vermont democrats has at last provided America with a seedbed of hope. To wit: the increasingly vulgar and theoretically challenged national left/right dichotomy can be replaced by a new American paradigm whereby liberty and community are once again united and the Founders' dreams reborn."
— **Frank Bryan, John G. McCullough Professor of Political Science @ the University of Vermont, and author of numerous books on Vermont history and town meeting**

"It's clear to anyone with a pulse that we're in terrible trouble: as citizens who need a polity, as humans who need a community, as animals who need a home. For the disillusioned, the dispirited, and the despairing: take heart! A seed of resistance is taking root in a place called Vermont. For the ready, the willing, and the able: take aim—the Gods of Empire can be defeated. *Most Likely to Secede*, with its intellectual clarity, its moral authority, and its quiet, fierce loyalty to people and place, will show you how."
— **Lierre Keith, co-author of *Deep Green Resistance***

"Madison and Jefferson would be proud of this book. Pray read it now. *Secede* is illumination in the age of unreason, a 21st century *Common Sense*, a crystal clear analysis of why size matters, and why we must create human(e) institutions to live and work within. Immensity is crushing us, whether the whopper is a multinational corporation, fast food, money center banks, the federal government, modern medicine, the military/industrial complex, the two political parties, or the media. The tyranny of concentrated power is tearing our land, culture and communities apart. If we restore autonomy on local and bioregional levels, the genius, gumption and generosity of American people can breathe and flourish again."
— **Paul Hawken, author of *Blessed Unrest* and *The Ecology of Commerce***

"Steeped in Jeffersonian decentralism, pro-democracy sentiment, and love of land, the mad farmers, sheep growers, and legal philosophers of Vermont have forged themselves into a force of truth. In *Most Likely to Secede*, they bring together their finest—knitting organic farming and yogurt-making with historical/economic argument for secession that goes beyond current concepts of "Left" and "Right." Whether you're from Rutland—or Alaska, Scotland, Quebec, the Congo, Kashmir, or the Iroquois Nation—read this empire-breaking book. It'll get you going."

— Chellis Glendinning, Ph.D., psychotherapist, author of *Off the Map: An Expedition Deep into Empire and the Global Economy*

MOST LIKELY TO
SECEDE

MOST LIKELY TO
SECEDE

**What the Vermont Independence Movement Can
Teach Us about Reclaiming Community and Creating
a Human-Scale Vision for the 21st Century**

Dispatches from *Vermont Commons: Voices of Independence* news journal

Edited by RON MILLER and ROB WILLIAMS

Vermont Independence Press
Waitsfield, Vermont

Published in 2013 by
Vermont Independence Press
PO Box 1121
Waitsfield, Vermont 05673
www.vermontindependencepress.com
ISBN: 978-1-60358-502-6

First Printing, February, 2013

CONTENTS

PART FOUR **Sovereignty and Secession**   207

The Mad Farmer, Flying the Flag of Rough Branch, Secedes from the Union

From the union of power and money,
From the union of power and secrecy,
From the union of government and science,
From the union of government and art,
From the union of science and money,
From the union of ambition and ignorance,
From the union of genius and war,
From the union of outer space and inner vacuity,
The Mad Farmer walks quietly away.

There is only one of him, but he goes.
He returns to the small country he calls home,
His own nation small enough to walk across.
He goes shadowy into the local woods,
And brightly into the local meadows and croplands.
He goes to the care of neighbors,
He goes into the care of neighbors.
He goes to the potluck supper, a dish
From each house for the hunger of every house.
He goes into the quiet of early mornings
Of days when he is not going anywhere.

Calling his neighbors together in to the sanctity
Of their lives separate and together
In the one life of the commonwealth and home,
In their own nation small enough for a story
Or song to travel across in an hour, he cries:

Come all ye conservatives and liberals
Who want to conserve the good things and be free,
Come away from the merchants of big answers,
Whose hands are metalled with power;
From the union of anywhere and everywhere
By the purchase of everything from everybody at the lowest price
And the sale of anything to anybody at the highest price;
From the union of work and debt, work and despair;
From the wage-slavery of the helplessly well-employed.

From the union of self-gratification and self-annihilation,
Secede into the care for one another
And for the good gifts of Heaven and Earth.

Come into the life of the body, the one body
Granted to you in all the history of time.
Come into the body's economy, its daily work,
And its replenishment at mealtimes and at night.
Come into the body's thanksgiving, when it knows
And acknowledges itself a living soul.
Come into the dance of the community, joined
In a circle, hand in hand, the dance of the eternal
Love of women and men for one another
And of neighbors and friends for one another.

Always disappearing, always returning,
Calling his neighbors to return, to think again
Of the care of flocks and herds, of gardens
And fields, of woodlots and forests and the uncut groves,
Calling them separately and together, calling and calling,
He goes forever toward the long restful evening
And the croak of the night heron over the river at dark.

 —Wendell Berry

for
THOMAS H. NAYLOR
1936–2012

MOST LIKELY TO
SECEDE

Introduction

Ron Miller

Vermont Commons: Voices of Independence was launched in April 2005. It began as a 12-page "journal" published bimonthly on newsprint, eventually expanding to 40 pages. *Vermont Commons* was distributed free on literature racks and display cases throughout the state, reaching a circulation of 12,000 copies at its peak in 2011. Its website has attracted 100,000 visitors per year.

This publication arose in the context of American politics under the administration of George W. Bush. In those post-9/11 years, the "war on terror," the erosion of constitutional rights, and policies favoring the oil industry and other corporate elites posed an alarming acceleration of the nation's already unfolding evolution toward flagrant imperialism. The U.S. government seemed deliberately oblivious to environmental and economic issues that many of us felt were increasingly urgent, from climate change to widening inequality, while the U.S. military presence around the globe continued to escalate.

In response, activists in Vermont began meeting in 2002 to discuss alternatives. These were not simply progressives offering partisan reactions to Bush policies but included old-fashioned (not "neo-") conservatives alarmed by the spike in government powers. Together they began to ask tough questions about the deeper forces that fueled the rise of a U.S. empire and the consequences that would likely ensue. They considered some radical responses, including the idea of separating Vermont from national politics altogether, a proposal championed by a retired Duke University economist named Thomas Naylor.

Naylor is recognized as the father of the Vermont secession movement. As early as 1990, he was writing about "downsizing" the United States because, he believed, both government and corporate business had become too complex, centralized, and powerful. He laid out his argument in the 1997 book *Downsizing the U.S.A.* (coauthored with William H. Willimon). Naylor, who moved to Vermont in 1993, thought that this small, community-oriented state could lead the way toward the dissolution of the empire, but it was not until the aftermath of 9/11 that he found an audience. In March 2003, just before Bush's invasion of Iraq, Naylor spoke to students at Johnson State College, telling them that the only way to prevent such wars was "to break up the United States into smaller regions, and the process should begin with Vermont declaring its independence." He recalls that the students were "stunned, but they got it. Their positive response literally provided the energy to launch the Second Vermont Republic," an organized effort to advocate for secession. He and other activists interested in secession began meeting ten days after the start of the bombing of Baghdad. In October, Naylor published *The Vermont Manifesto* and held a meeting, in collaboration with Bread & Puppet Theater, that drew fifty people.

In November 2004, Naylor joined with Kirkpatrick Sale, a well-known author on decentralist movements, to organize a gathering in Middlebury. The group issued the "Middlebury Declaration," a succinct manifesto for the movement (see Appendix, p. 241). Also at the meeting, Ian Baldwin, cofounder of Chelsea Green Publishing, met media activist Rob Williams, and they began discussing a publication that would explore issues of empire and independence. Baldwin explains the process that led to his involvement:

> After 9/11, the overnight enactment of the massive, unread Fascistic Patriot Act, the federal proclamation of "war without end in our lifetimes," the invasion of Afghanistan, and the year-long blatantly deceitful campaign to conduct a massive "Shock-and-Awe" invasion of Iraq, I found myself wholly alienated from my own country. By the end of 2002 I was considering the ex-pat option when a friend invited me to my first meeting with the secessionists led by Thomas Naylor. That meeting in March 2003, the second one held by Naylor to explore the secession option, proved decisive for my political development and my willingness to question every lie propounded by the federal government and big business through their mass media mouthpieces.

Williams's journey was similar:

> After the debacle of the 2000 and 2004 presidential "elections" (and I use the term loosely), and the imperial madness surround-

ing the post-9/11 tragedy—the USA PATRIOT Act's passage and the acceleration of imperial wars in the greater Middle East, Africa, and Afghanistan-Pakistan—I came to the conclusion that the United States was no longer a functioning republic but an out-of-control Empire neither accountable to its own citizens, nor capable of being reformed or "fixed."

In December 2004, Baldwin and Williams met with other activists, including Gary Flomenhoft, Rick Foley, Tim Matson, and Jacki Brook, and the group launched the first issue of *Vermont Commons* only four months later. The publication would be philosophically aligned with the Second Vermont Republic, but it was always an independent effort.

Throughout this book, when I as editor refer to "we," I mean the group of editorial board members, supporters, and frequent contributors who have been affiliated with the publication at some time during these eight years. I myself did not join the group until late in 2007, when my colleague in educational activism, Susan Ohanian, introduced me to Thomas Naylor, who in turn invited me to meet Baldwin and Williams. I have been a Jeffersonian decentralist for as long as I can remember, and I was not only discouraged by the excesses of the Bush administration but, in my career in alternative education, I had become disheartened by the successful bipartisan efforts to centralize and standardize educational policies in the United States. Over the years I had supported Libertarian, Green, and Vermont Progressive party campaigns, looking for the right combination of grassroots democracy, social conscience, and ecological awareness. This small group of Vermont activists, with their thoughtful, holistic, incisive critique of the politics of empire, came very close to what I had been seeking. I thought the notion of secession was, at least, a provocative way to awaken Americans from our complacency—a potent conversation starter, although I've never been convinced that it should be the centerpiece of our political strategy.

Indeed, *Vermont Commons* has not simply advocated for secession; it has provided a forum for exploring the roots of American imperialism and a range of possible social, cultural, and economic antidotes to it. We view the machinations of the U.S. government as part and parcel of a contemporary trend toward endless growth, consolidation, centralization, and domination by powerful institutions, including not only the state but also corporations and lobbying interests, the media, universities and school systems, the medical establishment, and, well, just about every aspect of modern life. *Vermont Commons* writers have argued that this emerging empire destroys as much as it creates, diminishes and despoils the natural world, impoverishes many while it enriches a select few, and imposes its will through exploitation and violence. The solution, we have argued, lies in a return to the local, the regional, the *bioregional*—to intimate and participatory forms of democracy and economic practices that respect the health and autonomy of our communities, as well as the integrity of the land and the biosphere.

From the start, *Vermont Commons* attracted nationally significant writers who were also concerned about these and related issues, including Bill McKibben, Wendell Berry, Robert Costanza, Peter Barnes, and James Howard Kunstler. Kirkpatrick Sale became a regular columnist. Other voices from within Vermont, such as the well-known political scholar Frank Bryan, John McClaughry, founder of the libertarian Ethan Allen Institute, and grassroots activists such as Amy Kirschner, Enid Wonnacott, and many others, also found this publication to be a congenial outlet for expressing their ideas.

The name *Commons* suggests that the essential alternative to concentrated power and empire is the community or the commonwealth—a shared endeavor to live in harmony with each other and with the larger "biotic community" as Aldo Leopold called the living world. As Peter Barnes defines this concept in his visionary book *Capitalism 3.0*, the "commons" includes "a set of assets that have two characteristics: they're all gifts, and they're all shared." These assets may be unearned gifts from nature (such as air, water, photosynthesis, seeds, forests), shared resources of communities (streets, libraries, marketplaces, law, money), or inherited cultural achievements (languages, sciences, religions, arts).

Barnes argues that contemporary capitalism's single-minded focus on private wealth and market-determined value has led to the denigration and ruination of the commons, a destructive process we must now reverse. "We have a joint obligation to preserve them. That's because future generations [and other species, as he points out elsewhere] will need them to live, and live well, just as we do. And our generation has no right to say, 'These gifts end here.' This shared responsibility introduces a moral factor that doesn't apply to other economic assets. . . . Assets in the commons are meant to be preserved *regardless of their return to capital*" (pp. 5–6, emphasis in original).

For Barnes, and for the *Vermont Commons* group, this "moral factor" demands that we temper the excesses of the global capitalist empire. This does not mean replacing private enterprise with some form of state socialism, but shifting both political and economic power away from massive institutions back to human-scale locations. As we look at the social and environmental effects of militant, triumphant globalized capitalism, we are urgently concerned about the quality of life, or even the possibility for survival, of millions of people and their communities, along with the other inhabitants of this planet. We believe that there is a desperate need to renew public appreciation for the commons and to adopt a more holistic approach to politics and economic life that values communities, cultural heritage, and the ecosystems that make life itself possible.

The core group of *Vermont Commons* editors and columnists believe a majority of Vermonters share these values. We recall that our small state has experienced a unique history, having established its political culture free of royal or colonial influences. In stark contrast to the imperial nation-building of the eighteenth century, the constitution and local practices of the Republic of Vermont (1777–1791) highly valued both the commons and democratic participation in politics. Vermont, although filled with industrious people, largely avoided the harsh social and economic consequences of nineteenth century industrialization. Today, an increasingly intrusive U.S. empire thwarts these qualities and values, and, if we desire to preserve them, we will need to make our state more politically and economically independent. The main purpose of *Vermont Commons* has been to explore what Vermont "independence" means and how it might be achieved. For many of its writers, this means rebuilding local food systems, developing renewable energy sources, inventing local and regional currencies and markets, and strengthening local governance, such as the New England tradition of town meeting. Yet many in this core group believe that even these measures will not suffice to resist the increasing domination of global and national forces, and that the only effective solution is for Vermont to separate from the United States empire.

The idea of secession strikes many Americans at first as completely outrageous. The last time it was tried in the United States, it was in defense of a slave economy and led to a horribly bloody and destructive war. Americans, particularly in the north, view "states' rights" and secessionist impulses through the historical lens of the Civil War. Besides, the U.S. Constitution that forged the states into a single nation is one of the signal achievements of modern history, is it not? To deliberately repudiate membership in the United States would be to enter into an uncertain future and seems inconceivable to most Americans, including most Vermonters.

But, we at *Vermont Commons* argue, the world is already descending into dark and uncertain times, hurtling into an even darker future if the course of empire is not arrested. In establishing the secessionist Second Vermont Republic, Thomas Naylor asserted that everything Vermonters hold dear is threatened by U.S. imperial expansion, and he challenged us to defend our values by withdrawing from this empire. He explained the justification for this radical strategy in issue #7 (Nov. 2005):

> Whether or not your state should consider seceding from the Union depends on your answers to the following eight questions:
> 1. Do you find it increasingly difficult to protect yourself from the debilitating effects of big government, big business, big markets, and big agriculture, who want all of us to be the same?
> 2. In addition to being too big, is our government too centralized, too powerful, too intrusive, too materialistic, and too unresponsive to the needs of individual citizens and small communities?
> 3. Has the U.S. Government lost its moral authority because it is owned, operated, and controlled by corporate America? Are national and congressional elections bought and sold to the highest bidders?
> 4. Do we have a single political party in America, the Republican party, disguised as a two-party system? Is the Democratic party effectively brain-dead, having had no new ideas since the 1960s?
> 5. Have you become disillusioned with corporate greed, the war on terrorism, homeland security, patriotic hype, the denial of civil liberties, pandering to the rich and power-

ful, environmental insensitivity, pseudo-religious drivel, and the culture of deceit?

6. Is American foreign policy, which is based on the doctrine of full-spectrum dominance, immoral, illegal, unconstitutional, and in violation of the UN Charter?

7. Does your state face the risk of terrorist attack and military conscription of its youth so long as it remains in the Union?

8. As a result of imperial overstretch, has the U.S. become unsustainable politically, economically, agriculturally, socially, culturally, and environmentally? Has it also become ungovernable and unfixable?

If you answered all eight of these questions affirmatively, then you have a moral obligation to lead your state out of the Union. It matters not whether you live in a Red State or a Blue State, the categorical imperative to secede is absolutely inescapable. This is a wake-up call to reclaim your soul—to decouple from a truly evil empire whose power knows no limits.

Even for those of us who are not yet fully convinced that we have a "moral obligation" to advocate nonviolent secession, Naylor's raising of this previously unthinkable strategy has provoked a great deal of intellectual ferment and soul searching. It forces us to critically examine our basic assumptions about the use and abuse of power in the contemporary United States and who we are as citizens. In these pages we wonder whether the United States has strayed so far from the republican ideals voiced at its founding that the time has come to rethink the 225-year-old compact that tied the destiny of our region and culture to a nation that has become a voracious and destructive global empire—something the Founding Fathers surely would not have wished, but which many of them foresaw.

Only eleven years after he shepherded the drafting of the Constitution, James Madison authored the "Virginia Resolution," complaining about the federal government's efforts to "enlarge its powers." What would he think about the national government today? Given what the U.S. corporate state has become, we might simply ask, "What would Madison do?" and we suspect that he would be horrified enough to call for another convention to give the nation a fresh start. The founders did not expect their document, laced with compromises addressing eighteenth-century issues, to meet twenty-first-century needs. A constitution that can be interpreted to treat global corporations as "persons" with inherent rights is surely overdue for an overhaul. But if none is forthcoming because of resistance by the entrenched power structure, what shall we do to preserve the rights of actual living people and their communities?

Meanwhile, even as we are grappling with philosophical and constitutional questions, the global industrial economy has produced serious tangible problems for the planet. Climate scientists and oil industry analysts, among others, have been sounding increasingly urgent alarms about global warming and resource depletion, most notably the approach of "peak oil"—the historical moment when dwindling petroleum supplies can no longer keep up with demand for inexpensive energy. *Vermont Commons* writers have taken these warnings very seriously; they are not placated by the politicians or mass media pundits who, in the service of corporate interests, counsel skepticism or defend the status quo. To us, climate change and peak oil are real, and very dangerous. They signal that the modern way of life *is not permanent* and that we had better start preparing for a simpler, more locally rooted lifestyle. As James Howard Kunstler put it in our second issue (May 2005):

> We are unprepared for this crisis of industrial civilization. We are sleepwalking into the future. The peak oil production event will change everything about how we live. It will challenge all of our assumptions. It will compel us to do things differently— whether we like it or not. . . . One huge implication is that industrial societies will never again enjoy the 2 to 7 percent annual economic growth that has been considered healthy for over 100 years. This amounts to the industrialized nations of the world finding themselves in a permanent depression. . . . The future is therefore telling us very loudly that we will have to change the way we live in this country. The implications are clear: we will have to downscale and rescale virtually everything we do. The downscaling of America is a tremendous and inescapable project. It is the master ecological project of our time. We will have to do it whether we like it or not. We are not prepared. Downscaling

America doesn't mean we become a lesser people. It means that the scale at which we conduct the work of American daily life will have to be adjusted to fit the requirements of a post-globalist, post-cheap-oil age. We are going to have to live a lot more locally and a lot more intensively on that local level.

Of course, predicting the future is a tricky business. It is not clear when, precisely, peak oil will occur (if it has not occurred already), or exactly what its consequences will be. But it seems supremely foolish to simply ignore the warnings we are receiving. As far back as 1972, in the classic research study *The Limits to Growth*, we were given evidence that industrial civilization's consumption of resources and outpouring of wastes *cannot continue indefinitely*. Whether the inevitable decline begins in 2014 or 2025 or 2032, we would do well to begin preparing now. *Indeed, much evidence suggests that the decline of industrial civilization has already begun.* The climate *is* changing and glaciers are melting. Food and fuel prices *are* increasingly volatile. The global economy *did* implode in 2008 and it is still in danger of collapsing with the slightest new provocation. *Vermont Commons* writers anticipated the 2008 crash from the earliest issues of the journal; they pointed out how the manipulative, nonproductive activities of Wall Street and other economic imbalances could only end in ruin for the Main Street economy. Perhaps there will be a partial recovery, but the evidence pointing toward a long-term, permanent decline of global industrial civilization continues to add up. It would be stupid to reject this evidence out of a stubborn conviction that our great institutions are immune to historical forces that have occurred repeatedly over the course of previous empires. Our empire is not unique in the face of these perennial forces. The United States is not as "exceptional" as many believe.

This book gathers writings from the journal that capture the essential points of our complex and holistic analysis. Many good and inspiring writings, especially those that were concerned with specific issues or ventures inside Vermont, have not been included. I have organized these selections by topic rather than by author or date of publication. First, the contributors explain what *empire* means and why the present U.S. corporate system can be considered to be an empire. Then we explore the various social, political, and environmental issues associated with this system, explaining why smaller-scale institutions could provide relief and hope. Next we turn to underlying principles, to the philosophy of decentralism that influences our critique of empire and our vision of a more local, community-centered world. Finally, we explain how the provocative strategy of nonviolent secession embodies this analysis and critique. It is not this book's purpose to convert readers to the program of secession, but instead to invite you to ask hard questions about the institutions that govern us and the effects they are having on the planet. We trust you will reach your own conclusions about what strategies can best meet the collective challenges we face.

PART ONE

Empire and Overshoot

The primary argument made by the writers in *Vermont Commons* is that modern political and economic systems have grown too large and overbearing. Governments, corporations, educational systems, global food supply chains, mass media, and other institutions are controlled by powerful forces that are distant from, and indifferent to, the diverse needs and preferences of citizens and their communities. In sum, the United States has developed into a classic *empire*—a massive, centralized concentration of power that dominates local economies, regional cultures, and other nations through military intimidation and economic exploitation.

The contributors to *Vermont Commons* are not asking how this powerful nation state ought to be ruled—whether by "liberal" or "conservative" principles—but whether its institutions should have so much power in the first place. We pose this radical, challenging question out of two major concerns, one moral and philosophical, the other quite practical and empirical:

1. Morally, the concentration of power is profoundly anti-democratic. It reduces individuals and localities to impotent, irrelevant ciphers in the vital decisions that shape society. At their worst, empires employ deadly violence against elements of their own population or other nations to further their aims.
2. Empirically, empires inevitably *overshoot* the resource base (energy, agricultural land, human, and cultural capital) that enable their growth, and the result has always been, and will apparently always be, *collapse*. For several reasons, most primarily the declining availability of cheap oil, we believe that the American empire is perilously close to a tipping point into collapse.

In this first part of *Most Likely to Secede*, Ian Baldwin, the cofounder of *Vermont Commons,* and other writers share concerns about the moral and political effects of empire and provide an overview of the challenge. The essays in this section should make it clear that the network of critical observers (we are not yet influential enough to constitute a "movement") is not a partisan crusade, nor is it obsessed with any particular issue. Although the next section of this book discusses specific problems individually, it is the totality of these problems, and their root causes in the overgrown and overly powerful institutions of the modern age, that concern the writers here.

Voices for Independence

Ian Baldwin

Issue no. 1 • April 2005

Why this journal, *Vermont Commons*? And why now?

Vermonters, Americans—indeed, all the world—stand at a widening divide. Not between red and blue, right and left, conservative and liberal, capitalist and socialist, and other such worn political coinage. No, we stand at a truly immense divide: that between our past and our future.

Behind us, an experiment in democracy whose energies are still robust, but whose framework—the modern nation state—teeters in all its towering immensity. Behind us stand the great achievements of the Modernist era, molded by one of history's great forces: centralization. Raw measures of power—governmental, military, scientific, economic, monetary, corporate—have reached levels of magnitude inconceivable a mere generation ago.

Once a merely "continental power," the United States has morphed into a colossus that spans the entire planet and has a finger in the affairs of all the globe's nations. Its corporations, banks, currency, media, laws, armies, navies, and covert operations rule the world's oceans, skies, economies, and its most potent political and cultural norms. Believing in its heavenly mandate, its supreme destiny, it has become a law unto itself among the community of nations, free as any empire before it to devour those whose wealth it craves, or whose rulers give it indigestion. Free under the banner of "regime change" to unilaterally act. To shock and to awe.

Was ever an empire different?

Like all those before it, however, this empire depends on abundant natural resources. Abundant means cheap. And it depends most of all on energy, specifically that derived from oil and natural gas. These fuel the empire's transportation system, its mechanized food system, and much of its industry, including a sizable portion of its electrical generation systems. Yet it is widely agreed that either now or in the very near future, the energy needed to run a modern empire—indeed any industrialized state of any consequence—is about to begin an inexorable climb toward being expensive beyond our experience and imagination. Indeed, it has already begun.

How do we respond to this? Human inventiveness is always ramped up by necessity, and never more so than when an entire system, whose foundations are always built upon beliefs, collapses. Only a slave to the idea of endless material growth will be paralyzed by fear and rage at the idea of its opposite.

Are we such slaves?

I think not. And so I believe we stand poised at something far greater than a mere "regime change," or a mere change of government, from Republican to Democrat or vice versa. We stand farther out from those tidy, familiar shores. We stand poised to reinvent ourselves.

Five years ago we would have been laughed out of court for trying to insist we Vermonters return to the small scale, to the gore, the village, the town, the block, the neighborhood. To the intimate. To plead for an escape from Big Brother, leering ever closer in our faces, incessantly reminding us that Terror lurks in our yards and that we must fight an Orwellian perpetual war that "will not end in our lifetimes" against an invisible enemy.

But now, in April 2005, and from this moment forward, there are reasons to hope. Fear, as one of our presidents cautioned, is our only real enemy. While the world shakes, and we with it, we need to turn to each other and open our hearts and minds. We need to speak and to listen, to hear and behold "voices of independence" that rise from the depths of everyone, regardless of education, status, employment, race, gender, creed, from all of us who live here, in this river- and hills-bounded place, our own immortal land: Vermont.

And that is what this new journal is about. How do we return to our roots, with all the new things we have learned in the course of a century, the good and the bad? How can we feed ourselves again; transport ourselves without having to wage wars to do it; light our homes without destroying the lands of others or divesting our children of a safe future? How do we shelter and warm ourselves without laying waste to the land around us, which gives us our peculiar soul as Vermonters; how do we heal and care for our sick without succumbing to debt beyond bearing; how do we educate our children without the gun of federal law leveled at our temples? In this journal we endeavor to explore those issues, and much more.

Our bag is full of questions seeking answers.

Can we be free again, bound by obligations to real, flesh-and-blood neighbors, harmonized by small-scale relations, nourished by community self-sufficiency, inspired by our own diverse and idiosyncratic creativity? Can we once again be satisfied by the small pleasures of subtle intimacies, day by day?

I believe we can.

The door is open.

The Collapse of the American Empire

Kirkpatrick Sale

Issue no. 1 • April 2005

It is quite ironic: only a decade or so after the idea of the United States as an imperial power came to be accepted by both right and left, and people were able to talk openly about an American empire, it is showing multiple signs of its inability to continue. Indeed, it is now possible to contemplate its collapse.

The neocons in power in Washington these days, who were delighted to talk about America as the sole empire in the world following the Soviet disintegration, will of course refuse to believe in any such collapse. But I think it behooves us to examine seriously the ways in which the U.S. system is so drastically imperiling itself that it will cause not only the collapse of its worldwide empire but vast changes on the domestic front as well.

All empires eventually collapse. Sumerian, Persian, Greek, Roman, Hapsburg, British, Soviet, you name them, they all fell, and most within a few hundred years. The reasons are not really complex. An empire is a kind of state system that makes the same mistakes simply by nature of its structure and inevitably fails because of its size, complexity, territorial reach, stratification, domination, and inequalities.

In my reading of the history of empires, I see four reasons that explain their collapse. Let me set them out, in reference to the present American empire.

1. Environmental Degradation

Empires end by destroying the lands and waters they depend upon for survival, largely because they build and farm and grow without limits. Ours is no exception, even if we have yet to experience the worst of our assaults on nature. Science is in agreement that all important ecological indicators are in decline and have been so for decades. As the Harvard biologist E. O. Wilson has said, after lengthy examination of human impact on the earth, our "ecological footprint is already too large for the planet to sustain, and it is getting larger." A Defense Department study last year predicted "abrupt climate change," likely to occur within the decade, leading to "catastrophic" shortages of water and energy, endemic "disruption and conflict," warfare that "would define human life," and a "significant drop" in the planet's ability to sustain its present population. End of empire for sure, maybe end of civilization.

2. Economic Meltdown

Empires depend on excessive resource exploitation, usually derived from colonies farther and farther away from the center, and eventually fall when the resources are exhausted or become too expensive for all but the elite. This is the exact path we are on. Our economy is built on a fragile system in which the world produces and we, by and large, consume. At the moment we sustain a nearly $630 billion trade deficit with the rest of the world. It has leapt by an incredible $500 billion since 1993, and $180 billion since George Bush took office in 2001. In order to pay for that, we require an inflow of cash from the rest of the world of about $1 billion every day. That kind of excess is simply unsustainable, especially when you realize that it is the other world empire, China, that is supporting it, to the tune of some $83 billion on loan to the U.S. Treasury.

Add to that an economy resting on a nearly $500 billion federal budget deficit, making up part of the total national debt of $7.4 trillion as of fall 2004. Nobody thinks that is sustainable either, which is why the dollar is losing value fast, and the world is beginning to lose faith in investment here. In just a few years the dollar may be so battered that the oil states will no longer want to operate in that currency and will turn to the euro instead, and China will let the yuan float against the dollar, effectively making this nation bankrupt and powerless, unable to control economic life within its borders, much less abroad.

3. Military Overstretch

Empires are by definition colonizers, always forced to extend their military reach farther and farther, and enlarge it against unwilling colonies more and more, until coffers are exhausted, troops are unreliable, and the periphery can no longer be controlled. The American empire, which began its worldwide reach well before Bush II, now has some 446,000 active troops at more than 725 acknowledged (and any number of secret) bases in at least 38 countries, plus a formal "military presence" in no less than 153 countries, and no less than a dozen fully armed courier fleets on the oceans. And now that Bush has declared war on "terror," instead of the more winnable war on Al-Qaeda we should have waged, our armies and agents will be on a universal and permanent battlefield.

So far that military network has not collapsed, but as Iraq indicates, it is mightily tested and quite incapable of establishing client states to do our bidding and protect resources we want. As anti-American sentiment continues to spread, and, as more countries refuse the "structural adjustments" our IMF-led globalization requires, the periphery of our empire will likely begin resisting us, militarily if necessary. Far from having the capacity to fight two wars simultaneously, as the Pentagon once hoped, we are proving that we can barely fight one.

4. Domestic Upheaval

Traditional empires collapse from within, as well as often being attacked from without. So far the level of dissent within the United States has not reached the point of rebellion or secession—thanks both to the increasing repression of dissent and escalation of fear in the name of "homeland security" and to the success of our modern version of bread and circuses: a unique combination of entertainment, consumption, drugs, and religion that effectively deadens the general public into a stupor.

It's hard to believe that the great mass of the American public would ever bestir itself to challenge the empire at home until things get much, much worse. It is a public, after all, of which a 2004 Gallup poll found that 61 percent believe that "religion can answer all or most of today's problems." According to a 2002 Time/CNN poll, 59 percent believe in the imminent apocalypse foretold in the Book of Revelation and take every threat and disaster as evidence of God's will.

And yet, it's also hard to believe that a nation so thoroughly corrupt as this, resting on a social and economic base of intolerably unequal incomes and property, will be able to sustain itself for long. The upsurge in talk about secession after the last election, some of which is deadly serious, indicates that at least a minority is willing to think about drastic steps to "alter or abolish" an empire it finds itself fundamentally at odds with.

Those four processes by which empires fall seem to me to be inescapable, in varying degrees, in this latest empire. And I think a combination of them will bring about its collapse within the next fifteen years or so.

Jared Diamond's recent book *Collapse* details the ways societies crumble and suggests that American society, or industrial civilization as a whole, can learn from the failures of the past and avoid such fates. But it will never happen, for a reason Diamond himself explains. As he says, in his analysis of the doomed Norse society of Greenland that collapsed in the early fifteenth century, "The values to which people cling most stubbornly under inappropriate conditions are those values that were previously the source of their greatest triumphs over adversity."

If this is so, and his examples certainly support it, then we can isolate the values that have been responsible for American society's greatest triumphs and know that we will cling to them no matter what. They are, in one rough mixture, capitalism, individualism, nationalism, technophilia, and humanism (as the dominance of humans over nature). There is no chance, no matter how grave and obvious the threat, that as a society we will abandon those.

Hence no chance to escape the collapse of empire.

Liberals and Conservatives
Relics of the Past

Thomas Naylor

Issue no. 12 • April 2006

When former Democratic vice presidential candidate John Edwards and Illinois Democratic Senator Barack Obama recently spoke to packed houses in Burlington, they provided glaring evidence that there is "nothing new under the sun" in mainstream U.S. two-party politics. Both delivered speeches laced with pseudo-liberal blather, Obama delivering a "call to action" similar to Howard Dean's 2004 "Take Back America" campaign. As Edwards and Obama recited one liberal Democratic cliché after another, a discerning listener couldn't help but be struck by how completely irrelevant the terms "liberal" and "conservative" have become in today's twenty-first-century world. Those who openly identify themselves with either of the terms are anachronistic and out of touch with reality.

Both liberals and conservatives claim to be individualists, all the while behaving as world-class conformists, who are consumed by affluenza, technomania, e-mania, and megalomania. Conservatives like big business, big military projects, and big prisons. Liberals are drawn to big cities, big social welfare programs, and big government, the same big government that is owned, operated, and controlled by corporate America, which they abhor. Liberals are indecisive moral relativists who tend to whine and believe that only the federal government can solve all of our problems. Conservatives, on the other hand, are tough-talking, mean-spirited, free-market zealots, who want to privatize everything in sight. They are often drawn to religious fundamentalism.

Many conservatives and some liberals support President George W. Bush's foreign policies of full-spectrum dominance and imperial overstretch, both of which are grounded in the doctrine of might makes right. They are big on revenge. President Bill Clinton proved to be a conservative Republican disguised as a liberal Democrat. He granted Republicans their every wish. Clinton called for more trade, more budget cuts, more privatization, more foreign investment, more mega-mergers, more computer networks, less government control, lower interest rates, and more economic growth. He wanted everything to be bigger, faster, more complex, more high-tech, and more interdependent—bigger markets, bigger trade agreements, bigger financial institutions, and bigger telecommunication networks. Every time his political ratings dropped, he would bomb some Third World country, and most Americans loved it.

Conservatives don't want anyone messing with the distribution of income and wealth. They like things the way they are. Liberals want the government to decide what is fair. Liberals believe in multiculturalism, affirmative action, and minority rights. Conservatives favor states' rights over minority rights. What liberals and conservatives have in common is that they are both into having—owning, possessing, controlling, and manipulating money, power, people, material wealth, and things. Having is one of the ways Americans deal with the human condition—separation, meaninglessness, powerlessness, and death.

To illustrate how irrelevant the terms "liberal" and "conservative" have become, consider the case of Sweden and Switzerland, two of the most prosperous countries in the world. Sweden is the stereotypical democratic socialist state with a strong central government, relatively high taxes, a broad social welfare net financed by the State, and a strong social conscience. Switzerland is the most free market country in the world, with the weakest central government, and the most decentralized social welfare system. Both are affluent, clean, green, healthy, well-educated, democratic, nonviolent, politically neutral, and among the most sustainable nations in all of history. By U.S. standards, they are both tiny. Switzerland and Sweden work, not because of political ideology, but rather because the politics of human scale always trumps the politics of the left and the politics of the right. Under the politics of human scale, a politics that trumps our now-outdated and useless "liberal-versus-conservative" dualistic mind-set, there would be but one fundamental question: "Is it too big?"

Our Land, Our Destiny

Vermont Independence Convention Keynote Address

James Howard Kunstler

Issue no. 9 • January 2006

When we think about the destiny of our land, there are a few questions we might ask: What do we mean by "our land?" What has been holding it together? Who are we? And who will we become? For about 210 years, we have been a federal democratic republic composed of more than a few states, eventually adding up to fifty. At times, the citizen's identity has shifted from allegiance to a particular state to the republic as a whole —as when Robert E. Lee, for instance, famously declared that he was first a citizen of Virginia. Lately the tendency has been for citizens to think of themselves first as Americans, and secondarily as New Yorkers or Virginians or Vermonters.

What has held us together—at least since the convulsion of the Civil War—is a common culture and especially the common enterprise of a great industrial economy. For much of our history, including the first half of the twentieth century, we were a resourceful, adaptive, generous, brave, forward-looking people who believed in earnest effort, who occupied a beautiful landscape full of places worth caring about and worth defending. Since then, lost in raptures of easy motoring, fried food, incessant infotainment, and desperate money grubbing, we became a nation of overfed clowns who believed that it was possible to get something for nothing, who ravaged the landscape in an orgy of wanton carelessness, who believed we were entitled to lives of everlasting comfort and convenience, no matter what, and expected the rest of the world to pay for it. We even elected a vice president who declared that this American way of life was nonnegotiable.

We now face the most serious challenge to our collective identity, economy, culture, and security since the Civil War. The end of the cheap fossil fuel era will change everything about how we live in this country. It will challenge all of our assumptions. It will compel us to do things differently—whether we like it or not. We are at or near the all-time maximum global oil production peak. We do not have to run out of oil to find ourselves in trouble. When world demand for oil exceeds the world's ability to produce oil, all the complex systems we depend on will destabilize. Everything from national chain retail, to the Archer Daniels Midland Cheez Doodle and Pepsi model of agriculture, to the arrangements for heating our homes and lighting our cities will begin to wobble. Some of these things will fail us and begin to change our lives. At the same time, we will be tempted to join a worldwide scramble for the world's remaining oil—most of which belongs to countries whose people don't like us—and the nature of this contest may be very violent.

Our suburbs will prove to be a huge liability. They represent the greatest misallocation of resources in the history of the world. The project of suburbia represents a set of tragic choices because it is a living arrangement with no future. And that future is now here in the form of the peak-oil predicament. Because they have no future, our suburbs entail a powerful psychology of previous investment that will prevent us from even thinking about reforming them or letting go of them. That's why Vice President Cheney said the "American way of life" is nonnegotiable. There will be a great battle to preserve the supposed entitlements to suburbia, and it will be an epochal act of futility, a huge waste of effort and resources that might have been much better spent in finding new ways to carry on an American civilization. We might, for instance, have invested in restoring our national railroad system, which we will need desperately, because no other project we might undertake would have such a profoundly positive impact on our oil consumption. But instead we will try desperately to make cars that get better mileage, so we can continue being car dependent and continue building out and elaborating the infrastructure for a living arrangement with no future—the subdivisions of the McHouses, the strip malls, the big box pods, the deployments of hamburger shacks and pizza huts.

In the service of defending suburbia, the American public may turn to political maniacs, who will promise to make the country just like it was in 1997, before we started having all these problems. In the course of this long emergency we face, life and politics are apt to become profoundly local. Many of my friends wring their hands over George W. Bush, whom they regard as the second coming of Adolf Hitler and who think the federal government will regulate every inch of their lives. I tell them,

in the long emergency the federal government will be impotent and inef-
fectual—just as they were after Hurricane Katrina—and that the federal
government will be lucky if they can answer the phones five years from
now, let alone regulate anybody's life. I tell them, life in America is going
to become profoundly and intensely local, and it will be the local politicians you'll have to worry about.

American life will become intensely and profoundly local because
the complex systems that hold this nation together are going to fail.
We will have to grow a lot more of our food in the regions where we
live. That won't be easy. A lot of our best agricultural land close to our
towns and cities has been paved over. A lot of knowledge has been lost.
We are going to have to reconstruct local economies, local networks
of interdependency—and that will not be easy given the methodi-
cal destruction of economic infrastructure to our communities by
Walmart and the rest of the national chain companies over the past
forty years. As these severe challenges arise, different regions of the
United States will cope differently. The Sun Belt will probably suffer
in equal proportion to the degree that it benefited from the cheap oil
fiesta of the past several decades—because it squandered its wealth in
building gigantic suburban metroplexes that have no future. Atlanta,
Dallas, Orlando, Charlotte.

The people in these places will be full of grievance and bewilderment,
and they may seek comfort in the romance of firearms in seeking to
defend the indefensible entitlements of their failing suburbs. The people
in Phoenix and Tucson will have dreadful problems with water, on top
of their problems with oil and the loss of cheap air conditioning. They
may not be able to grow any food of their own, locally. In Las Vegas, the
excitement will be over. The capital of a something-for-nothing culture
will be left to the wind, the tarantulas, and the Gila monsters. California,
the most tragic part of our country—because it was once the most beautiful and is now most lost—will have many of the previously mentioned
problems and the prospect of awful ethnic conflict.

I am describing a nation that may not hold together far into the twenty-
first century. I would like to be wrong about this, but it is hard to look at
the big picture and come up with a different set of conclusions. All parts
of the United States are going to endure hardships in the decades ahead,
but some regions or states may be better prepared, or just luckier. I tend

to be more optimistic about the future in New England, the mid-Atlantic States, the upper Midwest, and the Pacific Northwest (if it can escape the wrath emanating out of California). I include Vermont in this list, of course. This part of the country enjoys some advantages: an armature of towns scaled to the requirements of life in a lower energy world; a lot of good agricultural land; a civic tradition of responsible local governance; a set of regional collective character traits we associate with New England Yankees at their best: rectitude, discipline, perseverance, and allegiance to the community.

I'm personally not an advocate of national breakup or secession. I grew up with United States and I have been, until recently, pretty comfortable with the idea that we would stick together no matter what. But in the Long Emergency all bets are off for politics, economics, and social cohesion. Turbulence will be the rule, and we will have to do our best to make sure that the just prevail over the wicked, and that the weak are not trampled, and that the best that was in us as a people can somehow be rescued from the dumpster of memory.

PART TWO

Global Problems, Local Solutions

This is the lengthiest and most detailed section of the book. Although the writings in *Vermont Commons* reflect a general philosophical orientation and an overarching critique of imperialism as such, the publication has devoted many of its pages to concrete problems and practical solutions. These particulars not only help illustrate the substantive contrast between the agenda of centralized power and the vision of human-scale democracy, they are also the arenas where ideological programs are actually lived through and suffered. We can build a strong moral case against an earth-consuming empire, but the hard work of dismantling that empire will take place on farms, in banks, on Main Street, through innovative communications media and alternative learning environments, and other places of social and economic transaction.

This section contains seven topics: economics, money, energy, food, information, community, and resilience. Some of the categories are fairly conventional, while others require a bit of an imaginative leap to embrace the diverse issues they contain. This is not an attempt to create a fixed or arbitrary agenda; it is a panoramic sketch of the major themes and issues *Vermont Commons* writers have addressed.

ECONOMICS

One defining feature of the modern world is the dominance of *economic* values over all other moral and cultural considerations. The production and distribution of material goods, the amassing of personal, corporate, and national wealth, and the profitable utilization of the landscape and all the "resources" it contains, generally trump or completely displace other ways of defining a good and worthy way of living. Economists are the high priests of the nation-state, despite their contradictory and sometimes disastrously erroneous pronouncements. So we begin our analysis of empire by examining the economic values that shape it.

The triumph of economic values reflects several historical sources. One is a philosophical commitment to materialism—the assumption that solid physical entities are more real, more essential, than moral, psychological, or spiritual domains of human experience. Translated into popular culture, materialism becomes consumerism, an addiction to the ownership of objects. Our critique addresses this addiction and its philosophical sources. Thomas Naylor, before becoming an advocate for political secession from empire, rebelled against the assumptions of mainstream economics (his own academic field) and coauthored a pioneering study of the fruits of cultural materialism, *Affluenza: The All-Consuming Epidemic* (2001).

Another source of economic hegemony is the agenda of colonialism and globalization. The field of economics is as much an ideology as a science. The founders of classical economics claimed to be describing universal "market forces," but in important ways their ideas essentially rationalized the concentration of wealth in colonial powers such as Great Britain at the expense of colonized peoples. Economics is about power.

The following essays from *Vermont Commons* challenge the foundational assumptions underlying modern economic theory and practice. The three authors selected reflect somewhat different perspectives, yet they agree on at least one key point: Economic systems need to be turned away from their current single-minded focus on material wealth and become more responsive to other human longings and to the health of communities and the natural world. For this to happen, they must become radically more local, human scale, and democratic. These essays help us imagine how such an economy might function.

The Real Economy

Dr. Robert Costanza

Issue no. 10 • February 2006

Stories about the economy typically focus on Gross Domestic Product (GDP), jobs, stock prices, interest rates, retail sales, consumer confidence, housing starts, taxes, and assorted other indicators. We hear things like "GDP grew at a 3 percent rate in the fourth quarter, indicating a recovering, healthy economy, but with room for further improvement." Or, "The Fed raised short-term interest rates again to head off inflation." But do these reports, and the indicators they cite, really tell us how the economy is doing? What is the economy, anyway? And what is this economy for?

Conventional reports on these questions are rather narrow. The "economy" we usually hear about refers only to the market economy—the value of those goods and services that are exchanged for money. Its purpose is usually taken to be to maximize the value of these goods and services—with the assumption that the more activity, the better off we are. Thus, the more GDP (which measures aggregate activity in the market economy), the better. Likewise, the more contributors to GDP (such as retail sales and salaries paid to employees), the better. Predictors of more GDP in the future (such as housing starts and consumer confidence) are also important pieces of information from this perspective. Declining or even stable GDP is seen as a disaster. Growth in GDP is assumed to be government's primary policy goal and also something that is sustainable indefinitely.

But is this what the economy is all about? Or more accurately, is this all that the economy is about? Or is this what the economy should be about? The answer to all of these is an emphatic no. Here's why. Let's start with purpose. The purpose of the economy should be to provide for the sustainable well-being of people. That goal encompasses material well-being, certainly, but also anything else that affects well-being and its sustainability. This seems obvious and noncontroversial. The problem comes in determining what things actually affect well-being and in what ways.

There is substantial new research on this "science of happiness" that shows the limits of conventional economic income and consumption in contributing to well-being. In his 2003 book *The High Price of Materialism*, psychologist Tim Kasser points out, for instance, that people who focus on material consumption as a path to happiness are actually less happy and even suffer higher rates of both physical and mental illnesses than those who do not. Material consumption beyond real need is a form of psychological "junk food" that only satisfies for the moment and ultimately leads to depression, Kasser says. Economist Richard Easterlin, a noted researcher on the determinants of happiness, has shown that well-being tends to correlate well with health, level of education, and marital status, and not very well with income. He concludes in a recent paper in the *Proceedings* of the National Academy of Sciences that people make decisions assuming that more income, comfort, and positional goods will make them happier, failing to recognize that hedonic adaptation and social comparison will come into play, raise their aspirations to about the same extent as their actual gains, and leave them feeling no happier than before. As a result, most individuals spend a disproportionate amount of their lives working to make money, and sacrifice family life and health, domains in which aspirations remain fairly constant as actual circumstances change, and where the attainment of one's goals has a more lasting impact on happiness. Hence, a reallocation of time in favor of family life and health would, on average, increase individual happiness.

British economist Richard Layard's 2005 book, *Happiness: Lessons from a New Science*, echoes many of these ideas and concludes that current economic policies are not improving happiness and that "happiness should become the goal of policy, and the progress of national happiness should be measured and analyzed as closely as the growth of GNP." Economist Robert Frank, in his 2000 book *Luxury Fever*, also concludes that the nation would be better off—overall national well-being would be higher, that is—if we actually consumed less and spent more time with family and friends, working for our communities, maintaining our physical and mental health, and enjoying nature.

On this last point, there is substantial and growing evidence that natural systems contribute heavily to human well-being. In a paper published in 1997 in the journal *Nature*, my coauthors and I estimated that the annual, nonmarket value of the earth's ecosystem services is $33 trillion globally, substantially larger than global GDP. The just-released UN Millennium Ecosystem Assessment is a global update and compendium of ecosystem services and their contributions to human well-being. So, if we want to assess the "real" economy—all the things that contribute to real, sustainable, human welfare—as opposed to only the "market" economy, we have to measure the nonmarketed contributions to human well-being from nature, from family, friends, and other social relationships at many scales, and from health and education. One convenient way to summarize these contributions is to group them into four basic types of capital that are necessary to support the real, human-welfare-producing economy: built capital, human capital, social capital, and natural capital.

The market economy covers mainly built capital (factories, offices, and other built infrastructure and their products) and part of human capital (spending on labor), with some limited spillover into the other two. Human capital includes the health, knowledge, and all the other attributes of individual humans that allow them to function in a complex society. Social capital includes all the formal and informal networks among people: family, friends, and neighbors, as well as social institutions at all levels, like churches, social clubs, local, state, and national governments, NGOs, and international organizations. Natural capital includes the world's ecosystems and all the services they provide. Ecosystem services occur at many scales, from climate regulation at the global scale, to flood protection, soil formation, nutrient cycling, recreation, and aesthetic services at the local and regional scales.

So, how has the real economy been doing recently, compared to the market economy? The short answer is, not so good. How do we know? One way is through surveys of people's life satisfaction, which has been decreasing slightly since about 1975. A second approach is an aggregate measure of the real economy that has been developed as an alternative to GDP called the Genuine Progress Indicator, or GPI. Let's first take a quick look at the problems with GDP as a measure of true human well-being. GDP is not only limited—measuring only marketed economic activity or gross income—it also counts all of this activity as positive. It does not separate desirable, well-being-enhancing activity from undesirable well-being-reducing activity. For example, an oil spill increases

GDP because someone has to clean it up, but it obviously detracts from society's well-being. From the perspective of GDP, more crime, more sickness, more war, more pollution, more fires, storms, and pestilence are all potentially good things, because they can increase marketed activity in the economy.

GDP also leaves out many things that do enhance well-being but are outside the market. For example, the unpaid work of parents caring for their own children at home doesn't show up, but if these same parents decide to work outside the home to pay for child care, GDP suddenly increases. The nonmarketed work of natural capital in providing clean air and water, food, natural resources, and other ecosystem services doesn't adequately show up in GDP, either, but if those services are damaged and we have to pay to fix or replace them, then GDP suddenly increases. Finally, GDP takes no account of the distribution of income among individuals. But it is well known that an additional $1 worth of income produces more well-being if one is poor rather than rich. It is also clear that a highly skewed income distribution has negative effects on a society's social capital.

The GPI addresses these problems by separating the positive from the negative components of marketed economic activity, adding in estimates of the value of nonmarketed goods and services provided by natural, human, and social capital, and adjusting for income-distribution effects. While it is by no means a perfect representation of the real well-being of the nation, GPI is a much better approximation than GDP. As Amartya Sen and others have noted, it is much better to be approximately right in these measures than precisely wrong. Comparing GDP and GPI for the United States shows that while GDP has steadily increased since 1950, with the occasional dip or recession, GPI peaked in about 1975 and has been gradually decreasing ever since. From the perspective of the real economy, as opposed to just the market economy, the United States has been in recession since 1975. As already mentioned, this picture is also consistent with survey-based research on people's stated life satisfaction.

We are now in a period of what Herman Daly has called "un-economic growth," where further growth in marketed economic activity (GDP) is actually reducing well-being on balance rather than enhancing it. In terms of the four capitals, while built capital has grown, human, social, and natural capital have declined or remained constant and more than canceled out the gains in built capital. During the last four years, the decline in domestic GPI has picked up speed. While U.S. GPI was beginning to trend upward again at the end of the Clinton years, the policies of the Bush administration have led to a significant worsening of income distribution (thereby further decreasing social capital), an increasing depletion of natural capital, and worsening human capital through decreased spending on education and health and loss of jobs. And the Bush team has certainly not compensated for these negatives with a stellar performance in the built capital component (GDP). While the dollar incomes of some wealthy individuals may have improved over this period, the overall well-being of the nation has significantly declined. Further, the psychological evidence is that even the well-being (as opposed to income) of the wealthy individuals has probably not improved very much and may even have declined. From the perspective of the real economy, the country is in rapidly worsening shape.

Is the news all bad? No. We recently estimated the GPI of the State of Vermont and of Burlington, the state's largest city, and found that Vermont's and Burlington's GPI per capita had increased over the entire 1950–2000 period and is now more than double the national average. This was due to Vermont's attention to protecting and enhancing natural, human, and social capital in balance with gains in built capital—accomplished through the application of strong, local democratic principles and processes still actively at work in Vermont. The lesson from Vermont, and from similar analyses done at the regional level in other locales, is that there is significant variation across the country in trends in well-being and quality of life, and plenty of good examples we can learn from to improve the overall well-being of the country.

How can we apply these lessons to get out of the real recession in human well-being at the national scale that we have been in since 1975? Several policies have been suggested that would help to turn things around:

- Shifting our primary national policy goal from increasing
  marketed economic activity (GDP) to maximizing national well-
  being (GPI or something similar). This would allow us to see
  the interconnections between built, human, social, and natural
  capital, and build well-being in a balanced and sustainable way.

- Reforming the tax system to send the right incentives by taxing negatives (pollution, depletion of natural capital, over-consumption) rather than positives (labor, savings, investment). Recent tax reforms have decreased well-being by promoting a greater income gap, natural resource depletion, and increased pollution.
- Reforming international trade to promote well-being over mere GDP growth. This implies protecting natural capital, labor rights, and democratic self-determination first and then allowing trade, rather than promoting the current trade rules that ride roughshod over all other societal values and ignore all nonmarket contributions to well-being.
- Implementing local complementary currency systems to encourage more local economic activity and help build social capital. There are more than 4,000 local currency systems in operation today, including "Ithaca hours" in Ithaca, NY, and "Burlington Bread" in Burlington, VT. While these systems have so far not played a major role in local economies, the potential for their expanded use is huge.
- Further reforming campaign-finance laws so that the needs and welfare of individuals are more fully and accurately expressed in the national democratic process, rather than the needs and welfare of those who currently fund political campaigns.

As Tom Prugh, Herman Daly, and I have argued in our book *The Local Politics of Global Sustainability*, implementing strong democracy (as opposed to the weak and ineffective sham of democracy we currently see at the national scale) is an essential prerequisite to building a sustainable and desirable future. Ultimately, getting out of our twenty-five-year recession in well-being will require us to look beyond the limited definition of the "economy" we read about in the newspapers, and recognize what the real economy is and what it is for. We must not allow deceptive accounting practices—analogous to those that caused the Enron and WorldCom debacles—to paint an inaccurate and ultimately destructive picture of how "well" we are doing. Alternatives are available, but they need significant further discussion and research. With nothing less than our current and future well-being at stake, we can certainly afford to devote greater effort to learning how to adequately understand and measure it. If we want the things that really matter to our well-being to count, we must learn how to recognize and count them, and use that information to inform policy in a real democracy.

Economics of Scale vs. the Scale of Economics
Toward Basic Principles of a Bioregional Economy

KIRKPATRICK SALE

Issue no. 10 • February 2006

Economics of scale is what conventional industrial economies are all about, finding ways to more profitably and efficiently exploit nature. But the scale of economics is what the economics of the future must be about, finding ways to live so that healthy communities may foster a healthy earth. There are only two essentials to consider in coming at the problem of the optimum scale for an economy to produce and distribute goods and services: the natural ecosystem and the human community. An economy that does harm to the natural world—depleting resources, extinguishing species, producing pollution, piling up wastes—has grown too large; an economy out of democratic and humanitarian control— where decisions are made by distant corporations and a polity whose choices are beyond individual influence—has grown too large.

An economic scale optimum for the earth's systems would be based on conservation, stability, sustainability, recycling, and harmony. That means, for starters, an economy at a bioregional scale that more or less dictates the economy appropriate to it. An economy based on a watershed, for example, automatically considers downriver populations as well as headwater ones. The human constructs would adapt to the environment rather than be imposed, and human uses would be confined to those the bioregion allowed. In Vermont terms, it would be possible to think of the western watershed of the Connecticut River, with all the rivers running eastward from the Green Mountains, as a bioregion. Another bioregion would encompass the watershed to the west of the Green Mountains, to Lake Champlain. Dairy and general truck farming would naturally be at the heart of the bioregional economy, although if a truly ecological sensibility informs it those farms would not allow the disastrous waste runoff that now pollutes Lake Champlain and other waterways. Nor would they use artificial chemicals and fertilizers, nor allow factory farms of 1,000-plus cows and 100,000-plus hens.

An ecologically based agriculture would depend on solar power appropriate to the region, on human-powered machines, on organic pest-
management systems, perennial polyculture, and permaculture, with
markets geared to seasonal and regional foods. The economic scale desirable for the human community would be one in which decisions about the
economy—what is produced, from what resources, by whom, for whom,
how distributed, how recycled—are made democratically by towns and
bioregions. Most power would locate at the level of the community, where
we can imagine effecting basic economic justice: workplace ownership
by the employees, workplace democracy for decision-making, and workplace commitment to the surrounding populace—all the things that are
impossible with large scales and distant chain store corporations. And
here we come to an essential element of a stable economy that dictates
much of its scale: self-sufficiency. If Vermont's farms were part of a self-
sufficient economy, feeding the 620,000 people within its borders as its
primary mission, there would not be such a concentration on dairy farms
(and the resultant pollution problems), but a greater diversity of animal
products and crops, ultimately to the health of the ecosystems.

Self-sufficiency is operable only at a limited scale—say, bioregions
of 10,000 to 20,000 square miles—where humans can understand the
resources at hand, perceive and regulate the variants in the economy, and
ensure that production and distribution arc made rational and systematic.
In terms of population, too, there is a limit at which self-sufficiency can be
achieved. In research for my book *Human Scale*, I found that historically
self-sufficient communities with economies of some complexity tended
to cluster in the 5,000–10,000 population range. Urbanologist Gideon
Sjoberg has said that "it seems unlikely that, at least in the earlier periods,
even the larger of these cities contained more than 5,000 to 10,000 people,
including part-time farmers on the cities' outskirts." Even when larger
cities grew in the thirteenth and fourteenth centuries to 20,000 or even
40,000, they were typically divided into quarters—literally four parts—of
5,000 to 10,000 people.

On a modern American scale we might imagine a mixture of somewhat self-sufficient cities within more self-sufficient counties within
mostly self-sufficient bioregions within a totally self-sufficient state, and
then the economy of self-sufficiency might be quite complex indeed. Such
units would need to be guided by certain maxims to provide a full range

of goods and services, and they would need to adhere to them with some ingenuity. But the maxims are simple and thoroughly practical. They would include the principle of sharing at the community level, recycling and repairing (or at a more complex level, remanufacturing) almost everything, an emphasis on handicrafts and bespoke production rather than manufactures and mass production, using raw local (instead of imported) materials, nurturing local ingenuity without patent and copyright restrictions, and agreeing to abandon as unnecessary and undesirable almost everything manufactured at the factory level anywhere and anyhow. All of which is no more complex than the old New England adage: Use it up, wear it out, make it do, or do without.

What follows are what I take to be the essential elements of a philosophy that would guide a bioregional economy, which I have constructed from a wide reading in alternative economics, including E. F. Schumacher's great range of writings (particularly "Buddhist Economics" in *Small Is Beautiful*) mixed with various economic ideas expressed by the Buddha himself, and ideas I enunciated in the "Economy" chapter of my *Dwellers in the Land: The Bioregional Vision.*

1. All production of goods or services would be based primarily on a reverence for life, a biocentric understanding that includes animals, birds, insects, plants, trees, the living ecosystems, streams and rivers, forests and wetlands, hills and mountains, clouds and rains—fundamentally Gaia herself, understood as the only living, self-regulating planet in the galaxy.

2. All systems have limits and they must be learned and adhered to in every economic act; overuse, depletion, or exhaustion of a resource or species would be seen as a criminal act of violence; overproduction of a resource or a species, such as the human, would be seen as a criminal act of avarice and greed.

3. The primary unit of production would be the self-sufficient community, within a self-regarding bioregion, which would strive to produce all its needs, and essential political and economic decisions would be taken democratically at that level.

4. Consumption would be limited, for the goal of economic life is not the multiplication of wants but the satisfaction of basic needs.

5. Everything produced, and the means of its production, would embody the four cardinal principles of smaller, simpler, cheaper, safer—technology on a human scale, comprehendible, affordable for all, and nonviolent.
6. The only jobs would be those that enhance the worker, contribute to the community, and produce nothing but needed goods—and that means goods, not bads.
7. All people who wish to do so would work, for the purpose of work is not to produce things to satisfy wants but to nourish and develop the individual soul, aiming at fulfilling the highest nature of the human character, including identification with community and the satisfaction of its needs.
8. All economic decisions would be made in accordance with the Buddhist principle, "Cease to do evil; try to do good," and the definition of good would be that which preserves and enhances the integrity, stability, diversity, continuity, and beauty of living species and systems; that which does the contrary is evil. That is, to my mind, the essential moral and intellectual guide to a right and successful bioregional economics.

Local Living Economies
The New Movement for Responsible Business

JUDY WICKS

Issue no. 10 • February 2006

A socially, environmentally, and financially sustainable global economy must be composed of sustainable local economies. Yet, tragically, from American "Main Streets" to villages in developing countries, corporate globalization is causing the decline of local communities, family businesses, family farms, and natural habitats. Wealth and power are consolidating in growing transnational corporations that wield alarming control over many important aspects of our lives—the food we eat, the clothes we wear, the news we hear, and even the government we rely on to protect the common good.

By working cooperatively, locally owned businesses and conscious consumers can create an alternative to corporate globalization that brings power back to our communities by building sustainable local economies—living economies that support both natural and community life. Over the last ten to fifteen years, the socially responsible business (SRB) movement has made great strides in raising consciousness about the responsibility of business to serve the common good, rather than simply increasing profits for the benefit of stockholders. The triple bottom line of people, planet, and profit has become a new measurement of performance for a growing number of companies that consider the needs of all stakeholders—employees, community, consumers, and the natural environment, as well as stockholders—when making business decisions.

Yet, problems have continued to worsen around the globe. All natural systems are in decline, global warming is accelerating, wealth disparity is increasing, and wars over dwindling natural resources pose a growing threat. Clearly a new strategy for building a just and sustainable global economy is crucially needed. While the SRB movement has brought improvement in business practices for many companies, overall business success is still measured by the old paradigm of continuous growth and maximized return on investment. Stockholder expectations and a "grow or die" mentality move companies to expand their brands nationally, competing with and often eliminating community-based businesses around the country and globally. In the end, even progressive companies are often forced to choose undesirable exit strategies when they become too large for purchase by employees, family members, or neighboring businesses with a commitment to the local community.

The forced buyout of Ben & Jerry's, a movement leader and innovator of the multiple bottom line, by the international conglomerate Unilever during the fall of 1999 proved a wake-up call for those who had looked to that company for innovative leadership. Many other model companies in the SRB movement have recently been sold to multinational corporations, adding to the concentration of wealth and power that the movement was intended to combat—Odwalla to Coca-Cola, Cascadian Farms to General Mills, and most recently a large part of Stonyfield Farms to the parent company of Dannon yogurt. The sale of these businesses collectively demonstrates that companies committed to continuous growth and national branding, though financially successful and even environmentally friendly, end up detracting from, rather than contributing to, the creation of a democratic society where ownership, power, and prosperity are widely shared.

While there is important work being done to reform the corporate system by consumer groups and companies within the system, such as Stonyfield and Ben & Jerry's, a second front of the SRB movement has emerged. Rejecting the notion that corporate rule is inevitable, the Local Living Economy movement is building an alternative to corporate globalization—a decentralized global network of local living economies composed of independent, community-based businesses. The new movement focuses attention on issues of scale, ownership, and commitment to place, which the SRB movement has largely neglected. The Local Living Economy movement also demonstrates the importance of working cooperatively outside of individual companies, often with competitors, to build whole economies of triple-bottom-line businesses.

Businesses in local living economies remain human-scale and locally owned, fostering direct, authentic, and meaningful relationships with employees, customers, suppliers, neighbors, and local habitat, adding to the quality of life in our communities. Decentralized ownership spreads wealth more broadly and brings economic power from distant boardrooms to local communities where there is a short distance between business decision-makers and those affected by the decisions. Local living economies spread business models, not brands. Rather than expanding in the conformist, cookie-cutter style of the industrial era, entrepreneurs seek to diversify business ventures, creatively addressing the needs of their community through new business ventures that increase local self-reliance and sustainability. For example, a restaurant owner may start a retail store selling local food products, or a local ice cream company might join with local dairy farmers to start a yogurt company, rather than growing a chain or national brand.

Many new business opportunities lie within the "building blocks" of local living economies—local food systems, renewable energy, alternative transportation, locally designed and made clothing, recycling and reuse, green building, holistic healthcare, eco-friendly cleaning products, independent retail, local arts and culture, neighborhood tourism, and independent media. Addressing the deeper needs of their communities, local business owners can provide more fulfilling jobs, healthier communities, and greater economic security in their region. Success can mean more than growing larger or increasing market share; it can be measured by increasing happiness and well-being, deepening relationships, and expanding creativity, knowledge, and consciousness.

To provide sufficient capital for growing local living economies, the old paradigm of measuring success simply by maximized profits must also change for investors. Traditionally, investors seek the highest and quickest return on investment. But should we not also measure a "return" by long-term social and environmental improvement? In a living economy, investors seek a "living return"—one partially paid by the benefits of living in a healthy, vibrant community. By law, publicly owned companies are required to put the financial interests of stockholders above the needs of all other stakeholders. Therefore, even "socially responsible" funds, though screening out weapons manufacturers and tobacco companies, invest in a system that values profits over people and the planet. By choosing stock market investments, citizens take capital out of local economies and give more power and control to boardrooms in faraway places, where the well-being of local communities is not a priority. By investing our savings in community funds that loan money at affordable rates to small businesses, neighborhood projects, and housing developments, we receive a living return of improving the quality of life in our own communities.

Unlike publicly held corporations, independent companies share the fate of their communities and are free to make decisions in the interests of all the stakeholders. Local business owners are likely to understand that it is in their self-interest to run their companies in a way that benefits their own neighborhood and natural environment. Adam Smith's "invisible hand" of the market works well when the self-interest of the business decision-maker is clearly tied to the well-being of the community. Rather than depending on large corporations for basic needs, which gives up economic power and adds to the environmental costs of global transport, living economies produce basic needs—food, clothing, shelter, and energy—locally and sustainably. This builds community self-reliance, provides new opportunities for ownership and job creation, and keeps capital within the community. What is not available locally is sourced from community-based businesses and small farms in other regions and countries in an exchange that benefits the communities where products and resources originate.

Global interdependence is based on trust and mutual respect rather than exploitive resource extraction and sweatshop labor, and trade is facilitated through an intricate global web of small-to-small, win-win relationships that celebrate what it is to be human. Through global corporate domination, our Western business model, which takes more natural resources and gives off more pollution than the earth can restore, is being spread globally. Corporate monoculture has no sense of place, and the same chain stores and consumer goods are seen around the world. In a system of local living economies, cultural diversity flourishes, local languages are preserved, and what is indigenous to a region is valued for its quality, history, and uniqueness.

Lastly, and perhaps most important, large corporations have historically used militaries to protect their ability to exploit natural resources and cheap labor in less-developed countries, which is often the underlying cause of war. Through equitable and sustainable use of natural resources, local food and energy security, decentralized power and control, and celebration and understanding of cultural differences, local living economies will gradually build the foundation for lasting world peace.

Around the world, people are speaking out against the destructive role of corporate globalization in our lives—from indigenous uprisings in Mexico and farmers' strikes in France, to attacks on McDonald's in India, and mass protests in Seattle, Washington, Genoa, and Cancun. Many people, especially the young, have lost faith in business as a positive force and need a new vision for the constructive role business can play in our communities. Progressive business leaders are uniquely positioned to articulate this new vision, span the gap between the left and right, and direct the energy of concerned citizens, entrepreneurs, and young people toward creating a positive future for our world.

MONEY

Reorienting the current economic system toward local enterprise, community needs, and sustainability will require a multifaceted effort, from changing consumer habits to making major policy changes in the face of entrenched economic interests. Several *Vermont Commons* authors have focused on one aspect of this transformation that they believe to be particularly essential—the need to rethink the role of *money* in the exchange of products and services.

The nature of money is usually taken for granted; it is generally accepted as a neutral, objective medium for marking the value of economic goods. Further, even when it is considered, money proves to be a complex and abstruse concept, involving moral, political, and historical dimensions that defy easy resolution. Any comprehensive analysis of the present crisis, and any viable model of a resilient social order, must wrestle with these issues and provide a thoughtful plan for financing and mediating economic transactions. The articles in this section suggest places to begin this task.

Money and Liberty

Adrian Kuzminski

Issue no. 16 • Autumn 2006

The U.S. monetary system has been a scandal for a long time; whether it can continue much longer without intolerable social, political, and ecological consequences is an open question. Yet most Americans don't have a clue about it. "It is well enough that people of the nation do not understand our banking and monetary system," Henry Ford said, "for if they did, I believe there would be a revolution before tomorrow morning."

Our current monetary system, to be blunt, is an unjustified monopoly granted to private interests to create public money for their private profit. For this they charge the public usurious (extortionary) rates of interest, creating an economic system that unnecessarily transfers wealth from debtors to creditors as it forces often needless and wasteful economic "growth."

The idea that a national currency should be a debt incurred by governments (and therefore taxpayers) to private interests for their profit was first institutionalized with the Bank of England at the end of the seventeenth century, and subsequently developed in the United States by Alexander Hamilton and his successors. Under this scheme, the power to "create" money is granted as a monopoly to a central bank, like the Federal Reserve, which then lends the money so created back to the government at interest in return for government bonds. These bonds are then sold to commercial banks, where they form the collateral for loans to the public, at additional rates of interest. As the agent of the major private banks, the Federal Reserve not only regulates the economy by raising and lowering interest rates to control the money supply and to protect creditors but also guarantees the private banks' monopoly over the further creation of money through fractional reserve lending.

This system, now triumphant worldwide under the rubric of "globalization," with the dollar as the world's reserve currency, has made possible, perhaps more than any other factor, the relentless concentration of wealth into fewer and fewer hands. Yet this money system is mostly ignored by social critics. Crucial to this system is the power given to the central banks and the banking system in general to vary interest rates freely and without limit. Interest charged beyond administrative and risk insurance costs is usurious. Such usurious interest constitutes the income of the banking system, the profit from which goes to the private investors in that system, not to the public. This institutionalization of usury allows the banking system to skim off what is essentially a private tax in return for providing what should be a free public service. It creates a system in which money is scarce and available only at a steep price.

Most Americans believe the Federal Reserve is accountable to the public interest, but nothing could be further from the truth. Although the Governors of the Federal Reserve are presidential appointees confirmed by Congress, when we consider their long fourteen year terms, the byzantine and secretive traditions of the Fed, its lack of any other public accountability (apart from the Chairman's reports to Congress), and the strong Fed role played by commercial banks (who sit both on the Federal Open Market Committee, which sets interest rates, and on the boards of regional Fed branches), it is hardly surprising that the Fed has been able to enjoy a gloss of public accountability while evading public control.

Economic inequality is rooted in a maldistribution of capital. The only access to capital today for those without is to borrow money at interest. Anyone with a mortgage, a car loan, a student loan, or a credit card, is paying a hefty private tax to the banking and financial system for the right to use capital, which, as a public resource, should be freely and fairly available to the public. Being forced to borrow money at interest, individuals and businesses must pay off significant interest charges as well as the principal before they can see any of the fruits of their use of that money. Why should the banking system be allowed the monopolistic privilege, not only of creating money, but of charging excessive interest for the right to do so? Should not the creation of money, essential to the public welfare, be a proper matter for government, assuming democratic, publically accountable governments (which we currently do not have)?

This burden of usurious interest is the real engine behind economic "growth." Since borrowers must repay interest on top of principal before realizing any benefit from a loan, they are forced to additional labor and production. Money borrowed at 6 percent, compounded annually, will accumulate interest equal to the principal in only twelve years. This is insignificant at small amounts, but if I borrow $100,000 at 6 percent, it means I must pay my creditor a total of $200,000 within twelve years, which amounts to $16,666 a year. By contrast, at a nominal 1 percent interest rate, it would take 70 years before the interest burden equaled the principal, and it would cost only $2857 a year over that period to repay the $100,000 loan.

There is no reason that interest must be charged for the creation of money. There is no need to "rent" money from private bankers when we could just as easily create it ourselves at nominal cost. To do so would constitute a political revolution of the first magnitude. Traditional attempts to meet the challenges of social and ecological exploitation (socialism, communism, environmentalism) have failed insofar as they have not understood the underlying usurious monetary system that drives "growth." By contrast, nonusurious monetary policies in the hands of democratically accountable governments serving the public interest would be able, for the first time, to correlate the use of money with social needs.

The Constitution prohibits the states not only from coining money but from emitting bills of credit or making "anything but gold and silver Coin a Tender in Payment of Debts." (Article I, Sec. 10) Given the failure of Federal monetary policy, its ruinous effects in exploiting persons and nature, and its key role in creating great relative wealth for a few and great relative poverty for many, it is incumbent to insist upon a devolution of monetary policy to the local level, whether this occurs through reform of Federal monetary policy, through Constitutional Amendment returning monetary policy to the various states, or through the secession of various states from the Union. It is essential to this end to understand how a nonusurious, publically accountable currency might work.

The most thoroughgoing and ingenious system of such a currency was thought out before the Civil War by Edward Kellogg (1790–1858), and is perhaps stated best in his posthumous work, *A New Monetary System* (1861, reprint 1970). Kellogg was a forerunner of free bankers and populists who mostly missed, however, his central idea of a decentralized non (or nominal) interest currency. He proposed to establish local public credit banks, one in each county. These banks, Federally mandated but locally run, would offer nominal (1 percent) interest loans to resident citizens. Kellogg envisioned land as collateral, but credit worthiness could be based, as it is today, on one's potential earning power. Once lent out, Kellogg's public credit dollars would flow into circulation, providing the basis of a new currency, backed by the productive labor power of individual borrowers. Individuals and private banks would be free to reloan public credit money at higher rates of interest, but the availability of nominal 1 percent loans would undercut their ability to charge usurious rates.

The beauty of Kellogg's system is its decentralized self-regulating nature. Instead of credit issued on a top-down basis from a central bank to national banks, and then to regional and local banks, all charging usurious rates of interest for the privilege of borrowing money they create without effort, credit would be issued by local banks directly to local citizens without interest on the basis of the economic prospects of those citizens. These prospects would vary considerably from place to place, with some areas needing and creating more currency than others. But whatever currency is created would be equivalent to any other. The solvency of local public credit banks would be guaranteed by adequate reserve requirements, and the money supply would be stabilized by repayment of loans as they came due. The interchangeability of public credit bank notes would ensure a wide circulation for the new money.

Kellogg's public credit banks are a form of free banking, but done as an interest-free public service rather than as a private for-profit enterprise. Capital would become cheaply and widely available at local public credit banks to anyone minimally creditworthy. Students, for instance, could take out public credit loans instead of student loans. Public credit banks could offer no-interest credit cards. Homebuyers could take out public credit loans instead of mortgages. Small business (sole proprietorships and partnerships) could take out public credit loans instead of borrowing money from commercial banks. Corporations, however, would not be able to borrow from public credit banks, whose purpose is to serve the interest of flesh-and-blood citizens, not corporate entities. The latter would have to borrow on the secondary debt markets, at necessarily higher but still reasonable interest rates. No public credit currency would be issued at any other than the local level. National standards would determine uniform rules of creditworthiness, minimum reserve requirements, local public management, and a fixed nominal (1 percent) rate of interest. A local public credit bank issuing too many bad loans, or refusing loans to otherwise creditworthy citizens, would be subject to legal penalties, including closure and reorganization.

Notice the profound implications of Kellogg's money system. There would be NO controlling central bank, no centrally controlled issuance of currency. The banking system would be set on its head. A bottom-up system of capital creation would replace the old top-down system. Most fundamentally, credit would be made available to the general public at a nominal (1 percent) interest rate, instead of being made available selectively to large commercial banks at high rates, who in turn lend it to others at even higher or usurious rates. With interest eliminated as a factor in monetary policy, the principle engine of wasteful and compulsive economic growth would be eliminated. There would be no need to labor frenetically to overcome the interest burden. Economic investment would be possible on the merits of the situation, not on an abnormally forced rate of return. A sustainable economics would become possible, perhaps for the first time. And, not least, the widespread availability of capital to individuals (unknown since the closing of the Western frontier in America in 1890) would do much to overcome the vast and growing discrepancies of wealth that exist because of usurious interest rates.

Kellogg's model of a decentralized but democratically regulated monetary system is worth pondering, not only for financial and economic reasons, but for political ones as well. Democracy is necessarily a decentralized, face-to-face affair, and it cannot be successful unless its citizens personally enjoy relative economic independence in a relatively decentralized economy. For only then can they come together as equals in a free community. Most citizens today, however, are economic dependents, having been forced into debt peonage by usurious interest rates for most of the necessities of life (education, housing, transportation, etc.). Not being free economic agents, they cannot oppose the harsh and destructive economic system that oppresses them. A key step in developing such opposition is the realization that a decentralized, self-regulating, noninterest monetary system, of the sort outlined by Kellogg, can provide the basis for widespread economic independence.

Sovereignty and the Money Problem
A New Beginning

Charles Eisenstein

Issue no. 41 • Spring 2011

In the last several decades many independence movements around the world have been successful and the number of sovereign nations has vastly increased. Have these movements really achieved what they wanted? Or is the goal of political independence a kind of escape valve for aspirations that seek something deeper, something more substantial, than the symbols and trappings of the sovereign state? After all, many nations today find themselves to be sovereign in name only, their actions constrained by global politics and economics.

One of the most potent constraints on a nation's freedom to act is the global money system. In the Eurozone, for example, EMU rules dictate many economic and even social policies. Elsewhere, it is IMF conditions that do the dictating, or, in the case of large states with their own currencies, it is the bond markets. If a country implements policies that are perceived as unfriendly to investors, or as likely to reduce commodity exports, it is "punished" by capital flight, higher interest rates on its debt, runs on the currency, and so on. Like it or not, nations are forced to be more competitive: to cut wages and social spending, to orient toward commodity exports, to facilitate the exploitation of natural resources. No government, liberal or conservative, is immune to these pressures, which is one reason why liberal and conservative policies around the world have so converged as to become nearly indistinguishable. Even supposedly sovereign nations don't enjoy true self-determination.

Real political sovereignty requires economic sovereignty: local control over the exploitation and circulation of resources, along with a moderate degree of local self-sufficiency. Unfortunately, governments that defy international finance and seek to establish true economic sovereignty—for example, by protecting the domestic economy, limiting the exploitation of natural resources, and protecting workers and the environment—incur not only the above-mentioned economic punishments but are labeled "leftist" and subjected to political pressure, too. First their politicians are bribed, directly or indirectly, to adopt more "growth-friendly" or "free market" policies. Then, the government finds itself facing foreign-funded "democratic" opposition, hostility from the corporate media, or even a military coup, embargo, bombing, or invasion. Will a newly independent nation be exempt from the pressures that existing nations already face?

Whether it is a nation, a state, or a locality, political sovereignty is largely meaningless if its economy remains a helpless appendage of the global financial system. Today nearly every place is a colony, importing finished products that it is helpless to produce itself, and devoting its raw materials, skills, and/or labor power to the needs of distant markets. Fortunately, the financial and political system that enforces this status quo is in crisis. Its dissolution offers new possibilities for creating true local self-determination.

In theory at least, one of the most powerful ways to restore and protect local economy, and by extension some degree of political autonomy, is through local currency. Local currencies encourage businesses to source products locally and give them a competitive advantage against national companies that will not accept payments in local currency. Unlike dollars, which quickly get sucked away to corporate headquarters and Wall Street, local money stays local. The more businesses that accept it, the more useful it becomes, and the more businesses will want to accept it. In theory, once it reaches critical mass it should be self-reinforcing.

Yet local currencies still occupy a very marginal position in the economy. Most attempts at launching them founder within the first year or two. The reasons for their relative failure illuminate a future path toward authentic local self-determination. Anyone hoping to launch a local currency in a modern economy faces a Catch-22. Local businesses won't want to accept local currency unless they can use it to purchase labor, raw materials, or other inputs. For a local currency to thrive there must therefore be local producers who meet the needs of other local producers, who meet the needs of yet others . . . and eventually completing the circle. Otherwise, what often happens is that the currency accumulates in the hands of whatever idealistic enterprises choose to accept it.

In other words, to be successful, a local currency requires a functioning local economy, which is today a rarity because of the financial system that encompasses all. Without limits on capital flows, local producers are at the whim of global commodity prices. A restaurant might want to source food locally, but often the local farmer cannot compete with distant, subsidized megafarms enjoying high efficiencies of scale and market leverage. In short, local economies can only develop if they are financially protected from global commodity markets—for example, through a local currency with limited convertibility. But a local currency cannot be successful in the absence of a local economy. Catch-22.

To exit this dilemma requires a purposive political decision to nurture local economy. Local currency is a key part of this effort, which must also include local credit mechanisms, economic infrastructure, fiscal and tax policy, and so forth. It is particularly helpful if local currency is acceptable as legal tender for payment of taxes. (That is unheard of today; on the contrary, complementary currency transactions are subject to sales and income taxes payable only in dollars, forcing people to operate in the national currency whether they want to or not.) The successful local currencies that proliferated in the 1930s were issued mostly by local governments themselves. The reaction of central governments was uniformly hostile—understandably, since currency issue has become a key prerogative, perhaps a defining prerogative, of a sovereign state. Most local currencies were banned in short order.

The other circumstance under which local currency use becomes widespread is during times of social turmoil, war, or the collapse of the national currency. Then all kinds of informal currencies spring up: cigarettes, vodka, gasoline, gold, and so forth. In normal times, however, only the national currency is widely used.

Today it is becoming increasingly apparent that normal times are ending. We are witnessing the slow-motion disintegration of the financial system that has dominated our world for the past seventy years. In the wake of its collapse and the accompanying social turmoil, opportunities will arise to implement new kinds of money systems, rebuild local economies, and reestablish local sovereignty.

For a preview of how it might unfold, we can look to the Argentinian economic crisis of 2001–2002. Provincial governments ran out of pesos to pay employees and contractors, so they paid them in low-denomination bearer bonds instead (one-peso bonds, five-peso bonds, etc.). Businesses and their employees accepted them readily, even though nobody really expected the bonds would ever be redeemable for hard currency, because they could be used to pay provincial taxes and fees. Acceptability for payment of taxes enhanced the social perception of its value, and, as with all money, value and the perception of value are identical. The currencies circulated far beyond their region of issue. They revived economic activity, which had ground to a halt because, after all, people still had the capacity to produce goods and services that other people needed, lacking only the means to make exchanges. At the same time, Argentina's government repudiated its foreign debt, temporarily cutting it off from imports and increasing the need for local self-reliance. At that point the IMF stepped in with emergency loans to induce the country to keep its debts on the books.

In 2009, the state of California came within a hair's breadth of doing nearly the same thing. Faced with a budget crisis that rendered it unable to pay tax refunds and money owed to contractors, the state began issuing IOUs instead. Similar to bonds, these were to be redeemable for their face value plus interest at a later date, or they could be used to pay state taxes. The program was terminated after a month or so, as the state obtained short-term loans from banks. Although the IOUs were denominated in U.S. dollars, banks threatened not to redeem them, which would have made them into a separate currency. The episode shows that there are forces just below the surface pushing toward a different money system. It can happen nearly overnight. Unthinkable in normal times (i.e., the normality of endless growth, which will never come again), local, government-issued currency could soon become common sense.

At present we are living, if no longer in normal times, at least in the inertia of the habits of those times. Accordingly, local currencies still face an uphill battle, languishing without government support. Nonetheless, the efforts of local-currency activists over the past twenty years have not been in vain. They have created a model—many models in fact— to be applied when the next crisis erupts and the unthinkable becomes common sense. Already, cities and states are on the verge of bankruptcy. When, as in some cities already, there is not even the money to pay the firefighters, it may not be long before we adopt Argentinian and 1930s-style experiments on a wide scale.

But this is only a beginning. We face today a multiplicity of converging crises, not just economic. Of particular relevance to local sovereignty are the energy crisis and the ecological crisis, which call us to reduce our dependence on long-distance transport, and to produce and consume in a way that respects local ecosystems. In today's money system, producers profit by exporting their costs onto the social and natural commons, using up the wealth that properly belongs to all. This includes the soil, the aquifers, the land, mineral resources, biological diversity, and the capacity of air and water to absorb waste. While some of these forms of commonwealth, such as the CO2 commons, are global in nature, most are local or regional and should therefore be held under local or regional stewardship. In the current money system, that is nearly impossible, even for sovereign nations. The pressure exerted by global finance and the commodity economy to convert every possible bit of social and natural capital into money is too great to resist.

That is likely to soon change. Our money system cannot exist without economic growth; without growth, wealth quickly concentrates in the hands of the few, and social tumult soon follows. Today, growth is reaching its limits as the commons is exhausted and as human consciousness shifts toward a desire to protect and heal the earth. Local and bioregional governments will have a dual opportunity: to reclaim sovereignty over their economies and stewardship over the natural commons under their jurisdiction.

Ultimately, political sovereignty means very little if outside corporations can strip-mine a society's natural and social capital—its resources, skills, and labor—and export them to global markets. Meaningful sovereignty is economic sovereignty. As the tide of economic globalization peaks and reverses, we have the chance to regrow our social structures so that we become no longer mere inhabitants and exploiters of the cultural-biological regions in which we live, but their organic extensions, their lovers, protectors, and stewards. Isn't that what we are really seeking, when we speak of sovereignty?

Local Currency
A Revolution That Sounds Like a Whisper

AMY M. KIRSCHNER

Issue no. 16 • Autumn 2006

> When the French and Russian revolutions overthrew the estab-
> lished orders in their countries (in 1786 and 1917, respectively), they
> changed just about everything, but not their monetary systems.
> — Bernard A. Lietaer, *Of Human Wealth*

Vermont has a long history of challenging the status quo and being fiercely politically independent. As we look to the future, especially as the global economy forces new dependence, it is imperative that we strive for an economic independence to match our political independence.

Our economic system inherently requires competition and expansion. The need for an expanding competitive marketplace necessitates never ending growth and environmental harm, constant fear of economic loss, and the sad reality that many are left with nothing. Few are the people who see that we can change our economic system to reflect higher values: cooperation, stewardship of the environment, and an equal voice for all.

What would an economic revolution look like? It is imperative that we begin with how money works because that is a basis of what determines our economy. Greatly simplified, the creation of money occurs when banks issue loans to borrowers—the bank is not loaning money that others have deposited, as many people think, but is actually writing a check for money that did not previously exist. Since banks can loan more money than they actually have, needing only "fractional reserves," each loan is actually creating money. When banks issue loans, they charge interest. At current rates, for every $100 that is created, $106 is owed. Because of the economic system we have, at every moment of time more money is owed than is in current circulation. This means that there will always be economic losers and that for most people and businesses to meet their debts the economy must continue to grow. The never ending fear of failure to meet obligations naturally leads to competition and the belief that environmental stewardship and social equity are secondary to economic growth.

Another facet of our economic system is that money is global and can travel quickly worldwide. But with the advent of the global marketplace where dollars consistently seek out the highest rates of return, there are many projects that are in the community's best interest that are not funded because they are not profitable in the short term. Examples of these projects are investments in local food production, renewable energy, affordable housing, durable clothing, education and school infrastructure, and caring for the needy.

We have the ability to create a new system with new values inherent in it. A network of local and complementary currencies, whose money is created interest free, would dramatically alter our national behavior and culture. A wealth of dormant and disenfranchised capacity would be unleashed as citizens became engaged in maximizing creative utilization of already existing local resources. This is not a dream; it has happened thousands of times in the past and today there are over 4,000 local currencies now strengthening local economies around the world.

Imagine the local pride and feeling of empowerment that would be created if communities recovering from natural disasters could start the recovery by simply facilitating the exchange of needed goods and services through a new locally-based monetary system, thus harnessing contributions and abilities of their local citizens. Or imagine the boost to local farmers and merchants and the decrease in fossil-fuel usage if there existed a currency in wide use that could only be spent locally. Globalization and national currencies have tipped the balance in favor of large corporations and centralized distribution without accountability. By contrast, a local currency reempowers a community to issue credit to local businesses, institutions, farmers, and individuals to undertake projects that enhance local quality of life, reflect community values, and build long-term community wealth and well-being. Local currencies also bring back the competitive edge that favors local businesses, local decisions, and local identity.

Local markets cannot always be 100 percent self-sufficient. It does not make common sense for each locality to produce its own computers or automobiles, and dollars will always be necessary to buy U.S. postage stamps. However, we have gone too far in assuming that one currency and type of monetary system can fulfill *all* the needs of our community. We need multiple levels of currency for our multiple needs. We need local currencies, to increase local transactions at the retail and individual level and to create a new cooperative economy where communities can become more self-reliant by providing for basic needs like food, energy, healthcare, and personal services. We need a national currency to purchase items that cannot be produced here.

The Burlington Currency Project (BCP) envisions a network of local currencies throughout Vermont connected through an electronic "mutual credit clearing system" where businesses in Rutland or Montpelier or Brattleboro could accept their own local currency from their customers, deposit it in the electronic system, and then use that electronic system to order goods from their suppliers from other parts of the state. We envision a system to encourage informal care services that track hours of volunteerism (called "Time Dollars," currently operating in hundreds of communities in twenty-two countries) so that a high school student who "deposits" an hour mowing a neighbor's lawn over the summer can "withdraw" an hour's worth of tutoring at exam time. We envision the community frequently issuing the currency to create interest-free loans in order to fund projects and entrepreneurial ventures and making the repayment easier than bank loans in dollars that charge high rates of interest.

We believe that in order to have a significant impact on the community, we need to dream big. We will not believe that we have arrived until 10 percent of all Vermont's economic transactions are conducted with local currencies and all businesses use it, until city governments accept a portion of their property tax payments in local currencies and pay a portion of their employees' wages with it, and until it has become so ingrained in the local culture that citizens don't think twice about it and tourists come to experience it. There is nothing and no one to fight against in this movement. There is simply self-examination, education, discussion, and ultimately choice. It is a quiet and peaceful revolution one exchange at a time. It is people taking back control of their own destinies.

UPDATE (August 2012):

Burlington Currency Project ceased operations in 2007. As part of my Master's Thesis at the University of Vermont, I wrote a postmortem on the project that was published in the *International Journal of Community*

Research. The major problems were the accounting difficulties in attempting to switch a fiat currency over to mutual credit and the management and funding structures of the organization itself. (See: http://ijccr.files .wordpress.com/2012/04/ijccr-2011-kirschner.pdf.)

I am still working on the vision on a mutual credit engine to support Vermont businesses and citizens. In 2010, I launched the Vermont Businesses for Social Responsibility Marketplace program, which is an online business to business mutual credit platform for over 1500 local businesses. You can find more information at http://marketplace.vbsr.org.

There has been much more success and trading volume with the mutual credit model than with a paper-based fiat currency. While a paper currency is still desirable for day-to-day Main Street transactions, I would advise that the issuance of it be tied to mutual credit accounting.

The Buck Slows Here
Slow Me the Money, Vermont

Woody Tasch

Issue no. 35 • Spring 2010

We must bring money back down to earth.

It might have sounded far-fetched even a year ago. But today, surrounded by the politics of a trillion-dollar bailout, it has a different ring. It has the ring of common sense in a world that is coming to realize that there is such a thing as intermediation that is too complex and money that is too fast.

There is such a thing as money that is too fast.

Money that is too fast is money that has become so detached from people, place, and the activities that it is financing that not even the experts understand it fully. Money that is too fast makes it impossible to say whether the world economy is going through a correction in the credit markets, triggered by the sub-prime mortgage crisis, or whether we are teetering on the edge of something much deeper and more challenging, tied to petrodollars, derivatives, hedge funds, futures, arbitrage, and a byzantine hypersecuritized system of intermediation that no quant, no program trader, no speculator, no investment bank CEO can any longer fully understand or manage.

Just as no one can say precisely where the meat in a hamburger comes from (it may contain meat from as many as a hundred or a thousand animals), no one can say where the money in this or that security has come from, where it is going, what is behind it, whether—if it were to be "stopped" and, like a hot potato, held by someone for more than a few instants—it represents any intrinsic or real value.

Money that is too fast creates an environment in which, when questioned about the outcome of the credit crisis, former Treasury Secretary Robert Rubin can only respond, "No one knows." The buck, it seems, knows not where to stop.

So, we hold congressional hearings. We conduct SEC investigations. We undertake forensic accounting on the Madoffs and Lehmans and

AIGs of the world. Meanwhile, "Planet Finance," to paraphrase Niall Ferguson's words, "continues to dwarf Planet Earth." Even in this moment of financial uncertainty and economic contraction, trillions of dollars a day zoom through cyberspace, financing everything from smokestacks in Chongqing to parking lots in Las Vegas to frost-resistant fish genes in tomatoes.

What is to be done? First, we must acknowledge our addiction—and let us call it an addiction, this obsession with Buying Low and Selling High, this dependence on petrodollars, this insistence that a society composed of individuals who produce little but consume much can long be prosperous and fulfilled.

Then, we must recognize that there is no Money Czar who can arrest money's ever-accelerating trajectory around our ever-shrinking planet. No one person or group has the power to make the buck stop. But we can, we must come to realize, make it . . . slow.

A growing number of entrepreneurs and investors—Investors' Circle, the Business Alliance for Local, Living Economies (BALLE), the Transition movement, Slow Food — have already begun doing just that. These and other initiatives are supporting new ways of thinking about social entrepreneurship, local economies, and the centrality of cultural and biological diversity to economic health. They are early adopters in the shift from capital markets that maximize extraction and consumption to capital markets that prioritize restoration and preservation.

In this shift, we will need alternative stock exchanges for investors and entrepreneurs who are concerned about "slow, small, and local," and who are ready for an alternative to doing the same thing over and over again with their investment dollars, hoping for a different outcome. We will need a new generation of financial intermediaries who can steer meaningful amounts of capital to the soil of the economy, creating new benchmarks, new measures of investment success. We will need to affirm the centrality of local food systems to the health of our communities and bioregions. We will need municipal bonds dedicated to sustainable food enterprises. We will need to invest in small farms and create access for the next generation of organic farmers. We will need to accelerate the expansion of Community Supported Agriculture. We will need to build local processing infrastructure to reduce vulnerability to disruption of food supplies and minimize risks of widespread food contamination.

There are millions of jobs to be created here, and billions of dollars of slow returns—returns that don't sound so far-fetched in comparison to the risks associated with fast money. Not to mention the satisfaction, pleasure, and improved quality of life that comes from putting our money to work here, where we live, where we can see what it is doing, understand it, and benefit directly from that which our investment produces. If bailout billions are iodine in the wounds of global financial markets, and venture-capital billions are fertilizer for the consumer economy, let's set about the task of creating nurture-capital billions—a new financial sector for the twenty-first century.

ENERGY

One of the major global developments that galvanized the *Vermont Commons* group was the dawning awareness that petroleum production was approaching its all-time maximum extent and could, from this point forward, only decline, despite increasing demand in both advanced industrial nations and the rising economies of China, India, and other populous nations. Starting around the beginning of the new century, journalists and oil industry analysts including Thom Hartmann, Richard Heinberg, Kenneth Deffeyes, and Colin Campbell began explaining this phenomenon of "peak oil" and cataloging its very dramatic implications for the global economy, politics, and modern civilization itself. James Howard Kunstler (*The Long Emergency*, 2005), John Michael Greer (*The Long Descent*, 2008), and Heinberg (particularly, *The End of Growth*, 2011) argued convincingly that the end of cheap fossil-fuel energy would profoundly change every aspect of modern society. If their analysis is correct, the world economic system will be *forced* to abandon its aims of global domination and perpetual growth and yield instead to a more localized way of life.

The essays in this section demonstrate that energy issues are closely intertwined with the other concerns we are exploring. Money, food, governance, technology, imperial expansion, and even healthcare and cultural endeavors will be severely influenced when the cost of energy soars. Our call for a transition to a more localized, decentralized, resilient society is not only a moral vision but an eminently practical one. Peak oil exposes the deep structural flaws of globalized empire.

A skeptical reader may wonder: Is this for real? Or are we just conjuring the specter of peak oil as a scare tactic (similar to the global warming "conspiracy") to promote a countercultural agenda? Apologists for free markets, endless growth, and globalization dismiss peak oil writers as "doomers" and assert that capitalism, technology, and ingenuity will prevail. There is, they say, plenty more oil (and natural gas) to be discovered and extracted. Indeed, these essays were written before the recent expansion of "fracking" to tap a seemingly huge reservoir of natural gas that lies under American soil, and before ambitious new offshore oil drilling in the Arctic (which is, ironically, more accessible thanks to climate change) and off the coast of Brazil. However, the evidence and analysis provided in the peak-oil literature speak for themselves, and when we consider that evidence without having a significant financial and political stake in the corporate empire, it is quite compelling. I invite readers to explore this literature for themselves and reach their own conclusions.

Even if there are still untapped reservoirs of fossil fuels, another compelling body of evidence provided by climate research strongly suggests that we need to keep them in the ground rather than release their carbon into the atmosphere. As the Transition movement has emphasized, peak oil and climate change together constitute an extremely formidable challenge to business as usual.

Powering Vermont's Future by Embracing the Peak-Oil Challenge

CARL ETNIER *and* ANNIE DUNN WATSON

Issue no. 22 • Mud Season 2008

Oil. We're using it up like there's no tomorrow. But there is.

Why is it, then, that nobody wants to talk about peak oil? We're willing to discuss climate change; even send a tripartisan proposal to the governor in an attempt to move Vermont toward a less fossil-fuel driven energy portfolio. But the "P" word hardly ever gets any press. At what cost, this silence?

Peak oil, as many readers of *Vermont Commons* know, occurs when world oil production reaches its peak and starts declining. U.S. oil production peaked in 1971 and is now at about half of what it was then. The resulting gap between production and consumption has been filled by increasing imports from other countries; we now import about two thirds of the oil we use. The actual point at which the world's oil production will decline is in contention; what we do know is that, when world oil production begins declining, there will be no other oil-rich planet nearby to begin importing from.

Earlier this year, the U.S. Government Accountability Office released a report that concluded, "[T]here is no coordinated federal strategy for reducing uncertainty about the peak's timing or mitigating its consequences." Sadly, Vermont has no strategy either, and we are even more vulnerable than the United States as a whole. Vermont imports 100 percent of its oil and is at the end of a long supply chain that begins as far away as Saudi Arabia or Nigeria.

Why should we care? The cheap, abundant energy that has fueled Vermont's economy, heated our homes, and propelled us daily among home, work, and play is about to disappear—not the oil itself, but its affordability. As the era of cheap oil becomes a memory, activities that rely heavily on oil (transportation, agricultural imports, leisure travel) are likely to be scaled back or cease. Whole sectors of the Vermont economy are likely to disappear. How many people will fly or drive here to leaf-peep or ski, with gas at $5 or $10 a gallon and/or the world economy in a recession or depression?

Could natural gas, coal, nuclear power, and renewable energy plug the gap left by decreasing oil availability? Natural gas is also near peak; coal contributes more to climate change than oil does per Btu of energy; nuclear power, likely to remain part of energy portfolios everywhere, has no long-term solution to storing high-level waste and no solutions to the risk of weapons proliferation and terrorism; and renewables cannot provide the sheer amount of power that has been exploited by burning half the world's recoverable stocks of oil. (For example, hydrogen can be made by using electricity to split water molecules into hydrogen and oxygen. Powering a single daily New York–to–London round-trip 747 flight with hydrogen generated by this method would require 400 wind turbines the size of those recently approved for Sheffield.)

Such profound and imminent changes cry out for energetic preparation. Unfortunately, most people don't even know what peak oil is, and state leadership is not trying to educate them. We need to get the word out, to ride like Paul Revere to the corners of the state and shout "Peak Oil Is Coming!" Except our task is much more difficult than Revere's; the citizens on the roads to Lexington and Concord in 1775 already understood who the British were and what the consequences could be of redcoats on the march.

Unlike Revere, we need to prepare people by explaining to individuals and local groups why peak oil is important. It's especially important to talk to people who are willing to start writing letters to the editor, calling in to radio shows, and otherwise creating more awareness. Another way is to talk to leaders directly—both in government and in the private sector, including the press. This latter strategy—combined with the lack of response to peak oil at the state government level—has prompted the creation of the Vermont Peak Oil Report, being prepared by members of the Vermont Peak Oil Political Action Group with the intention of delivering it to the legislators early session 2008. We are cautiously optimistic about the results of this endeavor.

Once people are aware of the challenges associated with peak oil, possible responses vary. Some people simply despair. Among the constructive responses, most are aimed at finding more oil or oil substitutes, or learning to live with less. At their extreme, supply-side policies are aimed at continuing the steady growth in dependence on oil or oil substitutes. For example, drill for oil in the Arctic National Wildlife Refuge or turn coal into liquid fuel. Taken alone, supply-side responses are short-sighted attempts to fill an expanding void. The amount of new natural gas and oil production that must be brought on line by 2015 to compensate for declines in existing oil fields and meet business-as-usual growth is equivalent to ten new Saudi Arabias, or seventy-one Arctic National Wildlife Refuges!

Demand-side responses acknowledge that we humans exercise a lot more control over our demand for oil than we do over the supply of oil or its substitutes. Demand-side responses include such things as investing transportation monies into public transit rather than building new highways, and promoting local agriculture, which cuts down on the diesel-powered miles food travels.

Given the scope of the challenge, we're putting our money on the demand-side approach and in-state production of renewable energy. Since Vermont is 100 percent dependent on imports of fossil fuels, we also see a need for supply-side responses at the local or regional levels, not to continue growth in energy use but to provide us with an alternative to dependence on the global fossil-fuel marketplace.

"Relocalization" is the frame that most members of the Vermont Peak Oil Network have adopted to describe their work. Relocalization emphasizes strengthening social and economic communities close to home. It keeps the means and benefits of production and decision-making in the community, creating jobs and reducing the need for transportation of goods and people. For example, buy your food from local farmers and bakers instead of national chains that source ingredients from China. Heat your home with wood grown nearby instead of oil from the Middle East, and superinsulate your home so there's enough wood grown in Vermont to keep all of us warm. Instead of sending money out of state to fuel your car for a long commute, live close to your job and bicycle or walk there. Encourage the development of sustainable local enterprises within your community.

There are many sectors in which relocalization of goods and services makes sense and would reduce Vermont's demand for oil: land use planning; conservation work; natural resources management/restoration; organic food production/distribution; place-based education; public transportation planning/enhancement (including rail); sustainable forestry and related products (management/manufacturing/distribution); green building and design; energy conservation and efficiency; local entertainment; nontoxic clothing and textiles manufacturing (employing growers, artisans, weavers, seamstresses, and entrepreneurs); conflict resolution and local health services; emergency preparedness; community-generated energy; citizen government; intergenerational care programs; citizen media; and locally owned businesses and services of every sort. Relocalization strengthens people's ties to one another and the land; it elicits collaboration rather than competitiveness. Relocalization outwits peak oil, and a good many other things as well.

Cheap energy has allowed us to seek jobs and interests apart from our communities, reducing our time for community life. No wonder Americans are among the loneliest of the world's citizens. In *Deep Economy* (2007), Bill McKibben describes how self-reported happiness peaked in the United States in the 1950s and has declined ever since, despite a tripling of our national wealth. He blames much of the decline on the loss of contact with other people, which parallels the growth in automobile ownership and suburban sprawl. In Vermont, the additional pressure of local jobs disappearing creates its own special problems; dependence on distant jobs (and therefore cars) grew as job opportunities at home dwindled. New economic opportunities on a community scale are needed: good jobs, with dignity, right here at home.

Relocalization offers the opportunity to create economies and policies as if friendships and communities mattered, and gives individuals more control over the decisions that shape their lives. Supporting relocalization can also help people accept, even embrace, one of the keys to a transition to a postpeak world: buying and using less stuff. "Put down your Playstations and get to know your neighbors" could be a rallying cry. Or, as the Center for the New American Dream puts it, make time for "More of What Matters."

There is no magic elixir, no silver-bullet approach to the successful mitigation of peak oil. One doomed attempt at a silver bullet is what Richard Heinberg calls the "Last One Standing" response, a military-industrial grab for control of remaining resources. A better alternative is a combination of local responses, both individual and collective. Once people are aware of the peak-oil challenge, there are many things they can do immediately, like start growing more of their own food, insulate their homes, reacquaint themselves with their neighbors, install wood heat, build up their bicycling muscles, etc. But individuals alone cannot meet all the challenges; we need to respond collectively, through good policy, informed by and responsive to citizen input.

It's time to start a conversation about how we as a state are going to respond to peak oil. In Brattleboro, the selectboard has authorized an eleven-member Peak Oil Task Force to educate itself about the nature and consequences of peak oil, and to recommend mitigation strategies as appropriate. The Task Force is a logical and necessary extension on a continuum of community engagement that Post Oil Solutions, the local peak oil and relocalization group, has been involved with for more than two years. Such efforts have worked in other places. The city council of Portland, Oregon, appointed a twelve-person Peak Oil Task Force, which issued a report in March urging Portland to "Act big, act now." Recommendations included reducing oil and natural gas consumption by 50 percent over the next twenty-five years, and they include strategies for doing that. This is the type of fundamental shift in thinking that creates effective responses to the peak-oil challenge, and we hope that the Vermont Peak Oil Report will offer the same opportunity to Vermont.

We recommend that a Peak Oil Task Force be formed here in Vermont, to examine the consequences of peak oil for Vermonters and to recommend response strategies. It should, like the Governor's Commission on Climate Change, be drawn from a cross section of Vermont interests. It should also include many people already involved in relocalization efforts, who know what they entail and how valuable they are. Let's, as a state, recognize the scope of the peak-oil challenge and coordinate our strategies to mitigate its consequences. And, as individuals, let's take up our civic responsibilities and create resilient communities right where we live.

Peak oil is everybody's challenge.

The Way of All Empires

The United States on the Eve of Peak Oil

A book review of *Confronting Collapse: The Crisis of Energy and
Money in a Post-Peak Oil World* by Michael C. Ruppert

Ian Baldwin

Issue no. 35 • Spring 2010

For me, Michael Ruppert is the Paul Revere of our present moment in history. Revere risked his life to carry news and vital communiqués to the leaders of the burgeoning secessionist movement in Boston all the way southward to New York and Philadelphia. On his historic night of "alarming" the countryside en route to the Lexington homes of the secessionist leaders Samuel Adams and John Hancock, a sentry confronted him and asked Revere not to make so much noise. "Noise!" exclaimed Revere, "you'll have noise enough before long."

Like Revere before him, Ruppert is a dedicated, hard-riding messenger, who has risked his life to bear news vital to the survival of a society grown suddenly global. Of course, Ruppert's message is not about the dreaded approach of the redcoats, but a far larger, far more formidable, and yet strangely less visible, "enemy" known to some by the name of Peak Oil. Or, perhaps more accurately, Peak Oil and Peak Money.

Ruppert describes his purpose as an activist-writer thus: "to impart to as many individual human beings as possible the gut-level awareness of the magnitude of the crisis we face, and to enable those who do understand to prepare to face it, free of denial and with open eyes." It is fortuitous that a filmmaker of Chris Smith's consummate skill has given us a riveting hour-and-twenty-minute window into Ruppert's mind and soul in *Collapse*, which began as a project about peak oil and ended up as a film featuring the man who made the subject his cause célèbre.

Although he may not yet be a household name, Michael C. Ruppert's first book, *Crossing the Rubicon: The Decline of the American Empire at the End of the Age of Oil* (2004), a complex and labyrinthine tour of the multichambered basement of imperial power, sold more than 100,000 copies.

Rubicon became the Rosetta Stone for those who sought to deconstruct the most impenetrable, disguised machinations of power on the global stage and provided its readers with a veritable map of the post–9/11 world.

The phenomenon of peak oil has only recently gained consensus among a broad range of experts, despite being discussed and argued about for at least two decades. It is not about running out of oil, a common misconception. It is about running out of cheap oil. That is the peg on which the peak-oil story hangs. And it is quite a story. Ruppert writes early on in *Confronting Collapse*: "The edifice of human civilization . . . is built upon cheap oil." He then adds, "There is no combination of alternative energies anywhere . . . that will sustain the structure built by [cheap] oil and fossil fuels." It turns out the American Dream is negotiable after all. (Or soon will be.)

Unlike money, or credit, which may be and is being loaned into limitless existence by the central bankers 24-7, energy sources are bounded. And yet, as Ruppert insists, "Money has no value without energy to back it up." This essential and exquisite insight into the relationship between energy and money is either ignored or glossed over by nearly every economist who advises hapless governments, national and local.

"Energy, not money," claims Ruppert, "is the root of all economic activity . . . the equivalent of free slave labor for industrial civilization." And what a source of "free" labor it has been for those of us who have lived and live in the last and present centuries! One $2.69 gallon of gasoline yields us 500 slave hours of work, or the equivalent of owning three weeks' of slave labor. Anyone who commandeers the energy equivalent of a barrel of oil, for the moment priced at about $80, gets the energy-equivalent work of a human slave for two to three years—23,200 hours worth. Talk about cheap! However messy or proximate these slave-work analogies may be, they signify one thing for sure: cheap oil has meant boom times, and no nation has sucked up more of the black gold and enjoyed its oomph more than the United States.

Ruppert and other peak oil students believe that in 2005 the world economy climbed to the top of the bell-shaped curve that describes the useful life of oil (and practically any other nonrenewable resource located on earth). We humans now live atop the Bumpy Plateau, where global supply cannot be much expanded regardless of demand expressed by oil's price. The bumps on the world economy's road consist of price-driven dips down (a.k.a. recessions caused by "demand destruction") and rises (a.k.a. faux "recoveries," caused by massive inputs of central bank fiat money) that overall are making for a rocky ride for anyone who's not an investment banker.

The ride, and its eventual destination, matters not much to those Lords of the Universe who inhabit the warrens of Goldman Sachs, J.P. Morgan Chase, Citibank, the Federal Reserve, and the U.S. Treasury (as well as "too big to fail" banks elsewhere on the planet), for whom the laws of economic growth are more certain and reliable than the laws of thermodynamics (or any other science whose laws govern life), and who in the end are principally concerned to "make money on the way up and make money on the way down."

In *Confronting Collapse*, Ruppert reminds us more than once, during the course of his terse deconstruction of peak oil, that "Until we change the way money works, we change nothing." In the interim, we bear witness to the ravishment of our own wealth as ordinary Americans. "Simply put, more money can be made—more quickly—by accelerating decline, bankrupting the country, starving people, and selling off assets than by investing it in rebuilding under a new economic paradigm or by trying to soften the crash. . . . Financial markets have no long-term vision in the infinite growth paradigm. . . . The current economic paradigm will find that it uses less energy to make more money by driving things [assets, such as housing] down than by building them up."

At this juncture the hard facts of energy returned on energy invested (EROEI) raise their stony heads. According to Ruppert, "EROEI is at the heart of what sustainability means," the litmus test all new energy sources must pass (and few do). The search for the hard-to-find-and-hard-to-produce oil and other fossil sources of energy has already begun in earnest, albeit amidst confusing price signals. Demand decreases in the OECD countries (Organization for Economic Cooperation and Development) but rises in massive nations like China, India, and Brazil, as well as in oil-dense nations such as the Arab Gulf states, yielding a relentless net upward pressure on price.

EROEI now guides the calculus of energy enterprises and governments. If you have to invest $100 to get an $80 barrel of oil, are you going to do it? Not likely, even on spec. As for the oil fields already drilled, "Once it takes more than one barrel of oil . . . to extract one barrel of oil, an oil field is considered dead." More than 96 percent of all the oil used in the world to date has been used since the United States entered World War II. Earlier in the last century, when the oil boom started in earnest, one barrel of energy-equivalent oil yielded an astonishing 100 barrels returned. Kaboom! That same barrel of oil invested today yields a meager three barrels here in the United States. In Saudi Arabia, where one quarter of all the world's oil is estimated to lie, and whose reserves are a closely guarded state secret, drilling offshore has begun (despite Saudi assurances that its onshore storehouse is practically limitless). As for oil produced from shale, tar sands, and coal, from deep beneath the Arctic and other oceans, off Brazil's coast and in the Gulf of Mexico, such wished-for bonanzas are likely to yield EROEIs of 2:1 or less. A world built on such expensive energy will be profoundly, comprehensively different from the one built on 100:1 energy.

Entry onto the Bumpy Plateau has given us precious "transition time" to "power down" while not-yet-too-expensive energy reserves are available to repair and maintain the infrastructure that "lies at the heart of complex civilizations . . . without which civilization starts to break down." Plugging the leaks in the dikes that are our infrastructure gives us time to start the work of relocalizing our economies, plural. Make no mistake, Ruppert is "alarming" us, as did Revere in a similarly life-threatening situation 235 years ago, to relocalize our food and energy systems now, without delay. We must come to understand that "globalization," a term for the American Dream gone viral, "will die with ever-increasing [fossil] fuel costs."

Some peak oil analysts believe the Bumpy Plateau—our final breathing space or "transition-time"—may last for one or two decades, to 2015 or 2025 (or possibly longer). Ruppert is not among this sanguinary lot. In a personal communication he has told me 2010 could be the year when the global economy "goes over the cliff." I myself am agnostic on the timing, if not about the event itself. "The United States," he told me, "will be impossible to govern as a single nation. . . . There are only 13 combat brigades in the U.S. and these will not be enough to prevent chaos." Like Rome was, the United States will be caught with its troops scattered over the face of the earth fighting perpetual imperial wars on multiple frontiers where the last sweet crude still flows in a world grown ravenous for every last drop.

In a recent *Foreign Affairs* essay, "Complexity and Collapse: Empires at the Edge of Chaos," the historian Niall Ferguson suggests that empires are complex systems that "operate somewhere between order and disorder—on the edge of 'chaos.'" Following the theory of complex systems, Ferguson reminds readers just how fast actual civilizations do in fact collapse, contrary to the ex post facto narratives of professional historians. Rome—that is, the Western Roman Empire—fell "within the span of a single generation." That was a long time ago, when transportation and communication systems were almost infinitely slower than they are today.

The incomparable 300-year old Ming Dynasty's fall "from equipoise to anarchy took little more than a decade." The relatively modern Hapsburg, Ottoman, Romanov, and British empires all ceased to be empires swiftly. Closer in time to our own era was the former Soviet Union. "If ever an empire fell off a cliff, rather than gently declining—it was the one founded by Lenin," Ferguson notes. He concludes his essay by observing that, like it or not, the collapse of empires (and the civilizations they embody) "is sudden."

Ruppert thus hardly stands alone in his assessment of the precarious condition of the United States, and indeed of the whole of industrial civilization. Written in 2008, his new book contains many very specific and useful recommendations whose chances for adoption are now less than what they were when "change we can believe in" was a slogan that energized a plurality of voting Americans. However, in light of his ruthlessly sober observation that "recovery is what will kill us," do we have a choice—and a chance?

We do. We must confront the truth of peak oil and begin the long march toward radical relocalization of fundamental life-supporting economic enterprises such as agriculture, energy, credit and currency, education, security, and health, and toward the creation of a new economic paradigm that permits us to live in equilibrium with our natural Earth-given endowments, both renewable and nonrenewable, wherever we ourselves are located. And become sovereign in our own local domains.

Just as "union" was once necessary for nations, including our own, to survive and flourish in the wide-open, expansive energy era of the midnineteenth and early twentieth centuries, today's conditions, which are being determined by peak-oil-driven collapse, make secession the new survival zeitgeist, as inevitable as "union" was 150 years ago. Survival won't be in empires or regional hegemons but in the locales where we live as flesh-and-blood beings, growing our own food (no thank you, Monsanto), making our own energy (no thank you, ExxonMobil), assuring our own security (no thank you, Pentagon), making our own currency (no thank you, Federal Reserve), and issuing our own credit (no thank you, Goldman Sachs).

And thereby secede. Secede from the old paradigm and all that it enables, preeminently the thievery, murder, and wanton destruction of empire itself.

The Great Hydropower Heist
How Corporations Colonized Our Watershed Commons

DR. RICHARD FOLEY *with assistance from* HERVEY SCUDDER

Issue no. 18 • Spring 2007
Issue no. 20 • Fall 2007

From Vermont's founding as a Republic in 1777 until the early 1900s, its citizens were far more energy independent than we find ourselves now. The old-timers traveled and transported goods with an efficient blend of the original horse power and coal-fired steam trains. They heated largely with wood and built hundreds of small hydropower facilities—initially, mechanized mills that utilized raw waterwheel power and were later retrofitted with electric generators and complementary coal-fired steam-powered systems. Hence, the claim: "Hydro—the power that built Vermont." Now Vermonters spend roughly $2 billion every year on out-of-state fuels for transportation, heating, industrial applications, and electricity. More than $1 billion pays for imported oil and gas alone.

How did Vermont lose its energy independence? Why haven't we converted more of our potential "energy commons"—our sunlight, our wind, our forests, our rivers, our economy's waste products—into sustainable power sources?

The concept of "commons" goes back to medieval Europe where the law of the realm recognized that certain natural resources or "real estate" belonged to all the people, and that its ownership and access resided in the public domain for "the public good." American colonists carried this concept to the New World and built their villages around the "town commons" where they corralled their animals for safekeeping each night, and around which they built their meetinghouses, churches, homes, and businesses. The commons then functioned in colonial America both as the physical epicenter and philosophical keystone of the "public good." The physical commons has morphed into some "set asides" of natural resources that belong to the public, some more than others, at least theoretically. We're all familiar with state/national parks; internationally recognized offshore limits; public access to seashore, lakes, rivers; regulated access to aquifers, mineral rights, airways, and electronic bandwidths. The more prosaic forms of "public good"—like recognizing the value in keeping the village green for grazing animals—have evolved into a complex web of local, state, and federal government sponsored "public works" or "public services" that range from town water-and-sewer to transportation systems, healthcare, public assistance, and municipal electric utilities.

Stewardship, in this conversation, simply means the public's responsibility to maintain the health of the commons for future generations. And the public's track record reflects the full range of the human condition—from inspired care of sacred sites (e.g., declared wilderness areas) to utter neglect and abuse (most rivers in the United States at one time or the other). Vermonters' care of the Connecticut River watershed devolved from most respectful to shameful, before we earned our current reputation as a "green" or environment-friendly state. By the mid-1800s the new Vermonters had overlogged and then overgrazed by sheep farming the Connecticut watershed to the point where the land had lost its natural spongelike ability to absorb rainfall and release the water over time. As a result, unchecked runoff made the Connecticut River and its tributaries run wild after storms and in the spring, the floods repeatedly destroying railroad lines and inundating towns and farmlands. Damming many of the rivers for hydropower was not an option in the 1800s. So not until Vermonters reluctantly allowed the woodlands to grow back and made the transition to dairy farming in the second half of the 1800s did the watershed recover its ability to store runoff.

Experts agree that 60 to 70 percent of the Connecticut River's daily flow comes from the watershed's slow release of groundwater. Indeed, it has been Vermonters' responsible stewardship of the watershed—displayed in the popular images of pastoral Vermont's rolling mix of woodlands, farms, and small villages—that produces the "white coal," the hydropower potential of the Connecticut and Deerfield rivers.

Commercial interests also access the commons to extract natural resources, be it for farming, logging, mining, and so on. The inherent questions of extraction versus exploitation did not escape the settlers in North America. It can be argued that the abuses of the English-chartered corporations such as the East India Company and the Hudson's Bay Company triggered the American Revolution. The American colonists of all socioeconomic ranks—from laborers, small farmers, traders, and artisans, to the landed gentry—opposed these "multi-territorial" corporations that King George and Parliament used to exploit natural resources and human labor to extend their control over the British colonies. Having defeated English corporate imperialism, the revolutionaries did not grant executive, judicial, or military sectors the authority to charter corporations. Instead, they made certain that their elected representatives issued charters, one at a time, for a specific public purpose (building a bridge or dam), for a limited span of time (10–20 years), with the requirement that the project be turned over to the state or town at the expiration of the charter. A charter of incorporation was regarded as a privilege—and with that privilege came the corporate obligation to serve the public interest.

For the first half of American history, corporations served the public good at the pleasure of the granting authority. And so legislatures routinely revoked corporate charters, or allowed the charter to expire and corporations to be dissolved—at any time when the public's representatives determined that a corporation had failed the test of "serving the public good." Our early Vermont history is chock full of experiments in privately funded roads and postal services that ultimately failed to meet the criteria of the "public good."

What happened to this system of state control over corporations? In 1886, the federal government recognized "corporate personhood." Over the next 120 years, Washington coupled these newly acquired corporate-personhood rights and privileges with federal jurisdiction over interstate trade to erode state rights and state control over corporations.

The emergence of large, powerful corporations has heated up the debates around the commons versus corporations, public versus private, democracy versus development, socialization versus privatization. The question of what entity—public or private—would do the best job of delivering reliable, affordable electricity to Vermonters lands smack in the middle of this debate. It's a rhetorical question; the reality is that the private sector has basically controlled Vermont's electric power system over the past one hundred years.

Brattleboro and Windham County serve as a case in point; this corner of the state had achieved a high level of prosperity based on the small business model and a balance between economic activity—agriculture, transportation, retail services, and manufacturing—and the prudent utilization of the commons—properly stewarded graz-ing lands, woodlands, mineral springs, and the two major watersheds. All along the Connecticut and Deerfield rivers' numerous tributaries, several hundred water-powered mills, many with complementary steam plants, employed thousands and produced flour, textiles, and hundreds of different wood products from matches to chairs, as well as power-ing metal manufacturing machinery. Mirroring the age of water power in New England, a high point in decentralized, indigenous renewable-energy production, Brattleboro prospered, its practically self-sufficient economy exporting a wide range of manufactured goods to markets throughout the region.

It was natural then for people living along the recently tamed Connecticut to dream about harnessing its awesome power. In 1902 several forward-looking local businessmen promoted the idea of a hydroelectric station. Brattleboro's representative in the state legislature introduced a bill for the charter of the Connecticut River Power Company—CRPC, or what we'll call the "Power Company." The New Hampshire legislature gave its approval to a companion charter in 1903. The state charters specified that towns adjoining the flowage had the right to take power for street lighting and other municipal uses. The legislatures, in other words, empowered a private, for-profit company with powers of eminent domain and rights to water use because the legislators expected that the electricity would be distributed for public use and community benefit. Armed with the authority of the two state charters and backed by out-of-state investors, the Power Company incorporators, readily acknowledged as "town fathers," persuaded the public to support this enterprise.

In 1903, our local leaders and state legislators traded away a magnifi-cent slice of our commons for a promise. Well, how well did the deal shake out? While the local Power Company incorporators were sell-ing the Vernon dam project up here in Vermont, the Power Company's major players down there—wealthy Boston-based financiers—had recognized a growing power shortage in large industrial cities of east-ern Massachusetts. These utility speculators were looking to the rela-tively remote and untapped northern New England hydro resources. As the Vernon dam was being built, its output was upgraded from 12,000 to 28,000 horsepower, and other Power Company construction crews built hundreds of miles of transmission lines from Vernon to eastern

Massachusetts. This orientation of infrastructure flipped the switch. There was no way to direct significant power flow back to Brattleboro.

The Power Company's next major project, the Deerfield River System, was a monster technically and a monster ethically. The Whitingham dam dwarfed any existing New England dam. The Power Company drained much of southeastern Vermont and submerged thousands of acres of farmland, entire villages, and miles of roads and railways—all of which required expensive relocation. The Power Company augmented the dam work with additional transmission lines that linked the Deerfield dams with the Vernon dam, to further the goal of exporting the power south. The company promised a stable, affordable electricity supply while threatening potential customers with their financial and legal clout—to buy up water rights and dams from the mills on the Connecticut and Deerfield tributaries. In a final coup de grace to independent power producers, the Power Company refused to sign power supply contracts with local mills unless they agreed to sign over and/or destroy their dams and hydroelectric generators. Power Company crews went in and destroyed waterwheels and electrics with sledgehammers and crowbars. The net result was that hundreds of Windham County's water/steam mills lost access to their own inexpensive, local power— what we now call decentralized or "distributed" power.

Some might argue that Windham County and the Deerfield Valley never recovered from the invasion of the Power Company. Southern Vermonters experienced early on the "resource curse" that currently bankrupts developing countries that witness outside interests exploiting their resources to the detriment of the environment and indigenous people. As some humorists have pointed out, "Vermont is a third-world country, but the natives don't realize it." The aggressive energy moguls solidified their holdings to the point that by 1930, 95 percent of Vermont's consumers were held hostage to out-of-state Investor Owned Utilities (IOUs) that owned 99 percent of the electric power plants in the state. Vermonters paid "through the nose" for electricity. And worst of all, nine out of ten Vermont farmers could not get electricity! Today, TransCanada, a multinational energy corporation that makes its money largely from American consumers paying to have Canadian natural gas pumped across the border, and the new owner of the entire Connecticut/Deerfield hydropower system, is the latest investor to milk our Windham County "cash cows."

In 1909 the IOUs, not consumers' advocates, successfully lobbied for the establishment of the Vermont Public Service Commission (PSC), which later evolved into the current Department of Public Service and its complementary quasi-judicial agency, the Public Service Board. IOUs wanted the state to recognize them as "public utilities"—a clever misnomer for privately owned, for-profit entities. Secondly, IOUs wanted the PSC to supercede municipal authorities. Here the IOU lawyers and lobbyists really earned their paychecks. In one fell swoop, they maneuvered the state into removing local control and thereby shielding the IOUs Achilles heel. Instead of being burdened with dealing with hundreds of potential local "regulators" with clear allegiances to their communities, the out-of-state investors could focus all their resources on influencing one state regulatory agency. And early on, the nascent Public Service Commission was intentionally underfunded resulting in overworked, less-than-qualified personnel supported by IOU handpicked consultants.

To paraphrase architect and industrial ecologist William McDonough, regulatory agencies regulate us, the public. Not the agencies' partners, the corporations. Regulators decide what quality of service, at what cost, and at what level of toxicity we, the public, will have to tolerate. Arsenic and fluoride in our water, sulfuric acid in our rainwater, noxious particulates and unburned hydrocarbons in our air, genetically modified organisms in our food, radioactive strontium-90 in our atmosphere from weapons fallout. Exotic emissions from automobiles, refineries, power plants, pharmaceutical and manufacturing operations. So when you hear or read about "regulations," you may want to think carefully about the level of risk the regulations are imposing on you and your local community. "Regulator" is shorthand for the fox guarding the hen house.

As the Connecticut River Power Company's electrical power flowed south and east from the Vernon dam and the Deerfield River system of dams, the state legislature finally appointed in 1912 a Commission on the Conservation of the Natural Resources of the State of Vermont to look into the matter. The Commission recommended that the state control the export of electric power, much as Maine had banned exports in 1909. But the combination of the Power Company's and its IOU allies' lobbying efforts and public relations campaigns convinced the legislature to ignore the recommendations. A few years later spurred on by public outrage of the Vernon and Deerfield dams rip-off, the PSB made a second attempt to implement state regulation of exports. The Power Company challenged the order in Federal Court, which, in turn, ruled in 1919 that Vermont, or any state for that matter, had no jurisdiction over such interstate commerce as export contracts. The Federal Court's ruling rendered the State powerless to enforce the "public interest" intent of the original Power Company charter.

Many analysts agree that these watershed decisions triggered the longstanding, ongoing battle over Vermont's electric power exports. The decade of the twenties literally lit up America—demand of electricity doubled every few years—and ushered in the IOUs' ruthless campaign of monopoly and Enron-like manipulation, corruption, and outright thievery. By 1929 IOUs had bought out the lion's share of Vermont's patchwork of municipal and small private utilities and thereby controlled over 90 percent of the electricity generated and about 75 percent of the power distributed in Vermont.

Back in 2002–2004, our Brattleboro-based group NECSIS, the NorthEast Center for Social Issues Studies, put together a team of professionals who volunteered their time and talents to convince the State to purchase these "green" power sources, the dams on the Connecticut and Deerfield rivers—535 megawatts of combined capacity, or more than 80 percent of what Vermont Yankee supplies Vermont. A purchase that in one fell swoop would answer the Pro-Nukes' perennial rejoinder to the Shut-Down VY crowd: "And how do you propose to replace all that reliable, low-cost power?" Simple. With safer, more reliable, lower-cost, and infinitively more green and greenhouse-friendly hydropower. Our lobbying efforts paid off when the legislature invested $750,000 in an attempt to buy the dams outright. But Governor Douglas sold the deal down the river while the legislature washed its hands of the affair and went looking for other ways to "diversify the state's energy portfolio."

The vast majority of the world's remaining oil comes from the most unstable countries in the world. The Bush administration's reaction to 9/11 in the form of a more corporate-friendly, business-as-usual National Energy Plan (closed-door consultations chaired by VP Cheney) and the subsequent invasions of Afghanistan and Iraq opened the proverbial "Pandora's Box" and triggered a strong reaction from Vermont's culture of active grassroots organizations. More and more Vermonters have been equating their dependence on imported energy with the U.S. government's aggressive military policies. In the spring of 2003, eighty-one of eighty-three towns passed a Vermont Energy Independence resolution urging our state government and congressional delegation to encourage all sectors of the Vermont economy toward a sustainable energy future. In 2005, forty-eight of fifty-three towns across Vermont voted in favor of resolutions requesting that their state representatives use their executive and legislative powers to investigate the deployment of the Vermont National Guard to Iraq. On February 13, 2007, the Vermont House and Senate voted to press Congress and the president "to commence immediately the orderly withdrawal of American military forces from Iraq."

In addition, a spontaneous outbreak of self-selecting groups are initiating a wide array of direct action on the local level. In southern Vermont alone we can point to Brattleboro-based Post Oil Solutions, Windham Energy Coalition, Windham Environmental Coalition, District Heating Group, Vermonters for a Fair Economy and Environmental Protection, Brattleboro Climate Protection, Putney's Energy Committee, Springfield's Sustainable Valley Group, and Norwich's Sustainable Energy Resource Group. Most of these groups have been exploring the relationship between indigenous renewable-energy sources (wind power, small hydropower, wood chips, "cow power," basic energy efficiency, biodiesel) and the health of our local economies, especially around locally grown food. In short, Vermonters are stepping up their collective efforts to take responsibility for their dependence on the global fossil-fuel-driven economy and its enormous environmental and social costs.

Energy Crisis, Energy Opportunities

An excerpt from *Wanted: A Holistic Perspective on Vermont Energy*

GAELAN BROWN

Issue no. 33 • Winter 2010
Issue no. 39 • Winter 2011

Our world is in the midst of an endless list of crisis scenarios related to politics, the economy, credit, the environment, healthcare, security, human rights, energy, water, food, and the list goes on and on. Yet there is some reason for optimism, particularly related to our potential to transition to sustainable and clean energy systems. The world needs sustainable, decentralized clean energy as a foundation upon which communities can build sustainable, decentralized, and strong economies.

Unfortunately the only real progress for renewable energy in the United States is coming from a handful of states that have invested in a clean energy future, despite U.S. federal policy that dramatically favors centralized, monopolistic energy from oil, coal, and nuclear power.

This summary of a few of our national budget priorities during the past eight years is a good illustration of how Vermont and other states are being forced to spend their dollars on activities that have prevented the "green economy" from coming to life.

1. Subsidies for coal and oil industry: $75 Billion
2. Afghanistan oil gas war: $233 Billion
3. Iraq oil war: $706 Billion
4. Renewable energy subsidies: $12 Billion

Our national government's investment in the "green economy" this decade totals less than 1 percent of its investment in the fossil-fuel subsidies shown above. And so far, Obama has given every indication that his administration is all about continuity in these regards, versus change. Yes, there was $32 billion in the stimulus package for renewable energy and efficiency. That's more than ever before, but it is still peanuts compared to the trillions of tax- and inflation-dollars that have been committed for continued global military insanity and corporate welfare. A national clean-energy policy will continue to be "back-burnered" behind healthcare, the economy, and war.

How can we build an independent, sovereign, energy-independent Vermont, when our national government has bankrupted us? Vermont's economic and political independence will increase in direct correlation to how well we develop the foundation of our economy: sustainable, domestic energy. The good news is that market forces have made solar, wind, and biomass energy economically viable in Vermont, and Vermont has significant existing hydropower resources that could meet more than half of our electricity needs. The bad news is, we're attached to a sinking Titanic and we're not moving nearly fast enough to deploy the lifeboats, and our hydropower resources are currently owned by a Canadian company and not even connected to the Vermont grid.

Renewable energy can create strong, decentralized, green economies for Vermont communities. In turn, local economies so well-grounded will provide a foundation for an effective commitment to human rights and economic development that distributes food, water, and wealth more equitably and sustainably.

Our national government leaders, including those supposed champions of environmentalism such as Al Gore and Barack Obama, have given us only token gestures and a lot of empty rhetoric. Vermont's U.S. Congressional delegation is impotent in these regards. Most national politicians claim to support renewable energy, yet their priorities, as expressed by the subsidies they extend with our tax dollars, continue to support coal, oil, and military adventures; by contrast, they characterize renewable energy as "in need of more research to make it cost-effective."

We don't need new energy technologies. We just need the cultural and political will to invest in the transition and take the power back from the vested interests that today control our energy economy. Most people believe that solar, wind, and biomass energy systems are not yet cost-effective compared to fossil fuels. That's only because fossil fuels have been heavily subsidized for more than fifty years. The price you pay for electricity or heating oil would be at least twice as high if not for decades of heavy federal subsidies. In most European countries gasoline has cost more than $8/gallon for many years, and electricity costs are generally twice the U.S. national average ($.16/kWh vs. $.08/kWh in the United States). If today's renewable energy systems were deployed at a scale to cover a majority of our energy needs, the cost per kilowatt-hour from solar, wind or biomass would be less than unsubsidized coal-electricity.

Vermont is already a national leader in energy issues, with tremendous local energy resources within our borders. We have the capacity to become energy independent with aggressive investment in wind, solar, and biomass energy systems. Without the hopeless burdens we carry as part of the U.S. empire, we could create a sustainable, just economy.

We are the only state in the nation with a state-supported efficiency utility, and we have significantly reduced our energy use per person during the past decade. We could attempt to buy back our hydropower sites from the out-of-state corporations that Governor Douglas and the Vermont legislature allowed to purchase them. Nearly 30 percent of Vermont school children attend schools that are heated sustainably by high-efficiency boilers burning locally harvested woodchips and yielding low emissions. Vermont has enough standing biomass in the forest to sustainably heat every house in the state with wood without the forest shrinking, which would keep more than $700 million in the annual local economy instead of paying for out-of-state oil and propane. Vermont was the first state in the nation whose legislature passed a statewide "feed-in tariff" bill that forces utilities to pay favorable rates to producers of renewable energy (albeit with a conservative cap at less than 5 percent of our power needs, for now).

Vermont's business community has spawned many renewable-energy companies that are national leaders. Vermont probably has more clean-energy expertise per capita than any other state in the country. These companies include NRG Systems, Earth Turbines, and Northern Power Systems (the latter recovering from several rocky years, economically), all of them international leaders in wind turbine/measurement technology; Biomass Energy Resource Center, the nation's leader in biomass feasibility studies for district heating and power generation; groSolar, leader of the pack in solar installation; NativeEnergy, specializing in voluntary renewable energy credits (RECs) and carbon offsets that fund renewable energy projects; Vermont Energy Investment Corp., an international leader in efficiency programs and consulting that also runs Efficiency Vermont. And there are others beside.

Sadly for those who had hoped for "change," it appears that Barack Obama and the U.S. Congress will pay lip service but not much more to the development of a green economy, while continuing to push our resources into war and debt. Vermont's fastest path to a clean-energy economy is to build it ourselves by removing our federal burdens—for example, by seceding. Vermont's per household share of the cost of the U.S. war machine is $10,000 per year. This amount of money would cover the cost of installing enough solar power to meet 100 percent of our annual residential needs in less than three years. Without the cost of empire, we could then invest our hard-earned money in Vermont's priorities, including local, decentralized renewable-energy systems, instead of endlessly subsidizing the oil, coal, and military industries.

Here is the energy scenario that I see in Vermont, and the priorities that we should focus on developing:

1. Becoming more energy independent with renewable energy will create jobs, save us money, and give our economy a rock-solid, long-term foundation, regardless of the polarizing climate-change debates.
2. Vermont forests grow more biomass each year than it would take to heat every residential and commercial building in the state with modern high-efficiency woodstoves and wood-boilers that pay for themselves in less than five years while cutting annual fuel bills by up to 50 percent.
3. If we replace all propane and heating oil with sustainably harvested wood by 2020, Vermont will keep more than $1 billion in the local economies, and the average home will save at least $2,000 per year, while we create thousands of jobs.
4. We could reduce the energy demand from buildings by 20 percent through efficiency/weatherization, with investments that would pay for themselves in three years.
5. The critical missing elements in renewable energy are financing and access to the grid. A well-designed "feed-in tariff" that forces power companies to pay cash values to any electricity customer who feeds clean energy into the grid would create the investment-climate that would cause capital to pour into Vermont for renewable-energy installations, while actually

reducing our medium- and long-term power rates. Vermont's first feed-in tariff was limited to utility-scale installations. It must be expanded to allow any home, farm, or business to be paid a fair price for the power it generates, which is known as a "micro feed-in tariff."

6. Every Vermont property owner—residential and commercial— today has the option to produce all of their annual electric- ity with an investment in a net-metered solar electric system installed at their home/business, or as part of an off-site, group- net-metered project. Today's solar system prices translate to a retail price per kWh of less than 15 cents for the next thirty years without any Vermont tax subsidies. Most Vermonters are paying the power company more than that today. In Vermont, solar electric and solar hot water has a ten-year break-even point with twenty-plus years of free power after that, for any home or business.

7. A new nuclear power plant the size of Vermont Yankee would cost between $7 billion and $9 billion and would provide enough power to cover most of Vermont's total power use. But we'd be reliant on a dwindling global supply of increas- ingly expensive uranium, when Vermont Yankee already can't compete with Canadian hydropower. If Vermont invested $7 billion in distributed solar electricity that would generate 100 percent of Vermont's annual residential power requirement (about 50 percent of our total power demand) without any fuel costs for the next thirty years. Is there any question which investment makes more sense?

8. It would take less than 1 percent of our current open land being devoted to solar power to provide 100 percent of Vermont's net-annual electricity, including residential and commercial use (which translates to about 500 square feet of roof/ground space per home). Solar power does not provide a constant base load of energy, because it only works during sunlight hours, so Vermont still needs other sources of power like the New England grid or hydropower to provide the steady base load and cover solar's gaps. But on an annual basis, with net meter- ing we could produce all of our annual electricity needs (mean-

ing everyone would have an annual net-power bill of $0), with just 1 percent of our land being devoted to solar power.

9. It would also take less than 1 percent of our land to produce all of Vermont's electricity with wind power. But a wind-dominant energy portfolio in Vermont would require industrialization of the majority of our ridgelines. Because of our terrain, wind power has limited potential in Vermont unless we want to build industrial parks on our ridgelines. However, wind power makes a lot of sense for certain communities to explore what is known as community wind. Community wind means the turbines are locally owned and sized to produce power for local use. We could learn to love the view of wind turbines on a ridge, just as we love the view of the scarred mountainsides otherwise known as ski resorts.

10. Burning wood to generate electricity is horribly inefficient, except for district-heating systems that produce some electricity as a by-product. The only efficient use of wood to produce electricity is known as a "heat-led combined-heat-and-power system," where the plant operates primarily when heat is needed, with electricity as a by-product. Our biomass resources should be prioritized for heating needs and forest products, not electricity generation.

I suggest that policymakers and activist groups focus on these key questions:

1. What sustainable energy resources does Vermont really have, and what policies will encourage investment in developing these resources? (Hint, Vermont has no natural gas, uranium, oil, or coal, but we have lots of water, wood, wind, and sunlight.)

2. How can we finance our way toward energy independence, while saving money?

3. How do we reclaim our hydropower resources and put them to work for the benefit of Vermont, instead of for the benefit of transnational companies that sell our hydropower to non-Vermont markets?

FOOD

Everyone eats, and so we are all linked to the economic, environmental, political, and cultural issues surrounding food, whether or not we recognize these connections. During the past decade, an increasing number of people worldwide have become more conscious about the sources, quality, and environmental effects of their food. They are seeing how the globalized, corporate food industry causes extensive harm to communities and ecosystems around the planet. It puts small farmers off their land, pumps petrochemicals into the soil, introduces genetically modified "Frankenfoods" into croplands and diets, and transports agricultural produce thousands of miles, consuming huge amounts of energy, before it reaches consumers, excessively refining and processing our food along the way. Millions of people have begun looking for alternatives, and a popular movement for healthy, locally and sustainably produced food has begun to spread across the United States and elsewhere in the world.

Food activism encompasses numerous issues, from the astounding surge of obesity and diabetes, to peak oil's looming limitations, to the poor conditions of agricultural labor, to the corporate patenting—the confiscation for private profit—of genetic material, the very building blocks of life. At one end of the food movement spectrum, epicures and gourmet chefs are rediscovering the joys of local and regional ingredients, while at the other, activists for "food sovereignty" expose the blatant exploitation of farmers, indigenous populations, and colonized nations by powerful economic interests. The food movement shows up in the burgeoning popularity of farmers' markets and CSAs (community supported agriculture projects); demands for labeling, if not outlawing, genetically modified products; fair trade and migrant worker campaigns, Slow Food principles, heirloom seed preservation; and resiliency planning by community transition groups. Many writers, such as Michael Pollan, Marion Nestle, Eric Schlosser, and others, are examining the dangers of the industrial food system and exploring alternatives.

Vermont is one of the world's leading regions for the renaissance of local, sustainable, and healthful food systems, and *Vermont Commons* writers have frequently highlighted our agricultural innovations as examples. Yet the state still only produces a tiny portion of the food it consumes, and if national and international supply lines go down, it is estimated that we would only have enough to eat for a few days. Though Vermonters are diligently working toward resilience, we are still far from achieving it. In agriculture, as in the other areas of society we examine, a massive paradigm and policy shift is very much needed.

What Will You Eat if Vermont Secedes?

Amy Shollenberger

Issue no. 29 • Spring 2009

"What will you eat?" is a good question to ponder whether or not you support secession. In James Howard Kunstler's recent novel, *World Made By Hand*, food becomes a kind of currency after the governmental and economic infrastructure collapses. People in this story are forced to eat locally because they have little access to the outside world. Although secession is a much different scenario, it is worth considering what types of questions would need to be answered and what areas of the food system might need to be built up for Vermont to have true food security, and even food sovereignty.

In a July 2008 article in *Seven Days*, Bill McKibben suggested that the secessionist movement should "focus less on opposing tyranny and more on counting calories." I would suggest to you that these two focus areas are actually the same. We will not be able to count our calories more locally and regionally, the way McKibben (and I) would like to, until we openly name and then dismantle the tyranny of our corporate-industrial food system—which is supported by our government.

McKibben listed a few of the many folks here in Vermont who are working to build our local food system. However, as he mentions only briefly, the state Agency of Agriculture and the federal government are, in the best cases, supporting these efforts with little enthusiasm, and, in the worst cases, actively opposing efforts to build our local food systems.

Earl Butz, secretary of agriculture for Richard Nixon, reshaped America's food and agricultural policy when he urged farmers to "get big or get out." Even before that, however, a movement toward consolidated, industrialized food production was well underway. In 1906, Upton Sinclair published *The Jungle*, a novel that exposed corruption in the U.S. meatpacking industry. Although Sinclair's focus was on the labor conditions in the slaughterhouses and packing plants, the novel led to sweeping regulatory reforms focused on food safety.

These reforms did achieve a certain level of food safety; however, they also had a consequence of creating a system where small abattoirs and locally available meat are scarce because of the capital investment required to comply with all of the safety standards—which are designed to deal with the problems that occur when meat is processed quickly and on a large scale.

A similar history can be found in our country's milk-production system. In his book, *The Untold Story of Milk*, Ron Schmid shows us how competing interests fought to ensure the safety of our milk supply. Two doctors, responding to the real safety issues caused by the industrial revolution, came up with two different approaches. One created standards and certified farms to ensure the farmers and animals were healthy, the cows were on pasture, and basic hygiene and sanitation were routine. The other boiled the milk to kill any germs that had contaminated it. Because pasteurization had the added benefit of extending shelf life, it allowed the milk to be shipped greater distances—and the rest is history. Now, it is very difficult to process milk on a small scale (even if you want to pasteurize it), and even more difficult to sell it without pasteurizing it, because of the regulatory system that is in place and the costs associated with compliance.

In an October 12, 2008, open letter to America's next president published in the *New York Times*, Michael Pollan noted that "After WWII, the government encouraged the conversion of the munitions industry to fertilizer . . . and the conversion of nerve-gas research to pesticides. The government also began subsidizing commodity crops, paying farmers by the bushel for all the corn, soybeans, wheat and rice they could produce." This eventually led to Butz's encouragement for farmers to consolidate and to value production and efficiency above all else, and thus to mono-cropping and petroleum-based farming.

Pollan noted that we have a real opportunity right now because of a double crisis in food and energy. You probably have heard all about the energy crisis, but did you know—as Pollan reports—that in the past several months more than thirty nations have experienced food riots?

At this moment, there may be a chance to shift our policy and create a new food system. Pollan suggests that we move from a petroleum-dependent system to one that uses sunshine, which he calls a "new solar-food economy."

I agree with many of Pollan's suggestions, including expanding farmers' markets, creating agricultural enterprise zones, developing a "local meat-inspection corps," establishing a strategic grain reserve, regionalizing federal food procurement, and creating a definition of "food" that focuses on nutrition rather than on calories. Pollan's ideas are good places to begin for America's new president.

But what about us? Here in Vermont, what will we eat? What will our food policy look like? How can we work toward a secure and independent food system? I think we need to begin working on our state-level policy right now, in the same way that Michael Pollan suggests working on the federal system. Whether you want to secede and have Vermont be an independent nation, or whether you're not quite ready for that to happen yet, I would urge you to get involved in shaping Vermont's food policy.

This past summer, Rural Vermont conducted an online survey for consumers who were interested in local food. More than 200 people took the survey, and the overwhelming majority were interested in being able to buy local food and support local farmers. One piece of data that stood out to me was that the overwhelming majority of people taking the survey believed that the number-one way to support local farmers was to buy their products. I strongly agree that this is an important thing to do if you want to support local farmers (or any local business). However, I think it's also important to make sure that the policies in place encourage local production and processing on a reasonable scale, and also ensure that the farmers get a fair price for their products, so that they can make good choices for their farms, their land, and their families, rather than for their banks.

Here in Vermont, despite the amazing efforts of hundreds of people who want to support local and regional food systems, we still have gaps—gaps in poultry- and meat-processing capacity, gaps in food-storage capacity, gaps in some crops that could be grown here but aren't, gaps in research and development, gaps in milk-processing capacity. Although we are slowly filling in the gaps in our agricultural system, it is in spite of the policies of this state, rather than because of them. Where there has been success, it is largely because of the creativity and perseverance of the folks working on these issues, rather than the vision and foresight of our policymakers.

There are exceptions, of course. There have been good successes with the Farm to School program and Vermont FEED. Farmers' markets are strong, and many of them have EBT machines for food stamp customers. Last year, Vermont passed the "chicken bill," which opened up possibilities for farmers to direct-market farm-slaughtered poultry at farmers' markets and to restaurants. We're slowly expanding farmers' ability to sell raw milk directly to customers.

But these are relatively small steps. Rural Vermont has a vision for Food with Dignity—a Vermont local food system that is self-reliant and based on reverence for the earth. It builds living soils that nurture animals and people with wholesome, natural products, supporting healthy, thriving farms and communities. These communities in turn work to encourage and support current and future farmers, continuing our Vermont heritage. This abundant and generous way of life celebrates our diversity and interdependence. We want to achieve this vision because we believe farmers should have the first rights to local markets, and community members should have the first rights to locally produced food. We believe that farmers should get a fair price for their products, and we believe that, when these things happen, we are all healthier and happier.

Michael Pollan says we need to rebuild America's food culture by changing habits and diets, because we are used to "fast, cheap and easy food." Pollan suggests that in addition to working on food policy, we must work on food culture. He thinks that the new president should lead by example. He should take five acres of the White House lawn to plant an organic farm, which should be overseen by a farmer who would be selected with as much care and attention as the White House chef. Pollan also suggests planting gardens—lots of gardens—all over America. He wants us to plant gardens in every primary school, as well as at our homes, like the "Victory Gardens" promoted by Eleanor Roosevelt.

I agree that we should do these things; we should do everything we can to have more food produced in our home state, and I believe that these things are a matter of policy as well as culture. The state will need to create policy that encourages composting so that we can capture our nutrients and have fertile gardens. Towns could encourage residents to create neighborhood food councils the way we are now creating neighborhood energy teams.

The Second Vermont Republic could form a food council, too, to begin developing the ideal food policy for the new nation, if Vermont were to secede. This council could then work to have this policy implemented, whether we secede or not. The council could think about where people are more densely clustered, where the food is grown, and what sorts of infrastructure we must develop to grow, store, and distribute the food year round. What cannot be grown here that we need? How will we get it? What can we trade for it? What could we grow that we are not growing now?

For instance, if we are an independent nation, we could grow hemp. What sorts of processing facilities would we need for that, or for other crops? Where should we locate them? How can we encourage them to be opened? How will we train people to do this work? Where is the productive land that is not being used? How can we encourage its use? There are many beginning farmers looking for land; how can we connect them with the land that's available?

And, how can we begin thinking about ourselves as producers rather than consumers? I believe that this is the cultural shift that needs to happen. As long as we think about ourselves as consumers—people who use up resources—we will not succeed in achieving independence from the tyranny of the corporate-industrial food system. We must take responsibility at all levels and work to create a new system that adds health and value to our bodies, our soils, and our communities.

The Food Less Traveled

Enid Wonnacott

Issue no. 20 • Fall 2007

When I heard Michael Ableman, of the Center for Urban Agriculture, speak in Vermont last year, there was one statement he made that I have returned to frequently throughout the year—"pleasure is a better motivator for change than guilt." He continued, "How do we provide an invitation, rather than a harangue?" It is hard to determine what thing or combination of things motivates social change—this is a question that traverses disciplines, whether studying educational change or political change.

I have been interested in motivations for behavior change throughout my academic and professional careers—most recently, what will motivate kids to make different food choices in school; how can we most effectively impact child-eating behaviors? School food change has gained so much national attention, not because of the pleasure children will experience when they pull their first carrot out of the ground, but because of the increased incidence of type 2 diabetes and obesity. What determines which foods a second grader will choose when he or she gets to the end of the lunch line? Most likely, it will not be the school nurse's voice or their parent's voice or the memory of something they read; more likely, their decision will be influenced by the experience they have had with that food. Did they help plant those cabbage seedlings in their school garden, did they visit the farm and help harvest those potatoes, did they prepare a taste test for their peers in their classroom?

The Northeast Organic Farming Association of Vermont (NOFA-VT) has worked with Food Works and Shelburne Farms for over ten years on a collaborative project called Vermont Food Education Every Day (VT FEED). A focus of the project is to change the palettes of Vermont youth, so that when they get to the lunch line, they can choose food from farms in their community and they will choose those foods. It has always seemed commonsensical that if a school is within walking distance to a farm in their community, as many are in rural Vermont, then those schools should have a food purchasing relationship with those farms or at least other Vermont farms. Due in part to VT FEED's work, and to communities who were working on these efforts before VT FEED came along, there are now 75 schools out of Vermont's 300 public schools that are integrating the math, history, and science of local farms into their curriculum and purchasing local food for their lunch line.

I love that I can eat lunch at the Brewster Pierce Elementary School in Huntington that has been prepared with the vegetables harvested by the students from a neighboring farm, that the farmer has songs written about her by the students as part of an artist-in-residence program and that when farmer Sarah Jane comes to lunch she receives a standing ovation. I was, again, reminded of Michael Ableman when he said "I've seen chefs who prepare local foods receive mythical rock and roll status, it's time for farmers to receive the same." When adults think about their food choices, what is motivating them? What are the messages that influence those purchasing decisions? Consumer surveys say that "freshness" and "taste" are the predominant motivators, but factors such as the perceived health benefits, contribution to the local economy, and price are also influential. I think our greatest challenge and greatest strategy to influence food choices, as we have learned through our work with schools, is for individuals to experience food through growing, harvesting, preparing, or developing a relationship with that food and food producer.

The organization leading the crusade toward a new food culture nationally is Slow Food, "a non-profit, eco-gastronomic member-supported organization that was founded in 1989 to counteract fast food and fast life, the disappearance of local food traditions and people's dwindling interest in the food they eat, where it comes from, how it tastes and how our food choices affect the rest of the world." I was fortunate to attend Slow Food's Terra Madre in Turin, Italy, last fall. Accompanying the event was a celebration of regional foods called the *Salone del Gusto* where small-scale food producers come from all over the world to showcase their products, and the event is dedicated both to excellent food and to the extraordinary people who produce it. At the *Salone*, I tasted the wines from the Piedmont Valley and the prosciutto from Sienna (not to mention the molten chocolate . . .). All of these foods have a history and a story. A focus of the Slow Food event was to celebrate food traditions, to recognize foods unique to a region, and to create a connection to a place through the foods of that place.

One of the speakers at Terra Madre was Davia Nelson, a National Public Radio correspondent working on a program called "Hidden Kitchens," a series that explores how communities come together through food. Davia spoke about her experience visiting and chronicling all kinds of American kitchen cultures. She said that "America is in need of a movement—there was a peace movement and an environmental movement and now we are in need of a food movement." Similar arguments have been made during the current Farm Bill debates. Michael Pollan recently wrote that most Americans are not engaged in the process of creating the Farm Bill, that many people don't know a farmer nor care about agriculture—but we all eat. He recommended that "this time around, let's call it the food bill."

Of course Vermont is different, in that most Vermonters know farmers, and most Vermonters care about agriculture, but it begs the question, "How would our agricultural system be different if our country created a Food Bill or a Farm and Food Bill every five years?" As with other massive pieces of legislation, it is hard to get individuals engaged in the process of commenting on sections of the bill, calling their congressional representatives, or understanding the finer details. Having conversations with my peers about the Farm Bill reminds me of trying to engage individuals in the finer points of NAFTA (the North American Free Trade Agreement)—these are omnibus works that are hard to experience by individuals. NOFA-VT decided to go to where the people are this summer and have discussions about some of the details of the Farm Bill—we have tabled at places such as Hunger Mountain Coop and the Addison County Field Days. But, of course, the Farm Bill is not just about farms, it is about programs that impact farmers and reauthorization for nutrition programs that reach many Vermonters. And in our goals of influencing the food choices of children and adults in Vermont, we have to consider all of Vermont, and make sure that all Vermonters, including those with limited income, have access to fresh, local food.

It just makes common sense to circulate food dollars, as much as possible, within our local communities—the project gives terms such as "community economic development" and "relationship marketing" new meaning to me. Farmers' markets provide an opportunity for food consumers to purchase food directly from the person who grew that food—every individual who visits a farmers' market is engaging in a pleasurable food experience. That is what brings us back to a farmers' market or motivates us to renew our share in a Community Supported Agriculture (CSA) farm, or plant our own garden to nourish our family— we are predominantly motivated by pleasure. And because Vermont has more farmers' markets and CSAs, per capita, than any other state in the country, then I guess we can argue that we have the greatest capacity for pleasure!

The energy of the Localvore movement in Vermont confirms that Vermonters at a very grassroots and community level are harnessing our capacity for pleasure using food as a medium. Localvores are individuals committed to eating food within 100 miles of their home. Referred to as the "100 mile diet" in Canada or Locavores in California, they serve as examples of the emergence of a local food movement throughout the country. In Vermont, there are Localvore Pods organizing in communities to challenge and support each other to eat local foods for a day, a week, a month, or throughout the year. These learning communities are operating at a much more complex level than just planning for their meals for the week—in the Mad River Valley (www.vermontlocalvore .org), when a farmer's barn collapsed this winter due to the snow load, the Localvores held fund-raisers, supplied meals for the family, and organized work crews, and in, Brattleboro, Post Oil Solutions (www.post oilsolutions.org) is organizing a Localvore challenge and engaging the community in issues of climate change and peak oil. The Localvores meet quarterly to analyze Vermont's food transportation and storage infrastructure, to identify crops that we need in greater supply (grains, beans and oil crops), and to share community-outreach efforts.

Although many regions in the country are having the "local or organic" debate, fueled by high-profile stories challenging the emergence of organic food in Walmart and questioning the ethics of consuming food that has been transported so far when a consumer could buy those same products more locally, Vermont, fortunately, does not have to spend time on that discussion. The history of the organic movement in Vermont is a story of small farms, developing an infrastructure for local food sales and "food for the people, not for profit." In Vermont, organic is synonymous with local. Vermont consumers don't have to debate whether to buy an organic strawberry or a local strawberry, organic wheat or local wheat, organic cheese or local cheese—we can have both. Let's debate more meaningful topics, such as how do we build a vital food culture in Vermont? How can we support all Vermonters to have positive food experiences that influence their consumption and purchasing decisions? If I were creating an agricultural testament for Vermont, the first principle would be "Know Thy Farmer."

Putting the CSA Model to the Test

Robin McDermott

Issue no. 40 • Mud Season 2011

CSAs have become commonplace in Vermont. It is cool to say that you belong to one and even cooler if you belong to two or more. And, for the most part, farmers in Vermont have done a good job holding up their end of the bargain with Community Supported Agriculture models. So it is easy to forget the concept behind CSAs.

Most farms advertise CSAs as "buying into the farm," which is, in essence, what their shareholders are doing. Just like a Fortune 500 stock that goes up and down based on how well the business is doing (at least that's the way that it worked in the good old days), the value of a CSA share, or what the members take home from the farm on a weekly basis, depends on how well the farm is doing. For example, a couple of summers ago when early blight took out most of the tomato plants in the state, CSA members shared in that loss with the farmers; there were no tomatoes in most CSA baskets that year. Some CSAs make up for shortages by providing other veggies that are performing better on their farm (for example, kale, which thrived that year), but with most CSAs there isn't a contractual obligation on the farmers' part to provide any specific food or amount of food. Trust and reputation are usually the only guides that customers have in making a decision to invest in a CSA.

But even with small hiccups like the tomatoless summer, Vermont CSA farmers have been good at keeping up their half of the bargain. In fact, when a farm has a bumper crop of a particular vegetable, the shareholders will come away with extra veggies that week; that is how CSAs are supposed to work. Yet it's easy, as CSA shareholders, to forget that the periodic bounty that we look forward to picking up on a set schedule is not guaranteed.

It was easy, that is, until January this year, when a fire destroyed the barn at Pete's Greens in Greensboro. In addition to losing the wash house equipment, several tractors, numerous pieces of priceless vintage farm equipment, and the barn itself, which is the "heart" of a farm's operation, all of the storage vegetables and frozen meats that were allocated to fill CSA shares throughout the rest of the winter went up in smoke. This was a far more serious loss to CSA members than getting shorted on a couple of tomatoes. Before the fire department had squelched the last burning ember, members of the Pete's Greens Good Eats CSA received e-mail notification that their CSA pickup that day would be the last for a couple of months; there simply wasn't any food available to fill the weekly CSA orders.

But the e-mail also offered all of the shareholders a refund for the portion of the CSA that would not be filled in the coming weeks. Traditional financial investments simply don't work like this. Lehman Brothers stockholders had no such recourse when their stock lost its full value on September 15, 2008, after the company declared bankruptcy. My mother, who was heavily invested in General Motors bonds, didn't receive a letter from GM offering her a refund when a good chunk of her life savings became worthless as the company slithered into bankruptcy.

The unfortunate situation at Pete's Greens highlights the real value in CSAs and how Community Supported Agriculture is supposed to work. In these times of financial uncertainty, investing in a local farm makes a lot of sense. Sure, there's risk involved. You never know when weather conditions will cut a season short, an uncontrollable disease will wipe out an entire crop, or a greenhouse will be destroyed by a freak windstorm. But when you hand your money over to CSA farmers at the beginning of their season you can be certain that regardless of the challenges the coming growing season present, the farmers will be working their hardest to protect your investment. In fact, this deep sense of responsibility is why some farmers are no longer offering a community supported agriculture model for their farm. As one former CSA farmer told me, she would lie awake at night worrying about producing enough food to fulfill her commitment to her CSA customers. I don't think that the executives at Lehman Brothers or GM were kept awake at night worrying about us little guys.

CSAs are cool, and investing in a local CSA helps farmers get a strong start for the season when their cash reserves are at their lowest. While there are CSAs that start up throughout the year depending on their focus, most get going in the spring so the timing couldn't be better to consider how you might invest in a local farm this year. The NOFA

Vermont website lists more than one hundred CSAs in our state (see NOFAVT.org). If you grow your own vegetables, as I do, there are other types of CSAs that might make more sense. I belong to a flower CSA that I join in the spring and, in exchange, receive a beautiful bouquet each week throughout the summer and fall. I also join the High Mowing Seeds CSA each fall that gives me a 10-percent discount on my seed purchase in January. I couldn't imagine a better way for Vermonters to invest their hard-earned money.

The Case for Local Wheat and Bread in Vermont

Erik Andrus

Issue no. 25 • Fall 2008

April 18, 1775, Dijon, France: An angry mob gathered outside the shop of a wealthy miller suspected of mixing bean flour with wheat flour to cut costs. The miller was assaulted and his house and mill plundered for flour, then burned to the ground. In the weeks that followed, similar scenes followed at bakeries and mills throughout France. Everywhere, people were angry about the same things: flour was too expensive, often of poor quality, and bread, priced at fourteen sous nationwide, was unaffordable to many. At dawn on the second of May an angry mob arrived at the gates of Versailles, demanding action. Surprised and outnumbered, the commander of the palace guard managed to disperse the crowd with assurances that the king would lower the price of bread.

Louis XVI, however, was of another mind; he followed the counsel of Controller-General of Finance Turgot, who was adamantly against any government interference in the wheat commodity market. Instead, soldiers and police were posted at every wheat market, mill, and bakery to quell the theft and pillaging that were becoming rampant. Those who could not afford bread at fourteen sous would have to do without. The king's men clashed with the hungry and desperate during this ugly, decade-long prologue to the revolution known as the Guerre des Farines, or the "Flour Wars." The anger that led to the storming of the Bastille in 1789 was, therefore, a long time in the making. The Bastille itself was of no significance except that it was a symbol of a monarchy unable to ensure a stable food supply. Without bread on the table, there would be no governance.

Historically, predictable supplies of staple crops have been critical to all civilizations. When the crop is in trouble, so, too, is the state. In France, transportation issues and the brutality of the free market combined to precipitate a crisis. It's troubling that our present-day food supply system leaves us vulnerable on these same two counts.

For my bakery in Ferrisburgh, I buy some flour from a local mill that has increased its prices for organic flour from 40 cents to 80 cents per pound in the past six months. The increase is credited to rising fuel costs, the diversion of former wheat lands to subsidized ethanol production, and rising demand for grain in China and India. Prices are expected to continue to rise, and I have noticed that most bakeries nearby have already increased their prices substantially.

True, we still have very, very cheap food in this country, and we're a long way from a full-blown crisis, but I would argue that the time is right to take action, particularly when it comes to wheat and bread. As a lifelong lover of bread and a full-time wheat farmer and baker, the culture of growing wheat and the art of baking with it are both dear to my heart. But in Vermont, small grains—wheat included—are often overlooked. According to University of Vermont agronomist Heather Darby, Vermont plants only 500 to 700 hundred acres per year, of which half goes for animal feeds. Since we consume an average of about 150 pounds of wheat per person annually, this means Vermont is currently growing just eight-tenths of one percent of the wheat it consumes.

When it comes to wheat, we now are at the low point of a trend centuries in the making. Western growers have more favorable growing conditions (at least as long as their aquifers hold out), and cheap transport has made competition with them very difficult. In fact, since the completion of the Erie Canal, Vermont wheat has been losing ground. Yet I believe that we are poised for a real renaissance of the culture of wheat and other small grains in Vermont, and that such a rebirth has greater promise than liquid coal, biofuels, hydrogen cells, nuclear energy, wind towers, and the many other proposed solutions to peak oil.

Most remedies to declining fossil-fuel availability seem to assume that we will more or less live as we have been living, consume as we've been consuming. Common sense and observation of the world around us should warn us against placing too much faith in such assurances. The bottom line is, in our future, there will simply be less fuel, less travel, less stuff, less energy. Our primary challenge as a culture and as a people will be to unify to create a society capable of functioning under these constraints. I feel that Vermont is among the best places in the nation to undertake this challenge, that the physical makeup of the place we live in and our cultural makeup put us well ahead of the national curve.

I believe the lynchpin to thriving in a postpeak world will be grain.

I am talking about grain for eating, not making into biofuel. Grain fills bellies of people, chickens, pigs, and, from time to time, can supplement the grass-based diets of horses, cows, sheep, and other ruminants. Grain is a proven powerhouse for an agrarian economy. Before coal, before oil, grain fed the bodies of workers who got the job done with their muscles, and helped feed the hardworking animals who carried the loads. If we as a people can get over the inexorable fact that in the future we will have to get work done by hand, back, and hoof to a much greater extent, there will be hope.

If I had to name two additional resources we will need in place, those would be grass and wood. But in Vermont, we already have active stewardship of our pastures and woodlands. The grain is still neglected, but it is right at hand, ready to take its former place in our lives and on our tables. Grain is not a simple silver-bullet solution to peak oil but is a potential part of the complex, cooperative response that will be required of us. Grain culture cannot thrive without community. And it cannot thrive for long absent a diversified, ecological approach to agriculture.

Here at our farm in the town of Ferrisburgh, just outside the village of Vergennes, Vermont, we are engaged in an experiment of sorts, attempting to bring local wheat back to nearby tables using antiquated machinery and a large wood-fired oven. Ours is a new operation, and our journey thus far (open one year to date) has not been free of pitfalls, yet I think that there is promise enough in this model that others might care to duplicate or adapt it. I would offer our example up as a counterpoint to the technological-fix type of approaches to current problems. Significantly, our approach has essentially nothing new in it. It is just our combination of elements that is somewhat novel. Those who are ready to accept that sometimes the way forward is backward may be intrigued. Quite simply, our grain operation is everything the mass-market system is not: small scale, diversified, vertically-integrated, and local in scope.

Ten acres are used annually for grain production, chiefly winter wheat. At an average yield of one ton per acre, this makes for 20,000 pounds of wheat berries. If some bran is removed during milling, we may have 15,000 or so pounds of flour in total. To buy an equal amount of flour from our local mill would cost $12,000 at today's prices. While ten acres is not a lot of wheat, especially by Western standards, it is a lot to us. Those 15,000 pounds of flour represent a potential 15,000 loaves, which retail for about $3.50 each. So that's a potential $52,000 worth of income for the farm. I say potential because we have not realized this yet; miscalculation and inexperience lead to waste here and there, but we usually are able to clean up our mistakes and profit, however slightly, by them because we are diversified.

Occasional spoiled batches and overproduction are facts of the baker's life. But on our farm we have the luxury of dumping our mistakes to the beasts. This is never as satisfying as selling every loaf, but it is better than paying to haul garbage to the landfill. The animals' main purpose is to maintain the pastures that will rotate back into grain production in time, and also to fill the barn with a lovely manure pack that will fertilize the plots under the most intensive cultivation. Sustained cropping arguably cannot exist without animals to aid in nutrient cycling. In the conventional supply chain, wheat is trucked at least four separate times—from the combine to the elevator, elevator to milling facility, then to a wholesaler, and finally to the baker. The average article of food is said to have traveled about 2,000 miles to your plate, but this is probably too low when it comes to conventional wheat and bread. At our farm, from planting to baking, a kernel of wheat travels about a quarter mile. At no stage are we dependent on any input or process that our community hasn't the potential to supply. This kind of start-to-finish control means real local self-reliance and security. It is what Jefferson had in mind for us.

Baking transforms wheat from one of the most durable foods to one of the most perishable, with a shorter shelf life than baby salad greens! Marketing to immediate neighbors not only means fresher bread but also fosters a stronger bond between grower and eater.

Initially, we intended to market our bread within a two-town radius. Perhaps even that is too broad and will cost us too much in gas, so our current focus is our own town and those immediately adjacent. In time, as travel costs increase, operations such as ours with a strictly local focus may become increasingly competitive, providing they do not depend overmuch on inputs brought in from great distance.

Most Vermont towns have at least a little arable land here and there. If these fields were stewarded with care, and the resulting grain diverted to a nearby mill and bakery, the resulting thousands of daily loaves could provide Vermont with a major buffer from the remorseless national food commodity market. Just one ten-acre farm and bakery in each of our 251 towns could provide two loaves made from native flour each week, year-round, to nearly 37,000 Vermonters, a major dent in our food needs. Even if a crisis never comes, if we succeed in reviving and reinventing our historic culture of grain and bread, we would be the richer for it.

A Portrait of Food Sovereignty

A book review of *The Town That Food Saved*, by Ben Hewitt

RON MILLER

Issue no. 37 • Autumn 2010

When we feed ourselves, we become unconquerable.
—gardening author Eliot Coleman, to Ben Hewitt

Food is a logical rallying point for the localization movement. Agriculture is the most fundamental of all economic activities, because food is essential to life. Food self-sufficiency, as Eliot Coleman (and Thomas Jefferson long before him) suggested, is the basis for independence. The corporate centralization of our food system has turned us into passive, unskilled consumers, utterly dependent on the money economy and on the availability of cheap oil. In *The Town That Food Saved*, Ben Hewitt explains why this system is on the verge of breakdown, arguing that "our nation's food supply has never been more vulnerable. And we, as consumers of food, share that vulnerability, having slowly, inexorably relinquished control over the very thing that's most critical to our survival."

The Town That Food Saved considers the economic and social dimensions of relocalizing our food system. Hewitt, the popular "Greenneck" columnist for *Vermont Commons*, spent many weeks exploring the dynamic agricultural enterprises emerging around Hardwick, Vermont—successful young businesses such as High Mowing Seeds, Pete's Greens, Jasper Hill Farm, Vermont Soy, and others that have attracted national attention. Persistently inquisitive and thoughtful, Hewitt provides a balanced, carefully nuanced study of the community. While the emerging local food system is widely praised and "feels right," Hewitt wants to know why it is right. Questioning simplistic assumptions, he asks "What should a decentralized food system look like?" and examines the ironies and controversies that lurk below the media hype of the Hardwick phenomenon. For example, if the economics of small-scale production lead to high-priced specialty products beyond the reach of a working class town's citizens, can the system still be called "local"?

Hewitt gives readers an unusually intimate look at the people involved—the "agripreneurs" who have become media celebrities, as well as farmers whose families have grown food in this community for generations, and back-road homesteaders who have lived off the land for decades—because this is his own community and he knows these people well. The information he gained from extensive interviews is spiced with wry and candid observations of their habits and attitudes. Hewitt is a thorough and careful researcher who gives us serious sociological insights, yet he is also an engaging writer who fills this book with delightful wit and humor.

Hewitt places the quirky stories of Hardwick's people into the larger context of an economically strained community trying to gain independence from the corporate system. This is the most significant story Hewitt tells. He explains how industrial food appears to be cheap because so many production and distribution costs are externalized—that is, they are paid for by degraded soil and compromised nutritional value, and by taxpayers in the form of subsidies to agribusiness and oil companies, rather than directly by consumers. As well, there are economies of scale to centralized production—and Hewitt gives a good bit of attention to the problem of defining appropriate scale—but at least a local economy is circular, and profits stay within the community. One of the keys to Hardwick's success, writes Hewitt, is that its diverse agricultural businesses form a complete loop from seed gathering to planting and harvesting to compost. The system is relatively self-contained.

When the centralized economy implodes, due to resource depletion, ecological collapse, and financial chaos, this model of local self-sufficiency will prove to be vitally important. "If ever the chemicals and petroleum stop flowing, we will go hungry; we simply can't have 1 person feeding 140 of us without these inputs. . . . Chemical fertilizers and petroleum are to agriculture what easy credit was to the housing market, and we all know how that turned out." We will pay more for food, but as Hewitt suggests, we will be paying what this essential commodity is truly worth.

There is a political dimension to Hewitt's analysis, though for the most part he understates it. At one point, echoing the theme Eliot Coleman sounded, he asserts that "there's a bit of revolutionary lurking in every small-scale farmer," but he does not explicitly define the revolutionary politics of localization. This, I think, is what he is suggesting: A life rooted in land and community reflects "a desire to connect with something real and lasting." To pour one's energies into this strenuous and financially difficult way of life is to resist the role of passive consumer. To claim, through one's own effort, a life of self-sufficiency, is to refuse the seductive ease of mass consumption. It is a citizen's life, in the best Jeffersonian sense, one that is engaged with the life of nature and community; a citizen expects to participate in the world rather than simply to consume. And this, of course, suggests a more authentic democracy.

Toward the end of the book Hewitt acknowledges the local newspaper editor's lament that the Hardwick revolution has been brought about by a small number of prominent individuals pursuing their economic interests; in other passages he explains how some in the community feel alienated by the success and fame of the agrepreneurs. But ultimately Hewitt sees these as temporary flaws in the early, transitional phase of reclaiming local systems. He argues that a healthy food system has the potential to invite broad participation and reinvigorate democracy: "The participatory nature of local food systems holds tremendous power, not merely to secure and understand the cycle and source of our nourishment, but to reawaken a sense of responsibility for and toward the communities in which we live." Even after his thorough, critical inquiry into the Hardwick phenomenon, Hewitt concludes that it is a hugely important step in the right direction.

INFORMATION

For many years now, sociologists have been declaring that modernized societies have entered the "Information Age," meaning that through new technologies as well as an accelerating expansion of experience and expertise, we have immediate access to a prodigious storehouse of knowledge. There are diverse interpretations of this development in civilization; some argue that the explosion of information will liberate us from political repression, old-fashioned educational models, and humanity's general ignorance and prejudice. Other observers are much more cautious, if not worried, because they believe that the sheer *quantity* of information is eroding the *quality* (meaningfulness, moral orientation) of our shared knowledge. We may not have the capacity, or the time, or the inclination, to sift through the barrages of data that inundate us, leaving us as ignorant and prejudiced—and as subject to political manipulation—as ever, and maybe even more so than in times past.

While many *Vermont Commons* contributors are avid users and proponents of information technologies and social media, we are concerned about ways that powerful institutions—government, corporations, media, school systems, and universities — can manage information to promote conformity and complacency in the service of elites who run these systems. As these institutions have become ever larger, more centralized and pervasive, their power to shape public opinion and cultural norms has increased despite instant electronic access to the Internet and the world's store of information. To take one example, in place of a buzzing multitude of newspapers representing diverse perspectives, we now have a handful of huge media corporations that control most of the print media the public reads, as well as the radio and television stations that provide the "news" available to the bulk of the public. Another example: the authority of local school boards has been usurped by federal and state bureaucracies enforcing their "standards" of learning. In significant ways knowledge itself is becoming more centrally managed even as it wildly expands.

The articles in this section address three quite distinct realms: professional journalism, social networking via the Internet, and education. While the specific problems of each area require appropriately focused solutions, they are all related to the larger question about who controls information. Again, *Vermont Commons* writers assert that under the corporate empire, control has been seized by elites for their own purposes, and they argue that more diverse and localized access to knowledge is essential for preserving a democratic society.

(Un)Covering the Empire

Rob Williams

An excerpt from

Issue no. 9 • January 2006

The *Daily Prophet* is bound to report the truth occasionally, if only accidentally.

Headmaster Albus Dumbledore,
in *Harry Potter And The Half-Blood Prince*

During times of great upheaval—election fraud, militarism, "terror" attacks, corporate corruption, and war—it is sometimes useful to take refuge in the wisdom of stories told to us as children. In J. K. Rowling's wildly popular Harry Potter series, for example, the *Daily Prophet* (the wizarding world's newspaper of record) often serves as little more than a mouthpiece for the Establishment, stenographically serving up "news" that reflects the "spin" of the Ministry of Magic, while chipping away at the reputations of those who challenge the Ministry's power. Helped along by mentors such as Dumbledore, Harry and his young school-mates, wizards-in-training all, begin to realize that much of what passes for official "news" in the *Daily Prophet* is nothing more than carefully constructed public-relations propaganda designed to manipulate wizard hearts and minds.

Popular children's stories like Harry Potter often reveal much about the way the real world works. Remember the classic about the Emperor's New Clothes? Once upon a time, a rich and powerful emperor ordered snazzy new garments from a tailor with a sense of humor, an outfit consisting of nothing more than his birthday suit. The Emperor proved so taken with his new threads that he refused to acknowledge that he was *sans* clothing, parading about for the entire world to see. All of his loyal subjects, busy bowing and scraping, couldn't bring themselves to tell him the truth. The Emperor was naked. One person in the crowd—a lone child—refuses to wallow in this exercise in collective denial, decid-ing not to play along with the game. And that one child began telling others, who told others, who pointed it out to others, and soon—the story got out. The Emperor was naked. In a healthy and functioning democratic society, journalists must play the role of the child in that well-known fable. It is journalists who ask hard questions of the powerful. It is journalists who provide a rigorous accounting of the evidence as it presents itself. It is journalists who report truths about the way the world works, no matter how inconvenient or troubling. The empire is naked.

As the United States enters the twenty-first century, however, its third century as a so-called constitutional republic, most mainstream American journalists, out of fear, ignorance, or denial, refuse to acknowledge a simple fact about our great country: the empire is naked. The state of our "news" culture (and I use the term loosely) is deeply troubling. The United States is now the most powerful empire in the world. And, as citizens of the most powerful empire in world history, Americans had better know what the heck is going on. But when it comes to "news," Americans live in one of the most heavily censored societies in the world. "Censorship" in the United States, you say? Preposterous. (Note: we are conditioned from birth to believe exactly the opposite). Choices, we are told, define our media culture, unlike those oppressive top-down state-run regimes—Cuba, say, or the pre-*glasnost* Soviet Union—in which state-controlled media tell people what to think. We've got dozens of television stations, hundreds of magazines, thousands of radio stations, millions of web sites. Censorship? Don't be absurd.

Pay no attention to the fact that most Americans surveyed claim to get all of their news and information about the world from television. Or that we see, on average, more than 3,000 advertisements each day. Or that 90 percent of our media content is owned by one of six trans-national corporations. Or that millions of taxpayer dollars are funneled into dozens of federal agencies for the express purpose of subsidizing the manufacture of corporate-friendly "news" in the form of video news releases broadcast daily on millions of American TV sets without being identified as such. Or that big business spends more than 1 trillion dollars each year on powerful advertising, marketing, and branding campaigns that influence the ways we think, feel, buy, and behave. Just ignore such inconvenient facts. The empire is naked.

Project Censored

News Media Checking in at the ICU

Taylor Silvestri

Issue no. 39 • Winter 2011

A free press is essential to democracy. It writes history, shapes public opinion, and consequentially controls the future. If the people rule the press, they rule themselves. They are able to put whatever or whomever they want on trial—the murderer, the embezzler, the Wall Street executive, even the entire system of government.

But we know that democracy, in the United States, is dead. The power of many voices has disappeared, and, in its place, a single, centralized voice has grown. The people do not own the press and they do not rule themselves—the private sector does; it is that private sector, those corporate owners, that shapes public opinion. They write the history we teach to each new generation, and they dictate our future. It is because of this that less and less quality information is made available to the public. And now, after Obama's campaign built on hope for a democracy, we more often than not have none. We live with the same hushed journalism we fell victim to during the Bush years. In the United States, corporate media censorship fashions our view of the world. When offered filtered, poor-quality information, what is there to hope for other than an idea of a country idealized, but never experienced?

Into this unfortunate world, *Censored 2011* (Find out more at www .projectcensored.org) enters and offers up an alternative. Containing the top 25 non- or underreported news stories of 2009–2010, *Censored* presents news and essays that go largely unnoticed in corporate news media. As explained on Project Censored's website, stories are submitted by journalists, librarians, and concerned citizens and selected by judges, professors, and students trained in investigative journalism.

This kind of collaborative news generation has produced the theme of *Censored 2011*: the Truth Emergency. Described by contributors Mickey Huff and Peter Phillips as "our own media-generated fictitious reality show . . . addled by pseudo-events and the hyper-real," the Truth

Emergency is a subject written about in previous volumes, but never at such great lengths. For the first time, this year's *Censored* is divided into three sections, all in hope to greater emphasize the lack of purity in news and how it threatens democracy.

The first section, "Censored News and Media Analysis," contains a chapter that covers the top twenty-five censored news stories of this past year. Selected and analyzed for their relevance to the Truth Emergency, the stories submitted focused largely on five categories: "the Internet, corporate malfeasance, the military, health, and the environment." With eleven out of twenty-five articles, the military is covered most heavily. Articles about unresolved issues related to 9/11, increased military spending, and the "secret war" in Pakistan all offer information otherwise ignored.

One of the most unfortunate issues covered in this chapter concerns the indictment of four U.S. presidents and four British prime ministers. In 2009, Spain filed lawsuits against both George H. W. and George W. Bush, Bill Clinton, Barack Obama, Margaret Thatcher, John Major, Tony Blair, and Gordon Brown for war crimes, genocide, and crimes against humanity. All defendants were accused of aiding in Iraq's "intended destruction—that they instigated, supported, condoned, rationalized, executed, and/or perpetuated, or excused this destruction based on lies and narrow strategic and economic standards and against the will of their own people." After a reported 1.5 million Iraqi deaths, 500,000 of which were children under five, the charges were nothing less than reasonable. But due to pressure from the silent mainstream news and external forces, the Spanish government voted to no longer practice universal jurisdiction in Spain just one day after the case was filed.

But going to war is not all the United States has done against the will of its people. As reported in *Censored* story 6, U.S. tax dollars have gone to support and fund the Taliban. In hopes of protecting soldiers, payment is given to insurgents to gain safe passage through checkpoints in Afghanistan. The article reports that, "an estimated 10 percent of the Pentagon's logistics contract worth hundreds of millions of dollars are paid to insurgents as the U.S. government funds the very forces American troops are fighting." An example of such a contract exists with Host National Trucking, which oversees U.S. delivery of supplies to bases in Afghanistan.

These articles bring up points worth exploring: The United States started a war in Iraq and continues to fund terrorist groups in Afghanistan without the consent of its citizens. Manipulated by George W. Bush, Americans were led to believe 9/11 and the Iraq War were somehow connected, despite the absence of any realistic proof. On September 7, 2003, Bush stated in a national address that, "For America, there will be no going back to the era before September 11th, 2001. . . . We have learned that terrorist attacks are not caused by the use of strength. They are invited by the perception of weakness. And the surest way to avoid attacks on our own people is to engage the enemy where he lives and plans. We are fighting that enemy in Iraq and Afghanistan today so that we do not meet him again on our own streets, in our own cities."

All major networks have perpetuated this association by airing this speech and others like it. Fabrications such as Bush's can be classified as state crimes against democracy, or SCADs. Unlike conspiracy theories, which "speculate each suspicious event in isolation," investigations of SCADs approach events in a comparative fashion. Lance deHaven-Smith explains in chapter 6 of *Censored* that conspiracy theories promote belief in "widespread but unpredictable" crime among the political elite. Analyses of SCADs, on the other hand, holistically research suspect behavior that contributes to a long-lasting (and false) public impression of world events. These crimes are at the heart of the Truth Emergency, and kick off the second section of *Censored*.

Chapters 6 and 7, authored by Smith and David Ray Griffin, respectively, examine the events surrounding September 11, the most relevant SCAD in recent years. They do not assert that George W. Bush planned and executed all events of that day. They do not accuse the CIA of plotting to destroy all three buildings in New York City and part of the Pentagon. Instead, they offer compelling facts, scientific and otherwise. Despite the hasty and unsupervised cleanup of Ground Zero, chemical tests were conducted on some of the rubble. Samples showed traces of a compound called thermite. While it is not an explosive, thermite is most commonly used in grenades and controlled demolitions to expose metals to extremely high temperatures, thus causing them to catch fire. All the buildings went down at a free-fall speed. More than 1,000 architects and engineers agree that a building could not fall at such a speed due to the impact of a plane. Architects and Engineers for 9/11 Truth, an organization founded by Richard Gage (a member of the American Institute of Architecture) has obtained more than 1,300 signatures of architects and engineers demanding an independent investigation of the events of 9/11, citing the possible use of explosives as motivation. These scientifically based findings are often written off by corporate news media for fear of losing credibility, causing them to get no recognition by the general public.

But all of these issues, at times, can seem so distanced from us. Luckily, *Vermont Commons'* publisher, Rob Williams, is featured in "Project Censored International," the third section of *Censored 2011*. Designed to "lay out proactive paths of democratic possibilities for the future," this section serves as a positive conclusion to a largely negative book. If the Truth Emergency, a curtailed lawsuit, and evidence of SCADs haven't compelled you to pick up *Censored*, the entire chapter on secession should do the trick.

Williams explains how secession is the "dirtiest word in U.S. politics" due to its unfortunate association with the Confederacy. It is this association that most likely has caused a lack of media coverage, despite the fact that "thirty of our fifty states in our U.S. empire are home to active secessionist organizations." After explaining the reason and logic behind secession, and why Vermont specifically could benefit, Williams offers the *Censored* audience a set of guiding principles to help reinvent a journalism more suitable for this century.

Two principles in particular speak to the Truth Emergency in terms of a solution: provide news for people, not profit; and institute collaborative funding. If information is generated by and for the people, it is those people who control history. Also, we shouldn't strive for objectivity, but rather we should assert our power in subjectivity, and fully embrace our values and goals as a news media platform. In doing so, we are free to report on whatever we deem important. Nothing is written off as too dangerous. Thus we contribute to the solution, as supposed to being overwhelmed by the problem.

That problem is as follows: As media consumers, we are offered information and pseudo-information and expected to discern the difference. While it seems like a simple task, the truth is that it's nearly impossible without perpetually asking the question, "What stories aren't being told?" In a fast-paced society such as ours, there simply is not enough time to thoroughly question each piece of "news," and even less time to do independent research. That is where this book comes in.

Still, some direction when reading *Censored 2011*: Do so with a critical eye. Evaluate as you should any other source of news. Don't fall victim to cognitive dissonance but make yourself open to the truth. (All warnings, I believe, the good people at Project Censored would agree with.) It is with a sharp and careful eye that we will make tangible progress in the fight to find truth, purity, and reliability in news media.

Perhaps there is no better time than now to take the press into our own hands, to hold ourselves accountable for maintaining truth in our own lives. Read a variety of news sources—local, national, and international, left wing and right wing, satirical and tragic. Declare independence from the hyper-reality put forth by corporate news media and take responsibility for our own enlightenment. Assert our power as the antidote to the Truth Emergency.

Beyond Facebook
Building an Electronic Front Porch

An Interview with Burlington's Michael Wood-Lewis

Rob Williams

Issue no. 31 • Autumn 2009

Michael Wood-Lewis is the founder of Front Porch Forum, a social- and community-networking website primarily serving (thus far) Chittenden County. The following interview was conducted by *Vermont Commons* editor/publisher Rob Williams.

Thanks for talking with us, Michael. How would you describe Front Porch Forum for the average layperson?

In this era of super-busy people, Front Porch Forum (FPF) offers a way for folks to connect with their actual neighbors and build community. FPF hosts a network of 130 online neighborhood forums that blankets Chittenden County. Since our launch in 2006, more than 15,000 house-holds have signed up, including 40 percent of Burlington, the state's largest city. By conversing online with their clearly identified nearby neighbors, FPF members feel more tuned in to local goings-on, know more people better, and often get more involved in community events.

So, I have to ask. Why do we need Front Porch Forum in the era of powerful social networking sites, like Facebook?

Facebook is huge, and like most huge things it is powerful and does some great stuff and some not-so-great stuff. But why not build Front Porch Forum on top of Facebook's platform? More than 90 percent of my neigh-borhood subscribes to FPF, and 40 percent of Burlington. I think Facebook has about one-quarter of the United States signed up, which is amazing, but not amazing enough. FPF is not elite; that is, we want everyone who lives in a town or neighborhood to join. Our software is designed to be as simple and low-tech as possible. FPF works fine on dial-up. If you under-stand how to use plain text e-mail, then you're ready to go with FPF.

So low-tech is good. Are there other reasons to support FPF in the Age of Facebook?
There is a financial side. Facebook doesn't allow for a decent business model. I don't see how FPF could be financially sustainable on the Facebook platform. Facebook is also not flexible enough. FPF's most critical software elements are designed to work toward its mission of helping neighbors to connect and promote community. Some of these would be difficult or impossible to implement on a closed platform like Facebook. FPF on Facebook would be like a funky food vendor trying to ply her trade inside a tightly controlled corporate-owned mall. Give me Main Street every time.

So philosophically, it sounds like you are running in the opposite direction of Facebook.
We are. Philosophically, Facebook's mission seems diametrically opposed to FPF's. Facebook and most Web 2.0 social media sites are designed to maximize screen time for people; they want as many hours of your life as you'll give them before you shake off this mortal coil. FPF is designed to promote face-to-face time among people who live near each other, with the hope that that will lead to stronger and more vibrant real communities . . . the bedrock of our democracy. It would be difficult for FPF to succeed with its mission in a Facebook environment where you were encouraged to piddle away another hour via other Facebook bells and whistles every time you checked in with your neighbors.

And what about ownership of content?
Exactly. Facebook owns all content produced on its platform (or it will whenever it decides to assert that ownership). FPF wants to own its content and it doesn't want to be in the business of aggregating neighborhood-level content for Facebook to use at a later date for some other purpose.

Any other thoughts here?
Facebook can reinforce cliquelike behavior. Facebook is good for renewing old contacts and strengthening existing ones but doesn't do much for meeting new people who live near you. And, finally—bottom line, too— Facebook is the opposite of local; it's the online equivalent of Walmart and Starbucks. Facebook (and Craigslist, Twitter, Angie's List, Freecycle, etc.) is a huge international corporation that feigns local. In addition to dollars, the online economy is really sustained on contributions by

participants and by readers' attention. Facebook and its ilk suck online eyeballs and postings from other truly local Internet-based services, driving them toward extinction. Decentralized control of media, information, and communication is one of the great promises of the Internet. Facebook works directly against that hope.

Okay, so can you give us some specific stories illustrating how FPF has helped to build community in neighborhoods in Chittenden County?

Lauren Curry wondered if her town of Westford had a food shelf. So she posted a note to her neighbors on Front Porch Forum (FPF). When she learned that none existed currently, she reached out again via FPF to form a steering committee. Then it was through FPF yet again that they found food, cash, space, volunteers, and, eventually, recipients. Her neighbors delivered on every count! Now, one year later, the food shelf is critical in the lives of many town residents affected by the recession. And no government, foundation, or corporate money or leadership has been needed. Lauren wrote: "Thanks to FPF, having a community-wide conversation about how to address our local hunger problem was a cinch. With the help of rallying neighbors, we got our food shelf up and running in no time. Not a community meeting—or practically any public-oriented conversation—goes by without FPF being tossed into the mix. What a wonderful gift."

So what do you see in Front Porch Forum's future, three, five, ten years down the road?

We'd love to see Front Porch Forum grow across North America and beyond, region by region. We've been operating our service in our flagship neighborhood for nine years and more than 90 percent of the 400 households subscribe. People here say things like 'I can't imagine our neighborhood without FPF." It's simply become part of the infrastructure . . . like sidewalks, the newspaper, and the corner store. I'm eager to achieve that level of success in many, many places in the years ahead.

Thanks for talking to us, Michael, and good luck with your important work.

Thanks, Rob. We hope *Vermont Commons* readers will take the time to find out more about Front Porch Forum at www.FrontPorchForum .com.

FPF is designed to promote face-to-face time among people who live near each other, with the hope that that will lead to stronger and more vibrant real communities . . . the bedrock of our democracy.

UPDATE:

As of July 2012, Front Porch Forum serves nearly half of Vermont and is expanding. More than 40,000 Vermonters subscribe to FPF out of their 110,000-household coverage area.

Decentralizing Educational Authority

RON MILLER

Issue no. 28 • Mud Season 2009
Issue no. 31 • Autumn 2009

What does the word "education" mean to us? Does it refer to the state's power to shape the minds and attitudes of citizens to provide human capital for economic and political purposes? Or is education, instead, an intimate human encounter between caring elders and young people with their own aspirations and potentials?

If we believe that genuine education has more to do with the latter, then the hierarchical and authoritarian structure of our present system of schooling is absurdly inappropriate. Through much of the history of public schooling, but especially since the publication of the Reagan Administration's report *A Nation at Risk* in 1983, educational decisions have not been made by those most intimately involved in the educational endeavor—teachers, parents, or young people—but by technocrats pursuing their agenda of centralized social management. All important educational decisions are made by distant, impersonal forces completely out of human scale, turning teachers into technicians, parents into consumers, and young people into products. The standardization of teaching and learning through prescribed curricula and textbooks, and the obsessive pursuit of accountability through relentless testing, reflect the concentrated power of political leaders, corporate CEOs, influential foundations, and the mass media.

Policymakers are not concerned with the experiential quality of life or learning in schools, but only with measurable results, with "outputs," with the economic value of the nation's human resources. People don't much matter—systems do. Standardization endorses the ruthlessness and rootlessness of the global corporate system and insists that young people dutifully play their roles as producers and consumers to keep the system functioning. Standardization rewards robotic learning, not creativity or imagination or critical thinking or self-awareness or moral judgment or compassion or wisdom or loyalty to community or place.

This is not an education for democracy or human fulfillment, it is explicitly an education for empire.

Authoritarian educational policy is truly a bipartisan effort. The Bush administration's "No Child Left Behind" was followed by the Obama policy called "Race to the Top." While "No Child Left Behind" was a dishonest, deceptive term for a draconian policy of intellectual conformity (it should more accurately have been entitled "No Child Left Untested"), at least we can embrace its literal meaning, which is the polar opposite of "Race to the Top," as the goal of a truly decent and democratic education. To conceive of education as a "race"—a competition forcing schools, teachers, and students to contend for some sort of victory—is to poison the inherent human striving for understanding and meaning.

Defined as a competitive race, education is not a collaborative art of mentoring and nurturing the young, but a frenzied scramble to succeed according to some external measure of success—to reach some goal line established by those in authority. Teachers and schools are considered to be successful if students score well on tests. Period. The actual quality of their knowledge and understanding and the moral, emotional, and cultural meanings of what young people experience in schools are irrelevant and disregarded. Education is defined as mechanical academic performance, diminishing the possibility of providing a meaningful journey toward ethical maturity and democratic citizenship.

We need to ask, as Wendell Berry once did, *what are people for?* and the question that should follow from it: *what are schools for?* There is a fundamentally different way to define education, success, and the purpose of a life well-lived. As Berry and many others have described it, it is the way of authentic human encounter, collaboration, and fellowship, not the way of empire. It is the way of community, stewardship of place, and human scale. It is the way of decentralized power and authority, of partnership, not domination.

Numerous educational alternatives challenge the agenda of technocratic schooling. They give parents and students a wider range of learning options and engage them in meaningful ways in the decisions affecting their education. The alternatives movement represents the decentralization of educational authority. It redefines learning as an intimate, human-scale relationship through which young people are empowered to discover their own inner resources and their own unique relationships to the community. Young people thrive in these learning environments and come out brimming with self-confidence, multiple competencies, and a strong sense of purpose. They consistently prove that abstract, rigidly imposed standards are not necessary for equipping youth with essential life skills.

Let's consider a few examples already operating in Vermont. There are several Waldorf schools around the state, and each of them has attracted a community of parents and educators who seek organic, holistic, "green" variations on modern life, such as whole food, holistic healthcare, and a more deliberate connection to the rhythms of nature through festivals, stories, art, and other endeavors. These school communities give people who hold a transformative cultural vision places to share, refine, and practice their ideas. Another educational community thriving under the radar in Vermont is the network of "unschoolers"—families who believe that the most authentic learning takes place in daily life, when young people become engaged in the social and natural world around them and pursue their own purposes and questions. This practice promotes the sort of intellectual and civic self-reliance that our most visionary thinkers, such as Thomas Jefferson, Henry David Thoreau, and Ralph Waldo Emerson, considered essential to a democratic society.

A few years ago, an idealistic teacher named Tal Birdsey started an alternative school for young adolescents in Ripton, Vermont, called North Branch School. He tells its story, with delightful wit and penetrating insight, in his inspiring book *A Room for Learning*. We see how an authentic teacher builds a caring, loving community of learners. Every page, every incident and observation Birdsey relates, is a gentle but firm repudiation of technocratic schooling. "The first parents gravitated to the school," he tells us, because

> something entirely different could be made. . . .[C]urrent political debates about accountability or state funding fell far short of meaningful discourse about the education of children. These parents, no matter their income, education, or political views, were seeking education that involved something closer to the heart. In particular, they seemed to want something more

creative and free . . . in contradistinction to schools tethered to right, standards-based approaches or school officials bombarded with federal mandates to test (pp. 31–32).

A Room for Learning shows exactly what "something closer to the heart" looks like in education. Birdsey sees each of his students as whole persons, with their own challenges, inclinations, learning styles, quirks, and insecurities. Most of them have been "wounded by school" (as Kirsten Olson systematically documents in her compelling book by that title); they are afraid of ridicule and rejection, suspicious of adults who judge them and of peers who band together in cliques to exercise power. They are reluctant to open themselves to others, to test their own limits or pursue their deepest dreams. Birdsey tells how he created a safe, nurturing space in which these young teens could find and test their best, authentic selves. "I asked them to embrace the personal pronoun I so that we might come closer to what was sacred inside of them. Those truths—their truths—would bring us closer to what mattered" (p. 59). Ultimately, what really matters to Birdsey and his students is a community where everyone feels cared for, a community rooted in love. This, not triumph in the corporate race, is what people are for.

Educational alternatives promote participatory democracy. As described by Vermont's own progressive philosopher, John Dewey, "participatory democracy" means a society that encourages individuals to take an active part in shaping the social and political lives of their communities rather than entrusting decisions to policymakers and other elites. Dewey explained that education must encourage active, personally meaningful learning and critical inquiry; he argued that the coercive transmission of an authorized curriculum can only educate youths to become passive citizens in an authoritarian social order.

Educational democracy involves the redistribution of cultural power from the hands of a few policymakers to local communities, parents, teachers, and youths themselves. By repealing standardization and obsessive testing, we would enable those most closely involved in the learning process to determine their own educational goals and methods. In taking greater responsibility for education, citizens would participate more vigorously in shaping the intellectual and moral climate of their communities.

Decentralizing education would allow all families to find learning environments aligned with their values and with their children's personalities and styles of learning. Alongside progressive and culturally alternative places for learning, there would continue to exist schools (and homeschooling situations) that are more highly structured or academically oriented, or more concerned about moral or religious instruction. The educational alternatives movement transcends conventional liberal and conservative ideologies; the coexistence of diverse educational visions and experiments would nourish a more vibrant democracy.

A frequent objection to this goal of educational freedom is that it would surrender the public school ideal of a shared social purpose, a common good that transcends parochial interests (which Dewey also emphasized as a key element of democratic life). Wouldn't our society splinter along lines of religion, ethnicity, class, race, political belief, or petty local interests? If we allow people to gather in separate enclaves to practice their own educational philosophies, wouldn't this give a green light to all sorts of religious extremists, left-wing radicals, white supremacists, or tree huggers to freely teach the next generation their weird beliefs?

There are at least two ways to address this concern, both of which challenge the very basis of the technocratic model of schooling. First, we need to separate the educational task of mentoring young people from the political task of forging a democratic community in a diverse society. We need to get over, once and for all, the Platonic notion that the state should be molding children into citizens. When Jefferson proposed a system of public education to support the new American democracy, he sought to spread the intellectual tools of reason, skepticism, and critical inquiry among the population, not to establish a "curriculum" authorized by elite policymakers, especially one that promotes mindless celebration of existing institutions. (He would be horrified, I think, by No Child Left Behind.) When we put educational and political tasks in their proper places, we will see that children who have their developmental needs (such as the need to learn through play) and their individual learning styles well met are more likely to become thoughtful, caring, engaged citizens than those who are bullied and processed by the system of social engineering the technocracy has established. The proof is in the creative, active, generous, socially engaged lives of many thousands of alumni of independent schools and homeschooling.

The second answer to the fear of social fragmentation is to recognize that people will always identify with communities that share their beliefs and values, and that this is a basic, normal human need. Unlike a managed social system or a colossal nation-state, a genuine community provides the experience of communion with others; we become involved with people who know us, who understand and appreciate us, who share certain aspects of our identities. In a healthy democracy, as Tocqueville keenly observed in the pre-imperial American republic, there is space for these kinds of connections; they do not threaten the political coherence of the larger community.

Granted that a functioning democracy requires citizens to reach out to each other across partisan or parochial lines to find common ground and collaborate for a common good, the desire for cultural uniformity can be pushed too far, until it becomes oppressive, even totalitarian. Social engineering is counterproductive: By forcing everyone into the ideological mold demanded by standardized education, the state drives people to separatist enclaves and makes them suspicious of commonality. Standardization fans the flames of extremism, while honoring diversity invites participation in the larger society. There is a huge difference between a democratic sense of social responsibility and public spiritedness (which Dewey so thoroughly described), and the technocrats' goal of social control.

Rejecting the yoke of standardization and enforced conformity does not mean "privatizing" education, making it a commodity that only the privileged can afford. A democratic society must provide all its youths equitable opportunities for cultivating their unique gifts and achieving their potentials. It will surely be a challenge to publicly fund a decentralized system without standardized accountability, but that is a task we must take on. We need to figure out how to encourage educational democracy without invoking the awesome power of the national state to enforce some authorized model of cultural conformity. For when the state becomes an all-consuming empire, this power is dangerous indeed.

One vital goal of Vermont independence is an educational culture that respects and encourages learning on a human scale, that supports caring and loving communities of learning. National educational policy is one more reason why we need to challenge the burgeoning power of the American empire. Because Vermonters value genuine democracy, treasure individuality, and hold as precious the local land and community, we ought to decline the federal government's inducements to participate in any "race to the top."

COMMUNITY

One theme that implicitly pervades the writings in *Vermont Commons* is the notion of *community*. Local systems and institutions are preferable because they are rooted in communities. Local economies support the cohesion and health of communities. Governance is democratic to the extent that it reflects the values and priorities of communities. What does this word mean and why is it so important?

The dominant ideology of contemporary politics celebrates the individual. "Liberty" means the citizen's freedom from coercion or the consumer's freedom to choose in the marketplace. These individual rights are (presumably) protected by the formal mechanisms of the powerful state. This theory downplays the role of intermediary associations—more intimate groups of people who feel a sense of belonging, loyalty, and mutual concern, people who share common interests and participate in common endeavors. When *Vermont Commons* authors write about "communities," or "the commons" (a term embedded in the very name of the publication), they are emphasizing the neglected but vital importance of these communal identities and endeavors. They argue that individuals need something besides vast, formal institutions (elite governments, global corporations, impersonal medical and educational systems) to meet their most real needs, to nurture their sense of place, of meaning and identity. Wendell Berry's numerous writings, to give one inspiring example, express this understanding that people must *belong* to "a place on earth," to the land and its local culture, in order to fulfill their true callings. We can thrive only in the context of community.

To honor the human need for communal association is not "socialism" as that term is often used or wielded as an epithet. It is not the construction of another layer of rigid institutional control over economic or cultural life. Rather, it is the recognition that pure individualism or a conception of people as purely economic beings (i.e., consumers) leaves us in an existential and political void, without the cultural capital to withstand the concentration and abuse of power. It is the recognition that we do share essential resources—natural as well as cultural—which ought not be privatized or converted into commodities for sale. Our best interests, our highest purposes, are served by a balance of private rights and communal responsibilities. The rise of a global corporate empire has eroded this balance, and our task now is to restore it.

The National Healthcare "Debate"

Greed, Fear of Death, and a Vermont Alternative?

Thomas Naylor

Issue no. 32 • Stick Season 2009

Claims that the U.S. healthcare system is broken are by no means exaggerated. The United States has far and away the most expensive healthcare delivery system in the world. Our empire spends more than $2.5 trillion annually on healthcare, averaging more than $8,000 per person. Spiraling increases in the cost of health insurance impose an almost unbearable burden on employers and employees alike, as well as state and local governments. The possibility of the American healthcare system bankrupting the U.S. economy cannot be ruled out.

But contrary to what we have been told by President Barack Obama, Senator Bernie Sanders, and other big-government-spending politicians, there is no national fix to the United States' healthcare problems. First Lady Hillary Clinton inadvertently discovered this the hard way back in 1994 with her abortive attempt to sell Congress on a national healthcare system. She demonstrated conclusively that such a system was not politically feasible. Unfortunately, she did not appreciate the fact that a national healthcare system for 320 million people was beyond the scope of human possibility. Stated alternatively, no one knows how to design such a complex system.

The fundamental problem underlying the United States healthcare system is neither an economic nor a political problem, but rather a philosophical problem. In short, the U.S. healthcare system rests perilously on two principles: fear of death and greed. The demand for healthcare services in the United States is driven by our inordinate fear of death. We neither know when to die nor how to die, and few physicians are very helpful to us in dealing with these questions. The supply of healthcare services, on the other hand, is driven by the greed of providers, hospitals, pharmaceutical companies, and health insurance companies. When human greed exploits the fear of death, there is no limit as to how high healthcare prices can rise. For those who are fortunate enough to have good health insurance, the message is, "You deserve the best medical care money can buy, because you are entitled to live forever." So say physicians and pharmaceutical company television advertisements.

Those with good health insurance have access to a plethora of very expensive, high-tech medical services, including magnetic resonance imaging, ultrasound, nuclear diagnostics, complex multiorgan transplants, coronary-bypass surgery, artificial kidney machines, death-defying prenatal procedures, genetic enhancements, and gene splicing. Antiaging clinics offer everything from yoga, meditation, and mind-body medicine to growth hormones, sex hormones, melatonin, herbs, potions, and elixirs to delay the aging process. But to little avail. Joel Garreau's book, *Radical Evolution*, reports on a new breed of scientists who believe that advances in genetics, robotics, information technology, and nanotechnology will allow us to improve our intelligence, reinvent our bodies, and even become immortal. This new field of medicine is known as "transhumanism."

There are dozens of drugs and high-tech medical devices and procedures claiming to prolong life. We have become accustomed to an endless series of announcements on the evening television news reporting major breakthroughs in the cure of this ailment or that, only to be followed by a retraction six months later warning of risky side effects or questions on the efficacy of the drug or procedure. By widening the boundaries of illness and lowering the threshold for treatment, pharmaceutical companies have created millions of new patients and billions of dollars in profits. By exploiting our fear of disease and death, pharmaceutical companies have redefined mild problems and common complaints to serious illness and medical conditions requiring drug treatments.

So strong is the fear of death that it's not unusual for the wealthy who are terminally ill to spend their last months either on the Internet or flying from one medical center to another in search of a physician, a medical school, an unproven drug or medical procedure, or a high-tech silver bullet that will forestall the grim reaper for a few more months. The problem is that the number of options available to the terminally ill patient is often completely overwhelming. How does one cope with so many alternatives? Is this any way to live or die? Vermont writer Garret

Keizer refers to this phenomenon as "physician-assisted eternal life: the desire of the old to avoid death at any cost, especially if the cost can be passed on to another generation." But at the lower end of the income level, it's quite a different story.

The problem with national health insurance is what I call the "I've got mine, Jack" syndrome. Elderly patients who have paid their monthly premiums feel they are entitled to the best healthcare money can buy. They never think about the effect that a $100,000 hospital stay will have on other people's premiums. It's all about looking out for number one. Indeed, it's not uncommon for a senior citizen to boast after receiving notice of a large hospital bill paid by Medicare, "I'm really getting my money's worth." No wonder Medicare is almost broke.

To promote its cause the Alzheimer's Association recently issued a press release with the provocative headline, "10 Million U.S. Baby Boomers Will Develop Alzheimer's Disease." Virtually all of the attention bestowed on AD by the medical profession, academic researchers, and the National Institutes of Health treats this situation as though it were purely a medical problem: All we need do to cure AD is identify the gene causing the problem and then find a chemical compound to allay the effects of the troublemaking gene. Apparently it has never occurred to anyone that AD may simply be the body's way of protecting those whose lives have become meaningless from the despair associated with prolonged life. AD may, in fact, be a way of taking them out of their misery. Not only may there be no cure for AD, but even if there were a cure, what would be the psychological, social, and moral consequences of administering it?

Notwithstanding the predominance of Christianity in the United States, with its adherence to the belief in life after death, our culture promotes a Darwinian, survival-of-the-fittest attitude with regard to the extremes to which we are prepared to go to prolong our own individual lives. It matters not how much of society's scarce healthcare resources are consumed by prolonging my life for a few more months or years. I am the center of the universe. The rest of the world be damned!

Regardless whether a national healthcare system is publicly financed or privately financed, if it is driven by the confluence of greed and the denial of death it will be unstable and financially unfeasible. Any healthcare system that does not confront the moral, ethical, economic, and political implications of fear of death and greed represents an exercise in utter futility.

Obamacare is no exception to the rule. Not only is it too big, too complex, and too high-tech, but it tries to be all things to all people. Even if the Republicans in Congress do not bring it down, it's only a matter of time before it implodes. In a similar vein is the so-called single-payer healthcare system endorsed by the Vermont legislature—a health care system that will probably never see the light of day. Neither the governor nor the members of the legislature have a clue as to how much it will cost or how it will be financed. It's pure pie in the sky. No one in Montpelier ever mentions fear of death or greed.

For any healthcare system to stand a chance of working it must be highly decentralized so that patients, physicians, clinics, hospitals, and insurance providers are in community with one another. To be quite blunt, if I decide to have a nice $100,000 open-heart surgery performed on me, I must be prepared to face the other citizens in my community, who know I have spent $100,000 of the community's healthcare resources on myself. There must be a feeling of, "We are all in this together." My life may be important to me, but I am a part of a community in which others want to share in the pool of healthcare resources. Resources are finite and must be rationed by the community.

The Swiss healthcare system, unknown to most Americans, comes very close to achieving this ideal. The Swiss government requires everyone to purchase health insurance with their own money from one of 400 Swiss health insurance funds, some of which are private, others public. If individuals cannot pay for health insurance, then most Swiss cantons transfer funds to them. Ninety-five percent of the population is insured against illness. The delivery of healthcare services is decentralized to the canton or town level. The Swiss healthcare system works, and it works very well, as evidenced by Switzerland's high life expectancy and low infant mortality rates. Swiss healthcare is second to none. What are the lessons to be gleaned from the Swiss healthcare experience?

1. Single-payer health insurance may not be the panacea it is thought to be.
2. Whenever possible, healthcare insurance and the delivery of healthcare services should be decentralized to the community

level, where the community might be a town, a country, a
village, or a region in a state like Vermont.

3. With healthcare, as with other things, bigger may not be better.

My favorite hospital is the tiny nineteen-bed Grace Cottage Hospital located in Townshend, Vermont. Thanks to a very generous and supportive community, which includes devoted patients, committed volunteers, an amazingly talented, compassionate, and hardworking staff, and wonderful benefactors, Vermont's smallest hospital will soon celebrate six decades of saving lives, caring for the sick, helping those who are dying, and encouraging those who are well to stay that way. It's the Vermont way of living, staying well, and dying.

The United States could learn much from Vermont and Switzerland.

From Common Wealth to Common Property

Peter Barnes

Issue no. 10 • Feb. 2006

We all know what private wealth is, even if we don't own much. It's property we inherit or accumulate individually, including our fractional claims on corporations and mutual funds. When President Bush speaks of an "Ownership Society," it's this kind of wealth he has in mind. But there's another trove of wealth that's not so well known: our common wealth. Each of us is the joint recipient of a vast inheritance. This shared inheritance includes air and water, habitats and ecosystems, languages and cultures, science and technologies, social and political systems, and quite a bit more. Though the value of these manifold gifts is hard to calculate, it's safe to say they're worth trillions of dollars. Indeed, according to Friends of the Commons, their aggregate value probably exceeds that of everything we own privately.

There is, of course, a qualitative difference between private and common wealth. Private wealth is normally propertized, common wealth is generally not. You can sell shares of private stock and walk away with cash; you can't do that with shares of sky. We humans have a long tradition of enjoying gifts of nature and society without legally owning them. It would be sad to end this or any other good tradition. But in some cases, end it we must, for the following reason: much unowned common wealth is in grave danger. It's in danger both of physical destruction and of enclosure by private corporations (with the latter often leading to the former). Unowned air gets polluted; unowned genes get patented.

Because of capital's ceaseless quest to grow, anything valuable that isn't legally nailed down will sooner or later be grabbed or consumed. We could rely on government to protect our common wealth, but that would be to misplace our trust. Government is, most of the time, the handmaiden of profit-maximizing, cost-externalizing capital. Far better, when we have a chance, to lock up common wealth as common property, to be passed on, undiminished, from one generation to the next.

What are the advantages of doing this? Property rights are powerful human inventions. In essence, they're social agreements to grant certain people (owners) enforceable privileges. Once established, they're constitutionally protected and very difficult to take away. If private owners use property rights to protect their wealth, why shouldn't we as common owners do so, too?

Because property rights are so powerful, it's largely through them that economies are shaped. Feudal economies were based on large estates passed from lords to their eldest sons, alongside commons that sustained the commoners. As capitalism emerged, the commons were enclosed and a slew of new property rights were concocted, almost all designed to confer some advantage on capital owners. Common property—as distinct from common wealth, and from individual or government property— has a long, though little-known, history. Frequently it is property owned by a community—a tribe, a village, a people. Individual rights to share in the property depend on membership. If you're born into the community, your share is a birthright. Conversely, if you leave the community or die, you lose your rights. Shares aren't saleable to strangers as they are with corporate stock. Common property is normally managed as a unit on behalf of the whole community. Moreover, future as well as living generations are typically taken into account by the managers. A classic case is the medieval common pasture; its survival for centuries, contrary to the "tragedy" myth, is the ultimate example of sustainable management.

What forms might common property take today? The answer, as you might expect, is varied: conservation easements and outright ownership by land trusts, birthrights to property income (á la the Alaska Permanent Fund), "copylefts" that allow noncommercial reproduction (á la Creative Commons licenses), open access and "common carrier" guarantees, pollution permits, "time dollars," and more. Some of these rights would be tradable, others wouldn't. Management of the rights would be placed in the hands of trusts, nonprofit corporations, and hybrid entities of various sorts. Managers would be driven not by profit-maximization, but by community-based criteria. I'd nominate four to the top: (1) preserve common assets, such as gifts of nature, for future generations; (2) live off income from shared gifts, not principal; (3) distribute income from shared gifts on a one person, one share basis; and (4) the more the merrier.

Such common property rights would represent the "we" side of the human psyche, just as private property rights represent our "me" side. Both sides, I'd argue, need representation in our economy more or less equally. Common property rights would also manifest our connection to ecosystems, future generations, and nonhuman species, crucial interests that, at present, have no traction in the marketplace. While the main reason we need common property is to save the planet, there'd be ancillary benefits as well. These include nonlabor income for all, a more vibrant culture, and a less-distorted democracy. These benefits would arise because well-managed common wealth adds to well-being in ways private property can't. The bottom line is this: a true Ownership Society would protect both our private and our common wealth. George Bush isn't likely to build it, but, over time, we can.

Vermont's Common Assets
From Banana Republic to Sovereign Commonwealth

GARY FLOMENHOFT

Issue no. 33 • Winter 2010

Although the term "commonwealth" appears prominently in the Vermont Constitution, what does that mean? We have largely forgotten about the notion of "the Commons." How appropriate then, that Vermont Commons would run a series about the commons. Common sense?

When we think about the commons, perhaps we think of the town squares of yore, such as Boston Common, which once were grazing lands for cattle. The commons may seem like an archaic term in the modern age of privatization, corporatization, and globalization, but the commons persists despite the concept being largely ignored. The air we breathe, our ozone layer, and our climate are commons, currently undergoing drastic change. Public roads, sidewalks, schools, parks, lakes, beaches, bike paths, and hiking trails are all commons. The Internet is the global cyber-commons. Public museums, libraries, music, money, law, democracy, and fairy tales are all commons. We can't exist without the natural commons, and we all benefit from the wisdom of our cultural commons of accumulated knowledge.

When we think of the commons, perhaps we think of the Enclosure Acts in England during the fourteenth to eighteenth centuries that "enclosed" the common grazing lands and turned them into private property primarily for the benefit of sheep farming and wool-making. It has become the prevailing wisdom in capitalist societies that enclosure of the commons in private ownership of all natural and social resources is the best approach. But is this true?

It now seems apparent that unrestricted private ownership is an inefficient means of allocating resources and leads to environmental destruction, increasing inequity, speculation, and boom/bust cycles such as the recent S&L crisis, dot.com collapse, housing bust, and the ongoing Wall Street meltdown. On the other extreme, history shows that a system of total state ownership of "the means of production" is even worse. In short, a new economic paradigm (or perhaps, the revival of an old one) is needed.

In 2006, entrepreneur Peter Barnes wrote a book entitled *Capitalism 3.0*, in which he proposed a new paradigm by adding an economic sector called "the Commons" sector, managed by trustees. In this paradigm, society's common resources (the commons) are reclaimed for the public instead of privatized by corporations. Private enterprise continues as before, but commons trustees set sustainable limits on resource use, and property rights to the commons are allocated to the public. Resource users pay rent to the public for the use of the commons and are no longer able to privatize the unearned income from mere ownership of the resource. Ideally, with this increase in revenue there will be decreased need for taxation of earned income such as income, sales, or profits on productive activities. Trustees would collect revenue from economic rent on the commons and allocate it to restoration and protection of the commons, other public goods, and direct payments to citizens.

A working commons model currently in use is the Alaska Permanent Fund, where mineral rights are designated as belonging to the citizens of Alaska, and 25 percent of oil royalties go into the Permanent Fund, which pays dividends to all tax-paying Alaskan citizens. What's missing in this model is the investment in environmental restoration and alternative energy to replace oil when it is depleted. Several other governments—Alberta, Abu Dhabi, and Norway—have "sovereign wealth funds" flowing mainly from oil resources. There is no reason Vermont cannot have a sovereign wealth fund supported by its common assets.

Common assets are parts of the commons that have market value. They take two forms: natural assets and socially created assets. Natural assets consist of those parts of nature that no human being may rightly take claim for creating. These include fossil fuels like oil, coal, and natural gas, minerals like gold, silver, platinum, uranium, public forests, electromagnetic broadcast spectrum, water, the atmosphere, etc. Socially created assets include all those things created by society as a whole that, once again, no individual can possibly take credit for. These include the stock market, monetary system, Internet, land values, etc. Every state has a basket of common assets equal to or more valuable than Alaskan oil. Most of them have been privatized.

Property rights to some common assets are already owned by the public, but others are not. To take but one example, the electromagnetic broadcast spectrum, if it were leased annually instead of auctioned off, would be worth approximately $782 billion per year as of 2002 in the United States. The public already has rights to this spectrum through the congressionally passed Federal Communication Act of 1934.

Liquidity of the financial markets is a socially created asset worth about $51.2 trillion in the United States. Federal Reserve system banks have privatized seigniorage (the right to create money) to the tune of about $8 trillion per year.

The Internet was created by military research (DARPA) using taxpayer dollars, yet U.S. citizens receive no direct return on their investment.

Land values are socially created assets, as without population or municipal services, land is nearly worthless.

All of these socially and naturally created assets lend themselves to the creation of joint property rights, the collection of revenue, and the distribution of dividends. Distribution of revenue from common assets directly to the public has many advantages including fairness, efficiency, and freedom. The marginal benefits are greatest to the lowest-income citizens, yet no transfer payments are required.

One of the primary ways in which wealthy and poor countries differ can be found in their ownership and control of natural and social resources. Norway, Abu Dhabi, and Alaska all have major oil resources, and are relatively wealthy. Nigeria has massive oil deposits, Congo has gold, diamonds, cobalt, copper, and coltan, and yet these countries are desperately poor. Why? One reason is that wealthy countries with effective governments all exert sovereignty over their resources and collect resource rents and royalties for public revenue. The "Resource Curse" is due to poor governance. Poor countries' resources are often controlled by foreign corporations, local dictators, warlords, or militias, and revenue doesn't benefit the public. During the current economic slowdown, Norway is turning to its $300 billion sovereign wealth fund to cushion the blow to its economy, instead of using debt. Alaska residents enjoy a nearly $2,000 annual dividend from their $30 billion Permanent Fund, and Abu Dhabi's sovereign wealth fund is the world's largest at $800 billion.

In terms of its resources, Vermont resembles an economic colony more than a sovereign state—a banana republic without the bananas.

Our major minerals are owned by a foreign corporation (Omya), our groundwater is exported by out-of-state bottling companies (Coca-Cola and Nestle), our hydropower resources are owned by TransCanada, and 88 percent of surface-water withdrawals in Vermont are used by Vermont Yankee for cooling water at no charge. The federal government, meanwhile, has given away 98 percent of our "public airwaves" for free and allows private banks to create 93 percent of the currency with interest attached. Citizens and businesses are subject to taxation of earned income, which impacts job creation and economic productivity, while resource owners collect massive amounts of unearned income.

All over the world, countries are beginning to exert sovereignty over their resources, such as Ecuador over oil, and Bolivia over lithium. Can Vermont reclaim sovereignty over its natural and social resources, or will we remain a banana republic?

RESILIENCE

Contemporary economics and politics are concerned above all with *growth*. More wealth, bigger markets, more information, increased power of managerial control—these goals fuel the continuous expansion of the massive institutions of empire. As we have seen, the *Vermont Commons* critique of empire derives from both political and ecological considerations. Growth for its own sake weakens communities and local autonomy, and thus weakens democracy. And on a finite planet, relentless growth is a social and economic form of cancer that can end only by destroying its host organism—human civilization and thousands of other life forms on this planet. In our view, the aim of a well-functioning society and wise culture ought to be *resilience*—the ability to adapt harmoniously to changing environmental, economic, and social conditions—rather than growth.

Resilience is similar to the notion of "sustainability," in that it intends to maintain the delicate balance between human activities and natural ecosystems for an indefinite, ongoing future. But the term "sustainable" has been co-opted by all sorts of industrial processes and development projects that purport to continue business as usual with just a bit of fine tuning. "Resilience" is a more comprehensive and serious commitment to maintain the full, vibrant health of communities and ecosystems. It requires more of us than buying "green" (or greenwashed) products from the existing industrial economy; it demands that we become more active, engaged, and conscientious participants in economic activity— that is, citizens of the larger ecological community rather than merely passive consumers. This is a significant cultural and moral shift from self-aggrandizement (limitless growth of personal wealth) toward a greater appreciation of balance and simplicity, of harmony with the natural world.

As the following articles indicate, the idea of resilience owes its rising influence to the Transition Town movement and its founder, permaculture expert Rob Hopkins. The approaching realities of peak oil and climate change have caused alert observers, like Hopkins, as well as Vermont's own permaculture advocate, Ben Falk, to realize that in a post-fossil-fuel civilization, endless growth will no longer be possible. We will no longer be able to meet economic and social challenges by increasing industrial output or devising an endless array of new, energy-dependent technologies. This new era will demand flexible adaptation to ecological and geographical limits. Communities will need to live far more lightly and intelligently on the land, and aim to maximize well-being rather than financial profits alone. As we are already finding in developed nations, industrial-economy "jobs" begin to disappear when the limits to growth begin to be felt. Resilience, then, involves "re-skilling"—learning trades and crafts that enable us to live lightly and intelligently, using resources carefully and wisely.

The Great Re-Skilling

Inventing a Twenty-First Century Vermont

ROB WILLIAMS

Issue no. 31 • Fall 2009

The future is not what it used to be.
—Paul Valerie

Rob Hopkins, author of *The Transition Handbook* and cofounder of the international Transition Towns movement, uses a phrase to describe the collective processes required to move Vermont from a twentieth-century state powered by oil, natural gas, and other forms of cheap and abundant fossil-fuel energy, to a twenty-first-century state powered by a more diverse portfolio of energy sources—biomass, wind, solar, hydro, along with the deployment of energy conservation and efficiency measures. He calls this transition "The Great Re-Skilling."

It is a phrase I have grown to like—suggesting a broad and inclusive process by which Vermonters relearn and remember (literally—to reattach) place and community by rediscovering older and more traditional ways of doing things, and combining them with the best of twenty-first-century wisdom—all in the name of powering our homes and businesses, growing our food, and moving ourselves across our beautiful and rugged Green Mountain landscapes.

The Great Re-Skilling is not some quaint, romantic, or naïve notion. It is a vital and hopeful phrase describing what must happen in our Vermont communities right now, as the world confronts the reality of peak oil, the impending collapse of the dollar, and the implosion of the United States as the richest and most powerful empire in world history. The twenty-first century, in other words, is shaping up to be very little like the twentieth, and far-sighted Vermonters from all walks of life, all political persuasions, are beginning to embrace the Great Re-Skilling as a necessary and promising path toward a more sustainable and healthy future for our once-and-future Green Mountain republic.

The signs of inventing Vermont's future are all around us, and we've covered them in the pages of *Vermont Commons* for more than four years now. At the state level, grassroots organizations—the emerging Transition Towns movement, village energy committees, the Localvore effort, Rural Vermont, NOFA, Peak Oil Awareness, and dozens of other organizations—are providing Vermonters with the information and skills we'll need for a successful Great Re-Skilling going forward. Our annual food and energy conferences, county fairs, and events like Earthwise Farm and Forest's Northeast Animal Powered Field Days remind Vermonters of the importance of reconnecting with more traditional technologies (in NEAPFD's case, draft animals as energy sources). Members of our school and select boards and the state legislature are stepping up, too, supporting initiatives that move Vermont toward greater energy and agricultural independence for this new century—the feed-in tariff passed in Montpelier last spring being a prime example of a big step in the right direction.

But perhaps our biggest asset in the Great Re-Skilling is longtime Vermonters themselves, who harbor a wealth of knowledge and skills we'll all need moving forward. In my own four-town community in central Vermont's Mad River Valley, which didn't see the coming of electricity until the 1940s, I am surrounded by neighbors who can peen a scythe or sharpen a two-person lumber saw just as easily as they can reassemble the two-stroke engine on a Husqvarna Ranger or fix the intricacies of a New Holland baler belt. Having comanaged and worked on a yak farm for more than one year now, I am nothing if not grateful for their wealth of knowledge, patience, and good humor. Their families have lived here for generations, they know how to make our land produce, and most of all, perhaps, they understand the importance of community; their generosity and goodwill on behalf of neighbors, much of which happens under the radar and with very little fanfare, is inspiring.

"The best way to predict the future," computer wizard Alan Kay suggested, "is to invent it."

Designing Our Future in a Changing World

An Interview with Ben Falk

Rob Williams

Issue no. 23 • Spring 2008

Whole Systems Design, Inc., describes its work as "occurring at the inter-face of people and land—where the built and biological environments meet." Based in Vermont's Mad River Valley, Whole Systems Design integrates ecology, landscape architecture, site development, construc-tion, farming, education, and other disciplines. Founder Ben Falk holds a master's degree in landscape design and has taught at the University of Vermont and Harvard's Arnold Arboretum. *Vermont Commons* editor Rob Williams conducted this interview.

I read a recent article you wrote in which you stated "Climate change happens. Design for it." What do you mean by this?

We need to prevent climate-changing activities as much as possible if we are to maintain a habitable planet, no doubt. However, the climate's already changing, it always has, and it will continue to change, some-times radically, even without human influence. How do we design for this? Our work involves employing ecological design and perma-culture strategies to develop buildings, landscapes, and communities that can be resilient in the face of increased climate variations—longer droughts, hotter summers, colder winters, more intense wind and ice storms, increased pests, heavier precipitation events, etc. Our site-design and development work buffers regional climates at the site level (microclimate development); diversifies biological systems and inte-grates them with built systems; holds water in the landscape; develops the highest quality, most durable, and passive building systems; and employs many other techniques for dealing with the challenges posed by earth's changing climate and society's hyperdependence on dead-end resources.

You've spent some time thinking about how we might redesign Vermont in the face of what might politely be called our "carbon-constrained future"—dwindling access to cheap and abundant fossil fuel-energy. What are some of the most immediate challenges Vermonters face as we enter the twenty-first century?

Start with the big challenges we face today: climate change, peak oil, nukes in the hands of rogue organizations, a U.S. government prioritizing war over all other endeavors, dwindling reserves of fresh water and soil, etc. How might these problems play out in Vermont during the next few decades, and how do we respond? Calculating your carbon footprint is a nice exercise, but first take the 30-second "will-you-survive-in-this-place" test. Imagine your home in the following scenario:

The electrical grid is down and it's not coming back up because Vermont Yankee had a major malfunction and Hydro Quebec pulled the plug after deciding that Canada or states downstream needed more electrical power (and could pay more for it) than Vermont. You're out of heating oil and the delivery truck won't come—even if you could afford the $5,000 fill-up. It's January and an "Arctic clipper" is pushing minus-20-degree air into Vermont. The fridge is empty but you can't afford the $10/gallon gas to get to the store. The septic system is full and the truck won't come.

So let's talk about moving forward. How do we think outside the box here?

It's silly that we've put ourselves in such a precarious position, because there are a few simple and affordable systems that could, at the home scale, fundamentally change this situation for the better. One's called a composting toilet. Another is a big home vegetable garden, and gravity-fed drinking water. Another is twenty fruit trees and a half acre of nut trees. Another is a root cellar. Another, better insulation and a masonry heater, or at least a wood stove. For the minority of us who can afford it, there are solar hot water and electric panels.

At the macro level it's going to take investment by the public sector and those who can tip the scales of affordability for renewable technologies, local food systems, high-efficiency building systems, and the like: passive refrigerators, solar thermal panels, high-efficiency wood heaters, greenhouses, edible and highly productive landscapes. It's going to take substantial state incentives, private investment, and community/ watershed-level initiatives to make the postcarbon systems shift happen.

The nearly complete lack of readiness of our rural population to provide themselves with a basic measure of food, water, shelter, and fuel is an urgent public safety issue and is antithetical to democracy. If our educational institutions address this challenge, it will be through reorganizing their programs, at least in large part, to teach, as Abraham Lincoln put it, "the fine art of making a living from a small piece of land."

We also need to think clearly about how we ought to spend the remaining petroleum in our fossil-fuel savings account: We can burn petroleum only to burn more, like we are now. Or, we can use the remaining petroleum to establish energy, food, transport, and manufacturing systems that will durably function with little to no petroleum far into the future. Right now is the most affordable time to develop a sustaining economy for the future; it's only getting more expensive each week.

The logical planning question is this: what does a more localized future look like, without the destruction and hardship involved in the localization of the past? We need working examples of more sustainable food, fuel, electricity, and mobility systems at every scale in every valley and every village. If our rural places are to support decent livelihoods into the post–fossil fuel future, they will be organized to generate the most valuable nutrient- and calorie-dense foods and fuels per acre. This would necessitate the third, and possibly final, back-to-the-land movement. And this time it will involve everyone; it's going to take a lot more hands on the land to bring about a more productive land use. Many people will again be employed in the northern forests and fields. This shift requires unifying land preservation and conservation approaches with use-based strategies such as hunting and farming. It's possible for forestry and farming to greatly improve wildlife habitat and ecosystem health while offering abundant livelihoods for people. The father of modern conservation knew this; Aldo Leopold designed farms that grew wildlife in the early part of this century, but we didn't build on his work.

So what role might Vermont's landscape play in the development of a more sustainable,
more democratic society in New England and, perhaps, the "*Untied* States" as a whole?
I think there are four facts about twenty-first-century U.S. society that frame our thinking here:

1. We are 80 percent urban (without significant production resources in the form of farms, forests, mines, etc.) and 20 percent rural.
2. We use almost all of our resources remotely from their source.
3. These resources are produced and distributed via petroleum at every step.
4. These resources are evermore difficult and expensive to obtain as long as they are remote and require nonrenewable resources to source and distribute.

How do we turn this precarious situation into one in which our livelihoods are sourced from a more self-reliant and renewably powered regional and local economy?
Part of the challenge requires shifting from an import-based consumer culture into a generative "producer culture." This involves a reruralization of the Vermont landscape, which will be producing not only most of what our own citizens need to live but also producing many resources for larger population centers in our region like Montreal, Boston, and New York City—places that, due to their density, will continue to be sinks for most materials and energy resources (but providers of nutrients, information, and cultural resources). If we think ultradense urban centers will grow a meaningful fraction of their calories on rooftop gardens, we are hopeful but not realistic.

If we imagine what a more regionalized and sustainable society will look like in five, ten, or thirty years, we realize that rural areas of this country are going to be pressured into performing the role that nonindustrialized nations are performing today. The future success of rural societies is dependent upon the degree to which they develop regenerative working landscapes: places that produce more resources than they consume. Even Thomas Jefferson could not have realized the true extent to which the rural landscape of America will be the basis of its survival and success as a democracy. I think it's clear that a primary way to overhaul U.S. society's imperialistic underpinnings is through the redevelopment of a highly productive rural land base that is organized at more regional and local levels than the current global economy.

So, are you suggesting that we view Vermont as one large diversified, integrated, but decentralized farming/production system?

Yes, with an expanded idea of what the word "farm" can mean—farm as sustainable production system, a renewing economic system. Farming in contrast to mining. Today, even in Vermont, most agriculture, and especially most forestry, extracts more value from the land than it cultivates; that's mining. But this can easily change: Vermont is positioned to become a leading example of a cold-climate rural land–based economy. What kinds of planning and land use does this entail? Vermont would provide leadership in regenerative rural economic development by implementing a statewide diverse-yield planning process based on important questions such as:

1. What is Vermont most suited to producing? What are all the yields—from apples to venison, fish, freshwater, biofuels, squash, plums, hydropower, slate, renewable-energy technologies, chestnuts, tourist dollars, carbon sequestration, hardwood, information, methane, education, furniture? These are all yields that this state's physical and cultural resources are uniquely suited to produce.
2. What are the current and future markets for these yields—who and where are they?
3. How will we distribute these yields within the state and out of state?
4. Which region within the state is most suited to each yield? We would sector-ize the state into zones of use and production just like one would do with a profitable and well-managed farm.

Okay. So what kinds of projects would be most strategic in transitioning Vermont into a more locally reliant, productive landscape?

There are numerous initiatives that could be started tomorrow with great success if the social and monetary capital was ready to back it. Some of that capital is already emerging, as many of these projects simply represent profitable business investment opportunities. Reducing driving miles and roadway maintenance while increasing our ability to share capital resources and production systems—tractors, chippers, kilns, commercial kitchens, sawmills, and other light manufacturing facilities, for example—is perhaps the most important overarching strategy we can employ. This means resettling the villages and town centers. Most Vermont town "commons" are today virtually abandoned. If we're here in one hundred years, they will be bustling again. Rural landscapes can become highly functional through diversifying land uses and yields, maximizing crop and product integration, and minimizing input needs through increased efficiency, cycling of fertility on site, and other basic measures.

Other ideas?

Why not increase the value of Vermont's ski slopes by grazing Brown Swiss, Jersey, and other alpine-appropriate cows, goats, and sheep? They've been doing this in Austria for a long time. Why would we mechanically mow the state's steepest hillsides at an expense when the same land can turn a profit instead? Imagine our vast, public-mown turf areas transformed into fruit and nut orchards. We can generate 1,000 new high-quality jobs in the state in the span of a year, as well as stimulate the local economy and increase local food security by producing 100,000 pounds of fruit and nuts per year on lands that are currently mowed resource sinks. Part of a livable future involves replacing fossil-fuel–driven lawn mowers with human-powered shovels, seedlings, and jobs.

Why should we wait for another dust bowl or depression for state-supported land development? Vermont is positioned to show the nation what a New Deal for the twenty-first century would look like. We have time perhaps for one more big push like we saw in the 1930s. Imagine if the Works Progress Administration had established tree-based agricultural systems that would now be bearing trillions upon trillions of calories for use as food and fuel oils, carbon banks, wildlife production zones, and beauty. We could evolve the Current Use program to incentivize multiple outputs of our complex forests instead of only sawlogs and cordwood. We still call timber management plans Forest Management Plans. We've totally missed the forest for the trees and have let simplistic silviculture dominate the management of complex, multiple-yield woodlands.

When Vermonters move to create an independent republic, I'm going to nominate you for Secretary of Permaculture. How long will it take Vermont to reinvent itself as an independent republic, do you figure?

The degree to which we become more independent and free politically is highly dependent on the degree to which we get the two primary aspects of our interdependence in order: economy and policy. By "economy" I mean the basic needs: food, shelter, water, healthcare, energy, some mobility. I think the economic foundation of any place needs to be strong before a place can be its own polity. Can we imagine a desirable independent republic without a vastly more sustainable, more self-sufficient economy? Vermont imports almost all of its basic economic resources. Vermont becoming more independent politically would most effectively be preceded by Vermont becoming more independent and generative economically. Broad-scale regenerative land use is the foundation of enduring personal and collective freedom.

There's a lot of talk and some action about making this happen. Take Pete's Greens for example. This is a solid model of local economic health; they produce enough vegetables for about 1,000 people, I am told. Vermont has about 620,000 people. So at some point in the future the market will support 620 more season-extended, diverse vegetable farms. That's fantastically good economic news. That's an entire fiscal platform for a politician right there. "I will see to it that this state incubate another 100 organic farms equipped with passive solar greenhouses, per year, for the next six years." I can hear it now.

I can, too. But let's not wait for the politicians to lead. It is up to us to begin this work on our homesteads and in our communities. Any last thoughts?
With vision and planning, Vermont could manage the state's landscape as the first continental redevelopment project, in which the colonial settlement methods we've tried since 1492 would be overhauled and rebuilt to be more durable, more profitable, more collective, and more democratic. It is clear that the development of a local living economy is the most direct way to connect ourselves to one another, to rebuild and reinvent our culture, to celebrate the beauty of this place and our lives within it.

When the Ecofads Fade, Ditch the Carbon-Footprint Calculator and Pick up a Shovel

BEN FALK

Issue no. 35 • Spring 2010

2010: a few decades into the Green Dream. Sometime in the latter half of the twentieth century, upwardly mobile, socially conscious, academically educated professionals—those who could afford to—began to drive the commercialization of products and services that were healthier, less cruel, and more conserving of natural and cultural resources. The intent behind this movement was, and is, well-meaning. It grew out of an increased awareness of the destruction wrought by global consumerism and has sought to change that; in the words of the movement itself, to "make the world a better place through conscious consumption." People set out to reverse the course of destruction wrought by consumerism, through a different type of consumerism.

Decades before the Green Movement emerged, a similar political movement was embraced by even larger segments of the population. Progressive politicians and activists worked through the political process, legislating for increased social justice, revamping laws to clean up waterways, and regulating the processes of modern industry to better protect biodiversity and do less damage to Planet Earth in the creation of "products." Indeed, much of modern "progressive" politics can be seen as an attempt to minimize the damage wrought by the increasingly destructive ways citizens of this nation make their living. And with each decade Americans moved further away from domestic production toward an evermore globalized, colonial resource relationship, all the while exponentially increasing the take-make-waste capacity of each citizen.

No doubt this movement toward no-VOC paint, ecotourism, green building, CFLs, organic foods, fair-trade goods, low-flow fixtures, hybrid vehicles, and more stringent regulations slowed the rate of cultural- and natural-resource obliteration, but it has not reversed the trend.

These progressive consumer and political movements of the late twentieth century failed to change the underlying structure that gave rise to massive human-ecological unsustainability in the first place. Radical consumerism and its transference of value from two-thirds of the world's humanity to the richest third continued unabated, further bankrupting earth principal (biodiversity, soil, fresh-water and clean-air reserves), mining human capital (physical, intellectual, and emotional health of individuals and societies), and looting value from distant places and from future time periods.

Thus, despite these movements, the scope of human destruction continues to rapidly expand into the twenty-first century with:

- Greenhouse emissions of nations ratifying the Kyoto Protocol still on the rapid increase;
- Tropical rain-forest deforestation accelerating;
- Nuclear-waste production increasing;
- Species extinction accelerating;
- Climate changes happening faster than at any other time in human history;
- Resource-related warfare on the rise, with concomitant waste in money, energy, and lives;
- Overall biospheric toxicity increasing faster than any other time in the Holocene Period, and probably for quite some time previous.

Confronting the fact that the social justice and green movements (let's call them "surface movements") have not succeeded in changing the human trajectory away from perennial emergency toward a positively evolving, healthy, peaceful world forces us to recognize the structural forces that are at work. We start to see how surface movements have served largely to distract us ("let them have green products" instead of "cake"). The most meaningful forces determining the resource relationships between humanity and Planet Earth operate largely beyond the influence of these movements.

So how do we effect meaningful change, recognizing that our choice of dish detergent or fair-trade goods is not going to change the underlying drift toward deepening catastrophe?

Sometime in the twenty-first century the systems that had concentrated wealth in the hands of the few—the same systems that had become the most dominant social-organizing systems on the planet—began to disintegrate. A few generations of accumulating instability from the system's sheer scale and depth of injustice finally overwhelmed its capacity to contain its own fallout.

What if the same cultural process that stimulated the social-justice and green causes coalesced into a massive force and began to replace a consumer society with a society of producers based in decentralized, egalitarian, human-scaled, smaller units of organization? This shift is beginning to happen, starting from the home scale and working outward, to the neighborhood, village, city, and region. It's what the Transition Town movement represents.

Ask yourself what actions you can take to harness this transition away from a consumer society that belittles your own humanity to an organizing force that fosters individual empowerment—a liberating and enlightening cultural revival that replaces consumers with producers, hyperdependency with self-reliance. This is just the tip of the iceberg. Starting down this road opens the door to scores of other possibilities. The lifestyle of the producer can actually be far more stimulating, complex, and interesting than a consumption-oriented way of living.

Be Here Now, and in a Thousand Years
Toward A Tree-Crop Culture

Ben Falk

Issue no. 40 • Mud Season 2011

The average American moves 11.7 times in a lifetime.
—United States Census Bureau,
Geographic Mobility Report 2006

The best time to plant a tree is twenty years ago.
The second best time is now.
—Japanese Proverb

It's not surprising that we still call this continent the "New World." Relative to the first peoples in America, who have lived here for about 3,000 to 15,000 years, we just got off the boat. And so far we don't seem intent on staying. We were taught in school that the American Frontier closed in the nineteenth century, yet the same boom-bust cycle has continued into the twenty-first, shifting from the Appalachians, to the Prairie, to the West, to the Rust Belt, to Silicon Valley, and the Sun Belt.

Now—finally—we're almost out of both places to live and places from which to extract our living. Our distant sources of labor, food, energy, water, and rare-earth elements are running dry. Africa won't feed China for very long, nor can Canada and the Amazon feed and fuel the United States for more than a handful of decades. Though we fled from distant lands to America, we continue to live much like refugees, constantly moving from one place to another, never staying long enough to culti-vate the richest values possible in a specific place. In doing so we've traded uniqueness for the generic, culture for commerce. Even those of us who can afford to usually don't stick around long enough to harvest the fruits of our labor, nomads not seeking safety but "success."

Yet, we need the opposite kind of culture—a people that mean to stay.

Strangely, running out of places to go and resources to plunder may be what we need most. It's easy to wreck a place when you know you can move on to the next. Without another place to go, might we finally be forced to open our eyes to what's at hand? To gaze not at a distant horizon but at the ground beneath our feet? Then might we ask, "What can I do here? What can I make of this place?"

This transformation is inevitable and will happen whether we engage it or not; the earth is finite and we're spectacularly overshooting our resource base. This shift will also be not only personal but cultural.

"Staying" seems to be one of the key ingredients to a livable culture and to any civilization that can last beyond a few centuries, especially in the modern age. Rootlessness is simply not a viable operating system in a high-tech (high-footprint) world with billions of humans, and it begets a mind-set of conquest, a broken chain of cause and effect, not of accountability. Indeed "life, liberty, and the pursuit of happiness" seems hinged upon close feedback loops between action and consequence. That can only happen in a settled society, in cultures where "home" and community are central, where the individual is embedded in a long chain of generations, inheriting from those before, leaving for those who will come after.

Fortunately this pattern is hardly new. The instances in which human groups have sustained themselves in specific places for millennia occur where cultural and economic (resource) systems were organized not to maximize wealth for the individual but to grow and transfer value across human generations. Not moving to the next place has been the only way we've built wealth enduringly. This kind of value takes decades and centuries to develop: barns spilling over with the autumn harvest, apples stacked high to last through a winter, disease-resistant crops from hedgerow to hedgerow, towering groves of nut trees, abundant herds of game, lush pasture and sturdy animals, vigorous people mastering their work, cultural memory. Human culture can create all of these conditions—even thriving ecosystems. But it takes generations of people skillfully committed to each other, and to a place, to do so.

Our task, then, at the dawn of the third millennium, is to transition from a society based in mining the most value as quickly as possible to a long-haul culture living not on the principal but from the interest. So, how do we develop perpetual, interest-bearing systems from which we can live? We can start by looking at those places where human inhabitation has lasted millennia—and to those who dwelled and did not despoil their homes.

In difficult dry regions of the Iberian Peninsula a complex agroforestry system based heavily upon the interactions between an oak-and-chestnut overstory and a grazed understory (using pigs and small cows especially), called the Dehesa system, was devised. Grazing animals were rotated through the woodlands with animals thriving primarily on the produce of the trees. The nuts offered a wellspring of fat and protein from year to year, with no pruning, no fertilizing (other than animal rotations), little disease pressure, no irrigation, and no bare soil, no erosion, complete groundwater recharging/moisture retention. This kind of land use is the opposite of desertification.

The productivity of the Dehesa system has been found to be a higher per-unit-area than any version of modern agriculture in Spain, when accounting for all inputs and outputs. At the same time, the quality of the systems' outputs is superior to those of modern agriculture: chestnut-fed swine has long been regarded as one of the finest meats in the world, as flavorful as it is dense in nutrients, beyond comparison to grain-fed meats. The savannah-mimicking Dehesa silvo-pastoral systems were so widespread, evolved, and practiced for so many centuries that until the twentieth century many ecologists did not recognize the anthropogenic origins of these ecosystems. As the agroforestry practices of planting, cutting, pruning, and grazing waned in the modern era so, too, has the diversity of "wild" life in these woodlands, while springs dried up, soil-building slowed, and the region has become more arid, brittle, and less productive.

In what is now California, the Sierra Miwok, Yokuts, Chumash, and at least a dozen other first peoples developed perennial, fire-managed ecosystems that grew a stunning abundance of game along with medicinal plants in the understory of black oak–dominated woodlands. Peoples in California also developed systems based around sugar pine, hazelnut, and other masting and often exceptionally long-lived plants, using fire, transplanting, and selective cutting rather than grazing (having none of the domestic-able animals available in Eurasia). In the Sierra Nevada Mountains individual sugar-pine groves were often tended to by single clans, climbed and harvested for a dozen or more human generations (sugar-pines can yield rich pine nuts for 300–500 years). Imagine harvesting food from a tree that your great-grandfather planted, that your grandfather then climbed to harvest nuts from, that your father climbed and rested beneath, whose seeds your mother made a flour from to nourish you, that your son will feed your grandchildren from, that your grand-children, when the tree dies, will use the wood for shelter, the inner bark for medicines, the resin for fire-starter, the needles as incense in a cere-mony for the tree and for the lives which the tree made possible. Such is the life of a people who live close to trees, intentional in their legacy.

Over a period of at least one hundred human generations those dwell-ing in eastern North America guided the development of vast food forests. The Wabanaki, Algonquian, and Mahican peoples, the Abenaki, Huron, Iroquois, Manhattan, Massachuset, Narragansett, Penobscot, Seneca, Shinnecock, and others promoted an intergenerational food, fuel, fiber, and medicine ecosystem whose foundation was the mast-bearing tree: oak, walnut, hickory, chestnut, butternut, pine, beech, hazelnut (they did not yet have the apple from Asia).

The earliest European accounts of this land describe an open "park-like understorey, everywhere growing oake and walnut." These visitors thought they had encountered an unusually beautiful wilderness. But, as has become clear, this was no wilderness, but a continental-scale forest garden whose crops were trees, the game they sustained and understory plants. As in other regions of the world where cultures figured out how to dwell for thousands of years in a single place, the tools and techniques of choice were fire, hunting, selective cutting, promoting the largest, most-useful seeds, and dispersing them (think Johnny Butternut) and a deep awareness of seasonal cycles to properly time these activities.

Why are trees—especially nut trees—at the basis of these regen-erative land use systems and highly adapted human cultures? In the simplest terms, it has to do with inputs and outputs. A nut tree is simply more effective and efficient at converting sunlight and precipitation into value, over the long term, than any other technology humans have yet designed.

This becomes clear when comparing biological systems in general with nonliving technologies. Consider a photovoltaic panel or wind turbine. Each requires large and damaging inputs to generate single outputs. What are the inputs for a photovoltaic panel? Bauxite from which to smelt the aluminum frame, silicon and numerous other miner-als (many only found in difficult-to-access and a dwindling number of places on the planet), and myriad other mined and smelted metals and minerals. These all must be mined, transported, refined, transported again, then fabricated, then shipped again. All for one output: electricity.

What are the inputs required for a nut tree? An exchange between breeder and planter, transporting of the seed or seedling, some wood-chip mulch, rain, and sunshine. And time. What are its yields? Oxygen, soil, wildlife food and housing, moisture retention, carbon sequestration, air filtration, human food, stock feed, building materials, shade, windbreak, and beauty, to name a few.

The former resource path—the abiotic—provides us with a practical service at great cost. The latter, biological (or "soft") path creates an enduring and generative legacy of positive value. And whereas a solar panel or wind turbine or green building offers diminishing yields over time, a nut tree's output actually increases, for at least the first century or two of its lifetime.

Such is the power—and imperative—of biological systems: They are the only means we have of sidestepping entropy, at least for significant periods of time, on this planet. That's what tips the balance; it all comes down to capture, storage, and transfer. The best system is the one that can harvest the most sunlight and moisture, then store that value for the longest period of time while converting some of it into products and services that other living things, like humans, can use. And biological systems do this very well, while nonliving mechanical systems cannot.

In the modern era enough research has been done to quantify the advantage of cropping with trees over annual crops. Accepted yields for chestnut, for example, are 800 to 1,500 pounds per acre. That rivals modern corn production on deep-soil land. However, corn only produces such a crop with constant labor and fertility inputs each year while reducing the land's capacity to produce due to its erosive forces on the soil. A chestnut orchard, on the other hand, actually improves the land's (and climate's) capacity from year to year while it yields; it requires no bare soil or fertility inputs, and it produces hundreds of annual yields from each plant on marginal/shallow-soiled land (far more of the earth's cover type than deep-soiled land), while taking up less space than corn. As well, you can crop the same area with other species simultaneously: e.g., a chestnut orchard is also a pasture, also a game preserve/farm, also a place for understory berries and medicinals.

All in all you can grow about three to eight times the product value (protein, fat, carbohydrate, BTUs and other nutrients/values) via a tree-crop system like chestnut than an annual, input-dependent crop like corn, and you can do so while improving the land from decade to decade. Annual cropping, year after year, always leads to a ruined soil and culture. Mesopotamia, much of Greece, and many other empires were once forested; now they are deserts.

Despite abundant human cleverness we haven't invented a better way to store energy than a stack of firewood. We haven't yet devised a more effective means of capturing solar energy than by putting up a cow and hay in a barn through the winter. Biological energy harvesting and storage is what has allowed us to survive to this point, and our experiments of replacing biological systems with mechanical and chemical systems have at best been delayed catastrophes. We must rely on nonbiological aspects (the barn in the above example), but wherever we do we compromise the system and our own returns in the long term. The minute a barn is built it begins to decay. The famous comparison of a tractor with a draft horse highlights the entropy principle at work here: A tractor and horse are comparable in the amount of work they can achieve on a small piece of land, yet after a time the tractor dies and the horse makes another horse. Only life processes are regenerative. As such, our prospects for thriving on this planet depend upon our ability to partner with life forces.

Life, however, can be slow. Who can wait decades for a return on investment? Actually, most of us do already: pensions, Social Security, mortgages. A nut tree beats an IRA, hands down, on a strictly monetary basis alone (not counting all the side yields). Indeed, one could consider such an investment a "collective retirement account," maturing in 10–30 years and yielding ever-increasing returns for its first 100–200 years at least. Stone (nut) pines (which populate huge swaths of the Siberian taiga and are amenable to Vermont's climate and soils) often bear for 400 years. Go gamble on Lehman Brothers for a 100-year return.

Your apple tree, however, can easily do that. Planted for $100 and tended to at a cost of $50 per year, in your time the tree will yield roughly 50,000 pounds ($150,000 worth at $3/pound) of fruit in its first century— a total return on investment (ROI) of 2,841 percent and an annualized rate of return of 7.1 percent (almost exactly the same as a 50/50 bond/ stock portfolio over the last 100 years). If you didn't count your time pruning and harvesting, and chalked that up to family fun, your overall ROI would be 150,000 percent in 100 years. Over 50 years your A.P.R. would be 15.8 percent—not slow money.

Trees are one of the only financial instruments we can rationally depend upon for long-term returns on investment. Perhaps this is why humans have invested in trees for millennia and in banks for a brief moment in time. Unlike an IRA or Social Security, barring a lightning strike your family's nut tree carries a guarantee that the U.S. Treasury simply can't make (even if it wasn't bankrupt); it simply hasn't been around long enough.

One can find mature nut trees today that started yielding before the United States existed. Similarly, one can plant a tree today that will likely be bearing after this nation's life span is over. On the thousands of pounds of value falling from your tree year after year, you will pay not a cent of tax. The value is all for you—and for the squirrel, the owl, the soil, the groundwater, the climate, and your children.

Imagine inheriting a food forest. Imagine creating one. Planting season begins when the ground thaws and ends at leaf-out. Your inter-generational legacy can begin today.

PART THREE

Decentralism and the Vermont Tradition

Up to this point, the contributors to this volume have reviewed the multiple social, economic, and environmental problems they believe are caused or aggravated by the concentration of power and the activities of global empire. They have suggested that the deconcentration or decentralization of power offers possible solutions to these issues. At the very least, they argue that a more locally and regionally rooted democratic society will clear space for experimentation, innovation, and the diversity of responses that ecology shows is essential to the long-term resilience of species, including humans.

In this section, we explore the specific political philosophy of decentralism more deeply. In publishing these articles, *Vermont Commons* featured the views of two of Vermont's own leading political theorists—John McClaughry and Frank Bryan—as well as the seminal work of author Kirkpatrick Sale and the provocative historical analysis of Adrian Kuzminski. They show us that "decentralism" is not a momentary or quixotic response to specific realities such as George Bush's wars and constitutional abuses, but a long-established tradition in the United States and an essential component of Vermont's democratic heritage. Furthermore, these ideas have been cogently expressed by thoughtful European critics of excessive nationalism and militarism for well over a century. These thinkers are largely unknown in mainstream political discourse today but surely it is time to discover them.

Decentralism does not fit neatly on the left-right continuum; in fact it transcends conventional political labels. Some *Vermont Commons* contributors, such as McClaughry, are well-known conservatives, while others are distinctly progressive, even radical, in their orientation. What we hold in common, significantly, is a view that political and social values should be determined by communities and by polities intimate enough for people to discuss their experiences and beliefs in democratic forums. Some localities and regions will tend to prefer more "conservative" values, others will tend to the "liberal," while many will maintain a more or less fluid balance. What these writers generally loathe about the modern political system is the blanket imposition of policies by distant, powerful institutions that leaves little or no room for authentic democratic dialogue.

Vermont is widely seen as a quirky little enclave in the United States—one, for example, where an avowed socialist is enthusiastically elected to the U.S. Senate. It is no accident that the ideas explored in *Vermont Commons* are circulating here, inside Vermont. Democratic decentralism is strongly rooted in Vermont's unique history, and, as the nation has lurched toward imperialism over the last century, the contrast between its—and more particularly Vermont's—founding vision and present reality has grown evermore glaring. If the expansion of empire continues, it may even be necessary for democratic enclaves like Vermont to withdraw from it—that is, to secede—in order to preserve the well-being of their own citizens and communities. The founders of *Vermont Commons* and many of its contributors believe that that time has already arrived, and we will present their arguments later. First, it is important to fully understand the philosophy of decentralism that gives rise to such a dramatic position. In this section, then, we call attention to the vision of participatory democracy that presumably inspired the revolution of 1776 and the founding of the original Republic of Vermont one year later.

Left and Right

An Introduction to Decentralism

JOHN MCCLAUGHRY

Issue no. 24 • Summer 2008

Throughout human history, there has been a persistent yearning among ordinary peoples to live under comprehensible social, political, and economic conditions that afforded them shared customs and memories, agreed-upon standards of right behavior, recognized status, security against brigandage and invasion, and reasonable prospects for achieving economic security.

For millennia, the most promising route to this happy condition was incorporation into a larger, centrally controlled entity that offered security and profitable commerce, at the price of political subjection and taxation. Hence, the subjection and incorporation of Gaulish tribes into the Roman Empire, the entrance of the mini-kingdoms of Dark Age England into the unified nation of Alfred; the creation by independent cantons and colonies of Switzerland and the United States; and the submission of Indian principalities into the empires of Akbar and Victoria.

But equally persistent has been backlash against centralization, whether voluntary or forced. At first, centralism may provide tangible benefits. But over time, local sentiment comes to believe that "they" at the center are governing ignorantly or unfairly; "they" are in the grip of corrupt and greedy special interests; "they" think naught of our hallowed customs and traditions; "we" have little or nothing to say about it; "we" have been forced to send our wealth to the decadent center, and give up "our" soldiers to defend its imperial frontiers. This centrifugal tendency was first described as historically inevitable by the great Arab historian Ibn Khaldun in his *Muqaddimah*, published in 1377.

This anticentralization backlash naturally takes many forms, depending on which sort of centralization is complained of. It often is described as "decentralism," but that word generally connotes not so much a defined philosophy, as a label for arguments that sketch out resistance against the manifold ills caused by the centralization of power. Consider these varied examples of "decentralism": the Lutherans who walked out of the Roman Catholic Church; the "Velvet Revolution" that peacefully separated Slovakia and the Czech Republic; the jealously guarded economic independence of Hong Kong from Communist control in Beijing; the secession of the Austrian village of Woergl from that nation's failed national currency system; charter schools opting out of state public school systems; or naturopaths and ayurvedics rejecting the prescriptions of allopathic medicine.

To these examples must be added the secessionist Second Vermont Republic, whose adherents want to take the state out of George W. Bush's American empire. (Whether this secessionist ardor will survive a possible Obama presidency is an interesting question.)

All of these examples evince a determination of some group of people to "do things our way," independent of control from the center. History is rife with examples of cruel repression of decentralist movements—the Cathars come to mind—and, unfortunately, history is generally written to glorify the winners.

But despite the triumphs of Caesar, Alexander, St. Peter, Mohammed, Innocent III, Genghis Khan, Alexander Hamilton, Bismarck, J. P. Morgan, Lenin, and Franklin Roosevelt, the center rarely maintains its grip for long. And through the ages there have been numerous works written to explain, promote, and defend the decentralist impulse that breaks down that grip.

This impulse tends to take two forms. The liberal form tends toward the utopian: we're doing all this wrong now, but there's no reason why we can't redesign our world to usher in an era of happiness and prosperity! This version places great faith in the good nature of common people and their capacity to redesign their world if freed from the annoying and costly mandates from the corrupted center.

The conservative version, on the other hand, often offers a gloomy foreboding of creeping collectivism gathering all social, economic, and political power to the center, dragging society into a totalitarian dystopia. Somehow society must work its painful way toward mutually acceptable customs, governance, and ordered liberty.

The definitive universal work on decentralism, alas, has yet to be written. But here are a selection of works that together offer useful insights into the decentralist tendency.

Kirkpatrick Sale's *Human Scale* (1980) is as close to a classic as can be found. The central point of Sale's work is that when things grow too large, trouble inevitably begins. He examines the "burden of bigness," what happens when bigness overpowers the human scale in society, economy, and politics, and how it can be countered. Sale, a veteran of Students for a Democratic Society in its glory days of the 1960s, observes that government breakdown leads to "a resurgence of locally based forms, most often democratically chosen and scrupulously responsive, that turn out to be quite capable of managing the complicated affairs of daily life for many months, occasionally years, until they are forcibly suppressed by some new centralist state less democratic and responsive."

A work of special inspiration to me is Herbert Agar's *Land of the Free* (1935). Agar was the Pulitzer Prize–winning editor of the *Louisville Courier Journal*. His enthusiasm for a United States delivered from the evils of concentrated Finance Capital and its handmaiden Big Government is tied to the circumstance of the Depression years, yet the book exhibits a timeless Jeffersonian passion for distributed property ownership and protected liberty that, alas, is rarely emulated today.

Leopold Kohr is a name little known today, but his works have been published in at least five languages and have been an inspiration to many, notably Fritz Schumacher. Perhaps his most representative work is *The Breakdown of Nations* (1957). In it, Kohr points out that many of the world's problems come from political entities that are simply too big, and that such entities will inevitably fragment. With great wit and charm, Kohr makes a good case for a world of small translucent mini-states where the human spirit can flourish.

E. F. "Fritz" Schumacher is celebrated as the author of *Small Is Beautiful: Economics as if People Mattered* (1973). Schumacher became something of a cult figure in the 1970s, pioneering intermediate technology and new patterns of ownership (influenced by the UK Scott Bader Commonwealth plan). His essay on "Buddhist Economics," built upon a worldview of simplicity and nonviolence, was perhaps the most influential in this book, which is admittedly an uneven collection of lectures. George McRobie's *Small Is Possible* (1981) is an enthusiastic recital of people acting on Schumacher's ideas. A later and similar work is Richard Douthwaite's *Short Circuit* (1996).

Another German-born scholar with more libertarian leanings is Wilhelm Röpke. His most influential book is *A Humane Economy: The Social Framework of the Free Market* (1958). Röpke is not an advocate of decentralism *per se*, but his courageous commitment to a free society fighting to survive against fascism, communism, and the suffocating welfare state shines through half a century after he wrote. He is much in tune with Catholic social thought, which has always feared great concentrations of secular power as destructive to the human spirit and human community. Another valuable Röpke volume is *The Moral Foundations of Civil Society* (1948).

Similar to Röpke in his concern for the effects of mass society upon the individual is the conservative American sociologist Robert Nisbet. His most-quoted work is *The Quest for Community* (1953), which analyzes the human urge to re-create meaningful communities when overrun by the forces of centralized mass society. A similar but more optimistic work is Alvin Toffler's *The Third Wave* (1980).

A classic work of anarcho-decentralism, one that exerted a powerful influence on such diverse thinkers as Tolstoy, Gandhi, and Mao Tse Tung, is Peter Kropotkin's *Fields, Factories and Workshops* (1899). Though dated and derived from Russian experience, Kropotkin's readable and enthusiastic work paints a hopeful portrait of happy, self-sufficient, autonomous communities spread across the vast expanse of Russia.

Gilbert K. Chesterton was a renowned British author, a Catholic much influenced by Pope Leo XIII's encyclical *De Rerum Novarum* of 1895. He and his fellow thinker Hilaire Belloc founded a Distributist League to promote widespread ownership of property. Alas, the League never became a force in British politics, but Chesterton's witty writing—*What's Wrong with the World* (1910) and especially *Outline of Sanity* (1926)—made him a household word in the UK. Belloc's most prescient work was *The Servile State* (1912), well worth reading today for its analysis of the development of industrial society toward a few rich owners, a larger middle class of skilled technicians, and a vast body of unskilled laborers whom the state must compel to labor. Allan Carlson's *Third Ways* (2007) is a lively account of Chesterbellocian distributism and other family-centered economic movements. Especially interesting is his description of perhaps the most decentralist of all national governments, that of Alexander Stambolisky's Bulgarian Agrarian National Union. It was in power (under desperate circumstances) from 1919 to 1923 and expired when Stambolisky was murdered by the Communists.

For a clear statement of criteria for a free society, and an antidote to rigid ideologies of both Left and Right, Henry Calvert Simons' trenchant essay "A Political Credo" remains a classic. It appears as the lead chapter in his collection, *Economic Policy for a Free Society* (1945). While not an explicit plea for decentralism, it recognizes the importance of voluntary associations and distributed property, and the evils of collectivist centralization. If I were asked to recommend one short piece to a reader interested in acquiring a foundation for understanding U.S. social and economic policy, this would be that piece.

Modern political decentralists of the Left face a problem that does not much afflict their conservative counterparts. The Left is concerned that no self-governing locality makes doctrinal mistakes. Thus, Left decentralists tend to endorse lots of centrally established ground rules: no ecological damage, no racial oppression, full equality for women and gays, living wages and protection for labor, no Walmart and McDonald's, etc. Right decentralists—sometimes grudgingly—agree that there must be some overarching rules to prevent grassroots tyranny, but they are darkly suspicious of a Center imposing evermore-alien mandates on cultural communities seeking to evolve in their own way. For instance, the Right has little concern over locally prescribed manifestations of conscience, such as obligatory affirmations of faith and values, an established church, and exclusion of "undesirables" from civic life.

Two recent works from decentralist-oriented Leftist authors make serious efforts to avoid excessive centralist mandates upon local communities. Michael Shuman's *Going Local: Creating Self-Reliant Communities in the Global Age* (2000) synthesizes the arguments for why communities should resist the temptations of globalization and instead strengthen their economies through locally owned companies, import substitution, new community financial institutions, and smart local policymaking. He makes the case, from a progressive political viewpoint, for devolving political and economic power.

America Beyond Capitalism: Reclaiming Our Wealth, Our Liberty, and Our Democracy (2005) by my longtime friend Gar Alperovitz is a sweeping analysis of what's wrong with modern-day America—globalization, financial concentration, opulence, imperialism, etc.—and makes a well-argued case for creating a "pluralist commonwealth" in its place. Alperovitz founds his argument on the need for universal state-guaranteed economic security, an expansion of civil society, and (surprisingly) the necessity of people having more free time. True to the socialist tradition, his prescription requires a redistribution of wealth enforced from the center, but it abandons the Leninist insistence of totalitarian control from the center by a correctly thinking vanguard. Alperovitz has been thinking on this subject for forty years and has a very creative and inventive mind. His wide-ranging book deserves serious attention even from those who believe that a government made powerful enough to achieve such redistribution will inevitably use its power for inhumane and destructive purposes.

Finally, I hope I may be excused for mentioning a homegrown volume, *The Vermont Papers: Re-creating Democracy on a Human Scale,* by Frank Bryan and me (1989). This (if I may say it) interesting work proposes to decentralize Vermont into some forty self-governing shires, to which the state would devolve perhaps three-fourths of its present responsibilities. "Let forty flowers bloom" as an example to the nation and the world! With the passage of two decades, some of the policy discussion has become obsolete, but the basic decentralist philosophy and the description of the proposed Vermont shires remains valid and—Frank and I hope—still inspirational.

This quick tour of decentralist thought necessarily neglects many valuable English-language works by such authors as Paul Goodman, Ralph Borsodi, Andrew Greeley, Louis Brandeis, Allen Tate, Wendell Berry, Arthur Morgan, Jane Jacobs, Edward Goldsmith, Ivan Illich, Henry George, James Warbasse, Michael Zwerin, Herman Daly, Morgan Doughton, and James Robertson. It also overlooks two authors whose indispensable writings celebrate, among other things, the decentralist vision: Alexis de Tocqueville and Thomas Jefferson.

Centralism's apologists will always find an eager audience among those who seek to win supreme power, whether in government, finance, industry, labor, religion, education, and other arenas. The decentralist appeal to keep power and property widely distributed among people and communities has little appeal for the Alexanders, Napoleons, Hamiltons, Lenins, Mao Tse Tungs, and Nassers of world history. Thus, decentralism is never likely to become a reigning philosophy. Indeed, it is difficult to find any modern American politician who has made an explicitly decentralist appeal, untainted by the "states rights" defense of racial segregation. (The best recent candidate may be Ronald Reagan, but his accomplishments failed to match his inclinations and occasional rhetoric.)

But the decentralist tendency never goes away. Like grass growing up through cracks in aging concrete, the human urge to "bring things home where we can watch over them" is always likely to be with us. Perhaps the best we decentralists can do is constantly strive to give it room to flower.

The Decentralist Movement
A Third Way

KIRKPATRICK SALE

Issue no. 18 • Spring 2007

Just a few weeks ago I took seven large boxes of books from my library to give to the E. F. Schumacher Library just outside of Great Barrington, Massachusetts—books I'd gathered for years on decentralism, anarchism, community, separatism, and the like—and I was struck once again by the depth, tenacity, and importance of the movement to which I was contributing. For the Schumacher Society and its library were established to provide an intellectual and activist home for what we can call, loosely, the decentralist movement. This is the Third Way that has existed for a century or so outside the varieties of centralists, both conservative and liberal; a movement that has vigorously put forth cogent alternatives to the modern-capitalist industrial nation-state.

The Schumacher has most of the library and all the papers, speeches, and articles of Fritz Schumacher, the economist and philosopher whose work outlining the decentralist way went far beyond the notion of "small is beautiful"—however trenchant that idea may be—to include self-managed firms, Buddhist ("right livelihood") economics, intermediate technology, organic farming, alternative energy, and matters of scale in all human endeavors. But it also has the libraries and papers of a number of other decentralist figures. Among them are George Benello, a scholar and activist whose library emphasized worker ownership, alternative technology, and the Yugoslavian decentralized economy; Ralph Borsodi, the founder of the School of Living and keystone of the homesteading "back-to-the-land" movement in the 1930s; Richard Bliss, a teacher whose material concentrates on the quasi-anarchistic Catholic Worker movement and the English Distributists (who were also called leaders of "a third way"); Henry Geiger, for four decades editor of the decentralist weekly *MANAS*, whose copies are available online from the Library; Robyn van En, the creator of the Community Supported Agriculture movement; and Bob Swann, a cofounder (with John McClaughry, Ian Baldwin, David Ehrenfeld, and me) of the Schumacher Society in 1980, who for years acted as its president and guiding light, as well as serving as a leading theorist of land trust organizations.

That's an impressive group, and it argues that the decentralist movement has not only been wide-reaching and comprehensive but durable and impactful. No, it has not had the kind of support from the capitalist system that has created and sustained the conservative and neoconservative movements or the various do-gooding liberal parties and unions—largely because it generally stood opposed to large-scale corporate capitalism and the large-scale governments that were its handmaidens. So it has gone along with small and underfunded organizations, working in different parts of the country on different parts of the problem, sometimes without even knowing the others existed. But the point is that it has gone along, for more than eighty years (if we figure its modern beginnings with the Distributists and Southern Agrarians in the 1920s), and it is still to be found everywhere.

Let me see if I can distill the essence of decentralism, and its appeal.

1. Decentralism is the basic human condition. The community is the oldest human institution, found absolutely everywhere throughout the world in all kinds of societies. As Rene Dubos has pointed out, more than 100 billion human beings have lived on earth since the late Paleolithic period, and "the immense majority of them have spent their entire life as members of very small groups . . . rarely of more than a few hundred persons."

2. Decentralism is the historic norm, the underlying system by which people live even where there arises, from time to time, those centralizing empires that historians like to focus on and pretend are the principal systems of humankind. Empires are infrequent, do not last long, and are sparsely located. Yes, there was a Greek empire, for example, but it lasted effectively for fewer than twenty years; the real story of Greece is long centuries of decentralization, each city-republic with its own constitution, its own social life and cultural peculiarities, hundreds of separate communities that created the Hellenic civilization that is still a marvel of the world.

3. Decentralism is deeply American, from the anti-state Puritans, through the communalistic Quakers and Mennonites and religious sects, and on to the original colonies, independent bodies protective of their special differences and characters. The war that separated us from Britain was not a revolutionary war—we desired to have our own country, not take over Britain's—but a secessionist war. A unified state did eventually arise after it, the product of powerful banking and mercantile forces desiring centralized authority, but it was not especially centralist at that time, and even then contrary forces proved powerful, too. Emerson and Whitman and Thoreau gave voice to the old New England traditions of town-meeting democracy and parish rule. Utopians and communards like Lysander Spooner, Benjamin Tucker, and Josiah Warren gave voice to the yearning for community control and villages free from outside interference. In the twentieth century that tradition continued with the Country Life movement and other communal impulses; with Lewis Mumford and the original Regional Plan Association, devoted to a resurgence of regionalism; with the Southern Agrarians, determined separatists explicitly— and eloquently—opposed to the national government and its economic hegemony. And think of Henry George and the Georgists, Paul Goodman, Arthur Morgan and his Community Service organization, Ivan Illich, Gary Snyder, Helen and Scott Nearing and their Good Life Center, Wendell Berry, Thomas Berry, Chellis Glendinning and the neo-Luddites, Jerry Mander and the anti-globalists   well, the list could go on into the thousands.

4. Decentralism continues even now; it is alive and well in this country and around the world. I cannot say it is a dominant mode, anywhere, but I can point to all those ineradicable threads to be seen throughout the American scene: the wonderful bioregional movement, for example; the resurgent Indian tribal societies and organizations for tribal culture; the growth of worker-owned firms from 1,600 twenty years ago to more than 10,000 today; the phenomenon of cooperative businesses, which as of 2005 had revenues of nearly $1 trillion; the spread

of such efforts as community currencies, community land trusts (100 of them today, at least) and community-supported agriculture (1,140 farms) and local farmers' markets (4,400 in 2006); and the 250,000 private government associations housing more than 50 million people.

All of this is evidence that this great tradition, this basic human impulse, is still to be found in the United States, no matter how autocratic a power it has become. And in the rest of the world, as well. Separatism, of course, is a powerful force in almost every land, famously in Canada, Spain, Italy, France, and virtually everywhere in Africa, existing in a hundred splinter movements and "independence" parties and groupings wherever you look. The Soviet Union and Yugoslavia split up. Montenegro became an independent state in 2006; Kosovo is becoming one, in its own way. Catalonia gained significant autonomous powers in 2006, as did Aceh in Indonesia. More than 50 percent of the people of Scotland in a recent poll wanted complete independence from England, and that seems likely to happen within a few years. There it is: the Third Way. Ever powerful. And we—you—are a part of that great tradition.

Distributism
Beyond Capitalism and Socialism

KIRKPATRICK SALE

Issue no. 24 • Summer 2008

This column is adapted from an introduction to *Beyond Capitalism and Socialism*, a series of essays on distributism edited by Tobias J. Lanz and published earlier in 2008 by IHS Press (IHSPress.com), specializing in books on the social teachings of the Catholic Church.

Fritz Schumacher used to tell the story of the three professionals sitting around arguing about whose was the oldest profession. The doctor said that his was the oldest because God operated on Adam to remove his rib to make Eve. The architect, however, declared that even before that God built the world out of chaos. Yes, said the economist, but who do you think made that?

Yes, indeed, economists have made chaos, and they have done it on a worldwide, if not universal scale, and, for some reason, are richly rewarded for it. They have created a system, in both capitalist and socialist guises, that favors the using up of the world's resources at ever-faster rates, that encourages their processing in ways that produce pollution and waste, that puts wealth into ever-fewer hands in the countries of the favored few, that allows for great sickness, poverty, ignorance, and starvation across the world, and that celebrates every single one of what this culture knows as the Seven Deadly Sins. (For those of you who have forgotten the Church's teachings, those are pride, greed, lust, anger, gluttony, envy, and sloth. Yes, even sloth: for the couch-potato consumers.)

There must be a better way. And, of course, there is and has been for a very long time. It is a society based on small self-sufficient regions, empowered communities, vibrant neighborhoods, gainfully employed families, individual self-satisfactions, decentralized politics, local economies, sustainable organic agriculture, cooperative work, environmental humility, and careful nurturing of the earth. It is the way many people have lived, probably in most places and for most of the time, for the greatest part of the last eight thousand years, punctuated by some periods of empire and kingship, until the rise of capitalism five hundred years ago.

It was nearly a hundred years after the ravages of industrial capitalism had spread across the United Kingdom that a group of people in England began to talk about this sort of society, and they gave it the name of Distributism. It was a largely literary movement, with giants like Hillaire Belloc and G. K. Chesterton, and it set out in careful and inspiring terms what the good society would look like, giving a framework and a name to what had long been seen as an ideal, or at least more reasonable, way of life. It did not have a great deal of success, on the ground as it were, because of all the centralizing, big-government twentieth-century forces stacked against it, but it suggested the ways people might organize their lives insofar as those forces permitted it and the kind of world to be working for.

It was called Distributism because it held that in the ideal society ownership and property would be distributed as widely as possible, to individuals, families, and co-ops, and not in the hands of governments and corporations of either capitalist or socialist bent. It sought to work out the principles of late-nineteenth-century Catholic "social justice" teachings, as outlined particularly by Leo XIII's *Rerum Naturum* of 1891, in which he attacked the "excesses of capitalism" overtly as being responsible for the "misery of the working classes." Its solution was not so much the abolition of capitalism, the sort of thing that socialists were on about at the turn of the century, as the abolition of large institutions of capitalism and a return to an economy built on guild craftsmen, small family farmers, and village-level trading.

You may recognize in this many of the elements of agrarianism, a parallel movement largely in the United States, that similarly deplored the evils of industrialism and urged a return to a society based on small-scale agriculture. Its sense that farming and an interaction with nature are a moral good, foster family and village closeness and allow life on the human scale is carried over into most Distributist writing. Its classic statement, *I'll Take My Stand*, was published in 1930, around the time the Distributists were writing some of their most important books in England—for example, Chesterton's *The Outline of Sanity* (1927) and Arthur Penty's *The Elements of Domestic Design* (1930).

The Distributist philosophy is still alive today, though it is not always named Distributism, and so, surprisingly enough, are some of the actual elements of it, taking shape at the edges of the dominant society. To suggest but a few, there is the bioregional movement, deep ecology, farmers markets, community-supported agriculture, organic farming, homegrown gardens, local- and slow-food movements, alternative currencies, alternative medicine, alternative energy, intermediate technology (Schumacher was directly influenced by the English Distributists), Buy-Nothing Day, simple living, homeschooling, neo-Luddism, worker ownership, antiglobalization, anti–free trade, environmental interest groups, ecological restoration, eco-villages, land trusts, and land preservation. All of these would be welcomed by Distributists as living out their legacy.

What's more, if the predictions for the future prove to be accurate—peak oil and the end of long-haul transportation, global warming and the end of agribusiness—the world and its destructive capitalist/socialist economy will be forced to change radically and in the direction of Distributist principles. As James Kunstler puts it in *The Long Emergency*, when these crises hit, national and supranational economies will disintegrate, and the focus of society will have to return to the town or small city and its supporting agricultural hinterland. It will require us to downscale and rescale virtually everything we do and how we do it, from the kind of communities we physically inhabit to the way we grow our food to the way we work and trade the products of our work. Anything organized on the large scale, whether it is government or a corporate business enterprise such as Walmart, will wither as the cheap energy props that support bigness fall away.

And then, of necessity, the world will reconstruct itself on the lines of more human-scale, community-based, local-resource-dependent societies, something that the Distributists would recognize as what they'd been talking about all along.

The First Populist Republic

Adrian Kuzminski

Issue no. 28 • Mud Season 2009

Few Americans are aware that Vermont, the fourteenth state admitted to the Union in 1791, was not a colony like the others; it was a preexisting independent republic spontaneously created by its residents who rejected the authority of neighboring colonies, particularly New York, which had the strongest claim to its territory. In its fourteen years of formal independence, beginning in 1777, it very nearly fulfilled the textbook image of a society created voluntarily by free persons living in the state of nature—a favorite motif of seventeeth and eighteenth century social-contract political philosophers. In the United States, Texas, California, and Hawaii also enjoyed periods as independent republics, but Vermont's example reflects a greater equality of persons and resources. In the case of Vermont, in the face of a trend toward oligarchy in America—evident even in the eighteenth century—an egalitarian democratic community for a time found almost complete realization.

It's a story worth telling. New York had a claim to what became Vermont based on a 1664 British royal charter granting it the lands to the west of the Connecticut River north of Massachusetts. The same British royal government, however, subsequently recognized some authority over the lands of Vermont by the New England colonies of Connecticut, Massachusetts, and New Hampshire. In the 1740s the Governor of New Hampshire, Benning Wentworth, began to sell land in what is now Vermont to settlers mostly from New England. Wentworth's "New Hampshire Grants" were sold cheaply, partly because they lay in disputed territory. New York's titles to the same lands were monopolized by absentee speculators, while Wentworth's cheap titles went mostly to actual residents who moved in and cleared the forests and started farms and towns. With Native American populations drastically depleted, the settlers confronted a wilderness amenable to settlement; for them, it was a virgin land rich enough to guarantee ownership to anyone able to homestead it. Rarely in history have free resources been available to those willing to labor on them, without external obligations, as they were in early Vermont.

Content with having sold the Grants at a profit, Wentworth and New Hampshire showed little further interest in the lands west of the Connecticut River. New York, however, rejected the claims of those holding Wentworth's titles, insisting that its own title holders were the true owners of the land. In 1770 Vermont settler Ethan Allen, having witnessed the validity of New Hampshire grants denied in a New York court, organized an independent militia to defend the claims of those holding New Hampshire Grants: the Green Mountain Boys. This militia, which later fought in the Revolutionary War against the British—capturing Fort Ticonderoga under Allen's leadership—did so, not as part of the colonial union under the Continental Congress, but as an independent ally of the American colonists. Allen's resistance to New York proved, in the end, the vehicle of Vermont independence, which was formally declared at the Westminster Convention in 1777, after the Green Mountain Boys drove off invading New Yorker posses and sheriffs in a series of small hit-and-run battles near Bennington, Vermont.

What is relevant to us in this story, in addition to the opportunity for ownership of land free of external state or corporate power, is the radical democracy of the Vermont settlers. Indeed, the former informed the latter. They achieved, albeit briefly, a startling decentralization of political and economic power seldom seen in human history. Unlike the neighboring American colonies, with their links to Europe and their increasing hierarchical power structures rooted in the commercial seaport centers like Boston and New York, Vermonters in their hills were able to achieve widespread ownership of land as independent farmers and artisans without reckoning with an established wealthy elite in control of most resources, especially financial ones, as well as of the government. Vermont came into existence from the ground up, wholly on the local level, farm by farm, and town by town—as clear a case I can find of a free society founded in a state of nature.

Without any superstructure of preestablished authority controlling land grants, Vermonters were able to realize very largely the populist vision, which seeks to reconcile political freedom and personal private property in locally-rooted radical democracy. The essence of populism is the recognition that private property widely distributed (not concentrated in few hands) is the precondition of genuine democracy. Nearly all settlers were, or soon became, landowners, controlling enough land to be more or less self-sufficient. The economy operated on barter and personal credit, enforced by local courts presided over by locally elected judges and constituted by juries of local citizens. Real property functioned as reserve wealth, backing a state currency (some Vermont coins were minted in the 1780s).

The center of life and the ultimate sovereign authority in Vermont was the town meeting, open to all resident adult males, where all aspects of public life were debated and decided. As in ancient Athens, meetings were lively and sometimes contentious; officials seldom held office for more than a term. Official positions of authority were discounted, and the officers of the local militia were elected. Such radical democracy obviated the need for the traditional separation of powers. Separation of powers as we know it is designed to check each of the major branches of government—legislative, executive, and judicial—by providing recourse to any one of them against the others. It was developed by Madison and other founders as a way of controlling the abuses of oligarchy (which it has not done) while avoiding democracy. It also has the less noticed effect of confirming a considerable amount of unaccountable authority in each branch of government (and its divisions), thereby actually concentrating rather than disbursing power.

By contrast, a decentralized system of local democracies provides for another kind of separation of power: its breakup into numerous local governments. The basis of Vermont democracy, reflected in the works of Ethan Allen, is the doctrine of natural rights (not revealed religion or state authority). The essential natural rights for Allen are the rights of each individual to freedom *and* property. This early populist world was a pragmatic world, not one driven by ideology or religion.

What is crucial is the recognition by the first Vermont republic not only that democracy must be established in face-to-face local assemblies, or town meetings, but that these assemblies can maintain their freedom only by being confederated together in a broader representative body directly and wholly accountable to those assemblies. Direct democracy at the grassroots was characteristic of much of colonial America, but most colonial governments, with their royal governors, councils, etc., were not the unalloyed representatives of the grassroots, as Vermont was, but subject to varying degrees of control from above, a pattern which continued after the revolution and intensified after the Civil War. The unicameral legislature of the first Vermont republic was composed of representatives chosen by local communities to represent those communities. This is conspicuously not how modern legislatures work. They do not represent communities, they are not accountable to them, and their members are not chosen in face-to-face assemblies.

Instead state legislators as well as members of Congress are chosen invariably in mass elections by dispersed and atomized voters, in which largely preselected candidates are presented to a passive and manipulated public. Communities and their interests are by-passed in favor of largely symbolic and impersonal relationship—defined by mass propaganda and big money rather than personal experience—between the candidate and the voter. The private voting booth—often cited as the essence of democracy—is in fact its negation. Instead of casting a secret ballot in a town meeting for representatives personally known to me and my community on the basis of the problems facing my community, I am asked instead to vote in isolation for one or another media image on the basis of inane slogans concocted by power brokers and special interests. Large electoral districts lump together many communities and allow representatives to play off one against the other. Pork spending for local politicians who cooperate; neglect for those who don't. The result is oligarchy, not democracy.

The first Vermont republic was different; it was a true confederal democracy. As Michael A. Bellesiles puts it in his remarkable work *Revolutionary Outlaws: Ethan Allen and the Struggle for Independence on the Early American Frontier,*

> Vermont's constitution [of 1777] demands attention for the way it lived up to its theoretical assertions, creating the most democratic structure of its time. . . . The state's voters controlled every branch of government, electing the state's executive officers and judges, as well as representatives to the unicameral legislature. The governor and council of Vermont could not veto legislation. . . . To maintain civic participation, the constitution required public legislative sessions and forbade the passage of any bill into law the same year it was proposed, mandating its printing for

the public's information. . . . A septennial Council of Censors was to review all legislative and executive acts to ensure that the constitution was being fulfilled. . . . The Council of Censors could amend the constitution by calling a popularly elected convention allowing "posterity the same privileges of choosing how they would be governed" without resort to "revolution or bloodshed."

Bellesiles then adds the crucial point:

Vermont's leadership did not seek the approval of the people as an undifferentiated mass. Sovereignty lay in the distinct townships, which held the "unalienable and indefeasible right to reform, alter, or abolish government, in such manner as shall be, by that community, judged most conducive to the public weal." Finally, Vermont's Declaration of Rights proclaimed "that private Property ought to be subservient to public uses."

As Bellesiles nicely puts it: "The people of Vermont interacted with their state government through their community, not as isolated individuals."

Each community or town in Vermont with less than eighty free citizens got one representative to the unicameral state legislature, or General Assembly, and towns with more than eighty got two representatives (the largest town had less than 2000 in population). The Windsor Convention, which ratified the existence of Vermont, had fifty delegates from thirty-one towns. Vermont may be the only modern example of a system, at least in the United States, of direct representation grafted onto local assemblies, namely, the combination of direct local democracy with accountable representative bodies, something Jefferson envisioned in his "ward republics" as the completion of the American Revolution, and Tom Paine thought actually happened, or would happen, throughout the United States. It has not yet happened, but our current economic and ecological crises beg us more than ever to revisit our largely lost but more relevant than ever populist tradition.

Vermont, we should not be surprised, was unable to maintain the radical degree of democracy she developed in relative isolation. If she had supported Shays's Rebellion in Massachusetts in the 1780s, she might have sparked a second American revolution, this time directed not against the economic elites of London but those of the American coastal cities. And she might have preserved her own confederal democracy. In return, however, for considering an offer of statehood from the United States, the Vermont legislators by a narrow vote rejected Shays's overtures and Allen, who had been offered command of a revolutionary army by Shays, elected to stay in retirement at his farm.

Under pressure, Vermont caved in and gained recognition from the top down in 1791 as the fourteenth state from a national government and federal constitution seriously in conflict with the principles of her democracy. She conceded that her experiment in democracy would henceforth be limited and no threat to the larger monied interests of the land in their increasingly successful attempts to disassociate free individuals from their property. Still, Vermont has retained a degree of democratic spirit absent in most other states of the union, a spirit reflected in its election to the United States Congress in recent years of its only independent member and in a number of environmental, civil, and other reforms, as well as in a continued strong tradition of town meetings. And not least, the example of the first Vermont republic remains an important model for any future reform of our political system.

The First Vermont "Republic"
What's in a Name?

JAMES HOGUE

Issue no. 9 • January 2006

Republic: A system of government in which the people hold sovereign power and elect representatives who exercise that power. It contrasts, on the one hand, with a pure democracy, in which the people or community as an organized whole wield the sovereign power of government, and on the other with the rule of one person (such as a king, emperor, czar, or sultan).
> —*Black's Law Dictionary*, abridged seventh edition.

During the fourteen years between Vermont's Declaration of Independence (January 15, 1777) and its acceptance into the union (March 4, 1791), Vermont convened an elected assembly, adopted a constitution, coined its own money, operated a postal service, conducted military operations and diplomatic relations and trade, recruited and commanded its own militia, and wrote its own laws in a legislature elected at town meeting, where the people also elected the governor and his twelve member council. According to Ira Allen, Vermont from 1777 to 1791 proved a "free & Independent State Wholy unconnected with any Power whatever." (Letter to Alexander Dundas and Justus Sherwood, May 8, 1781.) Ira's brother Ethan called it a "neutral republic" in his letter to General Frederick Haldimand on June 16, 1782.

From the brothers Allen to the first historians such as Jared Sparks, then John Pell in 1929, through the romanticism of Frederick van de Water, to the recent scholarship of Michael Bellesiles, Vermont is referred to as an independent state and republic. Said Sparks of the Green Mountain Boys in his 1829 biography of Ethan: "Independence was their first and determined purpose; and, while they were neglected by Congress, and, like another Poland, threatened with a triple partition between the adjoining States, they felt at liberty to pursue any course, that would secure their safety." Sparks further states that many in Congress refused to interfere in Vermont's affairs, "affirming that Vermont was in fact independent, and had a right to set up such a scheme of government as she chose." This argument comes straight from John Adams, whose recommendation, delivered to "the Inhabitants of Vermont" by Dr. Thomas Young, led Vermont to form its own government early in 1777.

On May 16 1776 Adams wrote "That it be recommended . . . where no government sufficient to the exigencies of their affairs hath been hitherto established, to adopt such government, as shall, in the opinion of the representatives of the people, best conduce to the happiness and safety of their constituents in particular, and America in general." Adams' argument goes back to principles established by the Magna Carta of 1215, described in Blackstone as "the safety of the whole," and which Ethan called "the law of self-preservation," or the right of a community to exist. This right is also stated most clearly, and carried further, in the Vermont Declaration of Independence. Van de Water states, in *The Reluctant Republic* (1941), paraphrasing the sentiments expressed by the Allens, Jonas Fay, Thomas Chittenden, and the Green Mountain Boys, that "the land they had defended against the intrusions of New York should be forever theirs—an independent nation. . . . It must be, without qualification or higher loyalty, the property of the folk who now held it and their children and their children's children—a land of freemen, a republic."

Bellesiles, in *Revolutionary Outlaws*, points out the shocking words heard round the world in Vermont's Constitution: "That all men are born equally free and independent. . . . Therefore, no male person, born in this country, or brought from oversea, ought to be holden by law, to serve any person, as a servant, slave or apprentice, after he arrives at the age of twenty-one, nor female, in like manner, after she arrives at the age of eighteen." The Vermont Constitution of 1777 shamed the U.S. Constitution of 1787, which would not bring itself to reach the same, logical conclusion on the subjects of involuntary servitude and slavery. Make no mistake: the Vermont Constitution was powerful, and far more revolutionary than any before it. It was based on the Constitution of Pennsylvania and radicalized (traced to its root) by the Allens, Chittenden, and the Green Mountain Boys; and it represented true republicanism and anathema not only to the South but also to New York.

Bellesiles tells us of an even greater slap in the face delivered by Vermont to the entire colonial structure. The French historian Achard de Bonvouloir in 1778 wrote that Vermonters, led by Ethan, held all colonial charters to be void, their powers superseded by the will of the people. This means that Vermonters did not rely upon legitimacy from a superior authority, past or present, but rather in their own authority, granted to them by nature and nature's God. In the story of Vermont's independence, there are some fascinating incidents. Ethan took Fort Ticonderoga with the Green Mountain Boys, refusing to serve under the duly-appointed, would-be commander, Benedict Arnold. General Starke and Colonels Warner and Herrick refused to obey the orders of General Schuyler regarding the deployments of their men in the retreat from Ticonderoga. (This refusal led to their defense of and victory at Bennington and foiled Burgoyne's advance.)

The young republic attracted the secession of sixteen towns from New Hampshire and several from New York. This could not have been a decision that the towns took lightly. Vermont eventually surrendered these towns in order to join the union. That Vermont had the sole authority to surrender them is recognition on the part of Congress, New York, and New Hampshire that Vermont was sovereign.

Ethan Allen wrote, "I am as Resolutely Determined to Defend the Independence of Vermont, as Congress are that of the United States, and, Rather than fail, will Retire with hardy Green Mountain Boys into the Desolate Caverns of the mountains and wage war with human Nature at large." He's back.

Vermont's Genetic Code
Toward a Decentralist Manifesto

FRANK BRYAN

Issue no. 11 • March 2006
Issue no. 33 • Winter 2010

In his 2000 book *Bowling Alone: The Collapse and Revival of American Community*, author Robert Putnam ranked Vermont above all other states on his scale of "tolerance for gender, racial, and civil liberties." At about the same time, political scientist Tom Rice ranked Vermont first among states on a "civil society" measure published in *Publius*, the leading professional journal of American federalism.

Such rankings are not new. Praise for Vermont's unique civic virtue has been extensively documented. Vermont is an exceptional place regarding values most dear to those who appreciate humankind's need for a living nexus between liberty and community. Why is this?

The answer is critical to all those patriots committed to navigating Vermont's independence from the federal government. The answer rationalizes our instincts, electrifies our commitment, and sustains our courage. The answer lies deep in our sinews, our genetic code. Established by the Republic of Vermont in 1777, it arose from the first English constitution to outlaw slavery and to allow people without property to vote. The code was evident when Ethan Allen issued America's first Emancipation Proclamation—a "writ of freedom" for two African Americans (mother and daughter) found at Fort Ticonderoga, when it was captured by Allen in 1775, while gunfire from Lexington and Concord still echoed through the hardwood hills of northern New England. The code was recognized a year later by General John Burgoyne, who wrote in his diary while sailing down Lake Champlain to defeat at a place called Saratoga: "Vermont abounds with the most rebellious race on the continent and hangs like a gathering storm on my left."

This genetic code is called human-scale democracy.

But how was this code sustained over the two centuries that have since passed? How did it survive the second half of the industrial revolution—

the two most vicious centuries the world has ever known, ending with the hierarchical, totalitarian industrial horrors of Hitler and Stalin? Vermont escaped hierarchy and its attendant authoritarianism because of geography and climate. We were born cold, rocky, and isolated (the only New England state without an opening to the sea). The historian Arnold Toynbee, in his *Study of History*, dismissed Vermont as being above the optimal climatic area of the continent. He had a point.

During the heyday of urban industrialism, no American state had more people scrambling to leave than Vermont. This period is called Vermont's "dark age" by historians. In 1950, Vermont was the most rural state in America. We had a tiny state capital, the population of our largest city was less than 35,000, and a greater percentage of Vermont's citizens lived in places of fewer than 2,500 people than any other state. Vermont had been "left behind." This turned out to be a blessing.

In *The Vermont Papers: Re-creating Democracy on a Human Scale,* John McClaughry and I explained what we called the "leapfrog theory."

> Vermont never had what most Americans are longing to be rid of. [We] developed a unique set of historical circumstances that pivot around one critical event: the state leapfrogged urban-industrialism, ignoring the astounding transformation of American society that took place in the years between 1830 and 1960. The result is a state that is already free and clear of the twentieth century.

In short, the Dark Age "cocooned" Vermont. When the state entered the postwar period, it did so with its land green, its civil society preserved, its communities small, its democracy secure. Most important, its human-scale karma, its genetic code (while worn and tattered here and there) is still fundamentally intact. Vermont was the United States' best civil society because the variables that shaped it originally survived the twentieth century.

Why Vermont? The reasons abound. But fundamental to them all is this: None of the world's political structures (unitary states like France or federal states like America and its subunits, like Vermont) is more democratically governed at its roots than Vermont. Why is this so? Two words: town meeting. A bold claim to be sure. But true. Consider the words of Ferdinand Lundberg in his *The Myth of Democracy*, an exhaustive historical review of the absence of democracy in the world's great nations from ancient Athens to modern America. "Here [in the town meeting] more than anywhere else one finds democracy at work." In fact Lundberg notes that the town meeting is the only case of real democracy he has found, saying that when the Old World transplants in colonial New England created town meeting, it was "the first time ever in the history of the world" democracy was systematically practiced. And he might have said as well (with a tip of the hat to Maine and New Hampshire): no New England state still practices town meeting democracy—the real democracy the Greeks attempted but failed to realize in Athens—as well or as thoroughly as Vermont.

Thus it is that the fundamental reason many of us are joining together to discuss and promote the peaceful separation of Vermont from the United States is because of what we already are. We are at the core a real democracy and it is this grassroots democracy that now sustains the best representative democracy in America—featuring one of only two governors that must seek reelection every two years and a legislative body of 180 members representing less than 650,000 people. If the United States were comprised of fifty "Vermonts," the American Republic would be alive and well, not sinking into an abyss of disgusting politics, inhumane public policy, and increasingly authoritarian governance. And we would not be secessionists.

But it is equally true that the Second Vermont Republic will not survive as a republic (a representative democracy) without the strong foundation of real democracy that has sustained it for over two centuries. Vermont without town meeting might in some ways still be a good place. But it would never be Vermont

Let us therefore, as the first (albeit "unofficial") act of the Second Vermont Republic, agree to make sure that the Second Vermont Republic emerges with the single most important institution of the first Vermont Republic intact—alive, well, and growing in influence. It is what Jefferson called "the wisest invention ever devised by the wit of man for the perfect exercise of self-government." Town meeting.

The Cultivation of Our Own Tradition

ROWAN JACOBSEN

Issue no. 3 • June 2005

Those of us who lived in Vermont in decades past, and flew in and out of the state periodically, have all had a certain airport experience. No matter where your connection was for your flight to Burlington—Newark or Philadelphia or Cleveland—as you approached the gate for the flight home, you knew it was the Vermont gate without checking the Departures screen. There were still overalls and white beards. The dental care was spotty. There was no sheen to the crowd. You might have been flying to Albania. This isn't as true as it once was. In some ways, Vermont has caught up with the rest of the country, or, rather, the country has infiltrated Vermont. But it still holds. I still have no trouble distinguishing the Vermont gate from the others. There's a little less makeup, lower heels. People are more likely to be clutching books, more likely to wear their gray hair with pride.

Vermont's difference is even more profound when you enter the state by highway. An immediate sense of peace and well-being sets in, and it usually takes a few miles before you realize this is because the billboards are no longer blaring at you. Instead, the big green curtain has taken over. Vermont is simply different from the rest of the nation—geographically, politically, and culturally—and its difference can be felt at all levels of being. That is exceedingly rare in twenty-first-century America, and it alone may be enough of a reason to take extraordinary steps to preserve that difference. Not long before his death, in a letter to Second Vermont Republic founder Thomas Naylor, the eminent U.S. Ambassador George Kennan wrote, "All power to Vermont in its effort to distinguish itself from the USA as a whole, and to pursue in its own way the cultivation of its own tradition." I like that phrase a lot. The cultivation of its own tradition. It nails what may be the best argument for Vermont independence.

We live in a world that is virtually at war with tradition. Tradition is antiprogress. Tradition gets in the way of economic efficiency. And since we are tied into an economy in which dollars are the only acceptable measure of value (it's how we judge paintings, movie stars, hurricanes, and antiques), this makes tradition unjustifiable. Which means Vermont is in trouble. The National Trust for Historic Preservation just named the entire state of Vermont as one of the nation's most endangered historic places for the second time. That's because we can't justify our small towns, small schools, local agriculture, or traditional patterns of land use in terms of dollars alone. A community isn't worth a dime—at least, not on the open market. If we are to cultivate our own traditions—to let thrive those things that make Vermont unique—we need to detach from the national system.

So long as decisions about our schools, forests, and water are being made by senators from South Carolina, presidents from Texas, and judges from Chicago, Vermont's best interests are not going to be kept in mind. Why should they be? What makes sense for Miami or Des Moines does not necessarily make sense for Vermont. How can Miami and Moretown possibly both cultivate their own traditions under the same set of guidelines—especially when those guidelines are being set in a city at least 600 miles from both? Being part of a gigantic system gives one the illusion of participating in "big" and "important" events, such as wars and billion-dollar elections, but in reality it just allows us to take our eyes off the ball of the "small-time" local issues that have more direct presence in our lives, and that we can greatly influence.

I think it's a mistake to pursue Vermont independence as a protest against anything. It makes the movement symbolic, and the tremendous effort independence will take should not be wasted on symbolism. I don't care about "sending a message." What I do care about, deeply, is allowing all that is precious in Vermont to survive, and to thrive. Our village commons, our working farms, our loons and moose and thrushes. Our traditions of open-mindedness, self-sufficiency, and generosity. Movements started in anger spark great initial passion, then become lost when the spark flares out, or the target of the anger disappears. Movements started out of love have staying power. There's no question that the things that make Vermont Vermont are under increasing pressure from a variety of external sources. The question is what to do about it. Does Vermont make more sense, does it become more itself somehow, by going its own way? A simple test helps answer this. If Vermont had been an independent republic all along, would you now vote for it to join the United States? Of course not. It would be unthinkable. Which makes inertia the only true argument for sticking with the United States. And inertia has never been the Vermont way.

PART FOUR

Sovereignty and Secession

Finally, let us consider the radical strategy that many in the *Vermont Commons* circle believe is needed to escape from the grip of global empire—peaceful secession from the United States. This idea is of course highly controversial; even readers who otherwise agree with much of our critical analysis have difficulty accepting political secession as a remedy. Yet our critique of the imperial corporate state logically leads to a conclusion that if the system is beyond reform, our only recourse, if we wish to preserve democratic values and viable, human-scale communities, is to withdraw from it. We have argued that our most pressing problems result from the concentration of power in political and economic institutions, and secession is the most direct way to detach ourselves from the exercise of that power.

Secession is proposed as a nonviolent protest against the intrinsic violence of the imperial nation-state. Empires grow and assert their domination through coercive force. We abhor the concentration of power for many reasons, as we have explained throughout the book, but perhaps the most elemental reason for resisting imperial institutions is the violence they characteristically employ. This section, then, begins with two articles about the use of military force. Philosopher Donald Livingston, who contributed several extensive historical analyses of secession movements to *Vermont Commons*, here describes how the modern nation-state is an inherently violent institution, using force even against its own citizens to maintain its hold on power. And Vermonter Ben Scotch argues that this nation's founding ideals were lost as the United States became a "hegemon"—that is, an imperial power dominating the world through military might. All of the critics contemplating secession sincerely love the ideals that the United States claims to represent. They have regretfully turned to secession because they believe the United States has forfeited those ideals.

But isn't secession itself a violation of our founding principles? Doesn't the Constitution represent an enduring commitment, however inadequately accomplished, to ideals of justice, equality, human rights, and so on? Haven't previous American secessionists been motivated solely by racist ideology or narrow self-interest? These are important questions, and Livingston provided detailed responses in the journal. Here we present an abridged version of one of his articles, where he argues that until the Civil War (the name of which is itself open to question) it was considered legitimately American to resist the concentration of power in the national government. The Declaration of Independence was a manifesto for secession, not "revolution." Calls to secede from the newly formed United States did not begin in the south but right here in New England, with even some of the Constitution's framers questioning the political forces it unleashed.

Livingston calls this anticentralist streak Jeffersonian, and, indeed, many contemporary writers on secession invoke Thomas Jefferson's name in support of this perspective. Although Jefferson's own political career entailed a mass of contradictions (for example, the New Englanders contemplated secession in protest against *his* nationalist policies as president!), he has come to symbolize radical democratic opposition to concentrated power, and he famously proclaimed that governments *ought* to be altered or replaced as each new generation encounters a changing world. If secession violates America's founding ideals, then we'll need to count Thomas Jefferson as un-American.

Indeed, in *Bye Bye Miss American Empire*, a provocative and well-researched study of past and contemporary secession movements in the United States, Bill Kauffman argued that "We are a nation born in secession, after all, and of rebellion against faraway rulers." Secession "is radicalism deep-dyed in the American grain." It arises "from the belief that ordinary people, living in cohesive communities, can govern themselves, without the heavy-hand of distant experts and tank-and-bomb-wielding statesmen to guide their way." In essence, Kauffman shows that the principle of secession has much deeper roots than the "states' rights" justification for slavery: it is an integral ingredient of the democratic vision upon which the nation was presumably founded.

The articles in this section explain why and how Vermont should secede from the United States and suggest that this effort would not be an isolated incident because it reflects an active worldwide trend toward the devolution of the modern nation-state. We believe that this decentralization of power is a reasonable proposal, yet we also recognize that in the context of American history, secession remains controversial. Attempts by the Second Vermont Republic to network with other secession groups in the United States sparked a ferocious backlash among Vermont progressives. I will address these concerns in the Afterword.

The Violence of the Centralized State

Donald W. Livingston

Issue no. 24 • Summer 2008

The time has come for a third American Revolution. The first revolution occurred in 1776, when thirteen out of thirty British colonies in the western hemisphere seceded to prevent consolidation into an increasingly centralized British empire. John Adams, George Washington, and Thomas Jefferson were secessionists. The second revolution, the opposite of the first, occurred between 1861 and 1865 (the misnamed "Civil War") to create a consolidated American Union that could compete with the empires of Europe; a regime "one and indivisible" from which secession would be impossible.

After the so-called "civil war," what had been sovereign American states in a federation became little more than counties in an indivisible United States empire. It seemed to many observers that such an empire was a necessary instrument of human progress. But over time, it has become the greatest concentration of financial, political, and military power in history. It has divided the globe into five military districts and seeks "full-spectrum dominance." In such a regime—by virtue of its sheer size—the ancient republican ideal of human-scale societies living under laws they themselves have made is no longer possible. The third American revolution would be a reenactment of the first: secession, not from the British Empire, but from the United States, which has emerged as the most powerful empire of the twenty-first century.

There is every reason to think that democratic secession by referendum in the twenty-first century United States would be peaceful, unlike that in 1861. During the nineteenth century, states competed for territory in colonies and in Europe. During the Napoleonic wars, France had invaded Germany as well as other states. And Germany would later invade France. But that age is over. Few countries today show an interest in acquiring new territory by force, either by acquiring colonies or by taking their neighbor's territory. There are other avenues to attain power and influence. Polls show that a majority of Scots and English support the secession of Scotland. Should Scotland secede, would London launch an invasion to force them back into the UK? It is highly unlikely. The same is true of Quebec seceding from the Canadian federation. We live in a different age.

Yet there remains a deep and mysterious prejudice against secession. It is generally assumed, without argument, that large centralized states are a good thing and that any division into smaller states (Vermont seceding from the United States, for example) would be a bad thing. Article VII of the U.S. Constitution ordains that only nine states are needed to form the United States. The steady addition of states up to fifty was not viewed as a bad thing. But the secession of eleven states in 1861 to form a federation of their own was suppressed by the bloodiest war of the nineteenth century.

Why the prejudice against secession? The answer, famously stated in Thomas Hobbes' *Leviathan* (1651), is that large centralized states are thought necessary for peace, security, and prosperity. Systems of small states, so the thinking goes, inevitably yield petty quarrels and endless civil wars in a territory. The only way to prevent this is by creating what has come to be called "the modern state," a central government with a territorial monopoly on coercion.

From this logic it follows that, once established, a modern state cannot be divided by secession. It is "one and indivisible." Within the territorial monopoly on coercion, individuals are free to pursue their life plans in a civil condition. The larger the territory, the greater the sphere of individual liberty. Consequently, to talk of the territorial division of the state through secession is to raise the horrible specter of anarchy and to throw into question the very possibility of individual liberty.

The first problem with this self-congratulatory picture of the modern state as providing the best conditions of peace and security is this: Such a vision overlooks the violent history of the modern state's origins. A vast centralized state such as France or Germany did not and could not have originated at that size and scale. All political order begins small. Large states are nearly always the result of conquest or usurpation. Medieval Europe was composed of thousands of independent and quasi-independent political units. As late as 1700, the region known as Germany was composed of more than 200 countries and some 50 free cities. By 1828, monarchs had forcibly consolidated all but 38. By 1870, the whole was unified into a single monster state. This violent process of unification through a policy of "blood and iron" was well underway in the mid-seventeenth century when the modern state system was first acknowledged in international law. It did not reach North America, however, until the late nineteenth century.

The American Civil War, probably the most morally sanitized war in history, was not a holy crusade to abolish slavery—as Americans deeply need to believe—but a typical nineteenth century war of "unification." Prior to Lincoln's invasion, America was not a modern nation state, but an inchoate federation of states that had delegated only enumerated powers to the central government: mainly defense, inter-state commerce, and foreign treaties. Had this nineteenth century war of "unification" been fought with today's population, it would have resulted in more than 5 million battle deaths and perhaps twice that number wounded and missing.

Wars of "unification" and large-scale state-building were viewed in the nineteenth century as progressive movements, creating islands of peace, individual liberty, and prosperity in an anarchical world. Subsequent history has suppressed the high moral cost of building large, centralized modern states. To this, one might reply that once established (and however violent its origins might have been), modern states have been distinguished by two features: liberty and prosperity. But is this really true? Large-scale modern states consolidate vast financial, political, and military resources. This creates a dynamic center of power that inevitably falls into competition with surrounding states and leads to war. The rise of the modern state has gone hand in hand with expanding the scale, intensity, and destructive power of war.

The large-scale state system was created by monarchs over a period stretching from the fourteenth century to the French Revolution. Everywhere the story was the same: each king searching for more territory, revenue, troops, and a more efficient administrative system to make his realm "one and indivisible." As the forced consolidation of smaller political units into larger ones grew, so did the size of the king's armies and the scale of war. The battle of Poitiers, the most important of the fourteenth century, engaged 50,000 men. Three centuries later the number of troops available to monarchs had changed little. The battle of Nordlingen in 1648 engaged 65,000. This battle ended the Thirty

Years War, making possible the treaty of Westphalia, which historians fix as the beginning of the modern state system. This more efficient and expansive form of centralization was called "absolute monarchy." It was praised for the peace it enforced within the state's territory, but it also enabled the king to extract more men, resources, and revenue from his realm than ever before. Armies would now triple in size over what they had been for the last three centuries. The battle of Malplaquet in 1709 would engage 200,000, as opposed to the 65,000 at Nordlingen only sixty years earlier.

As monarchs fine-tuned their territorial monopoly on coercion into an evermore efficient machine for extracting resources, resistance appeared in the form of a discourse of liberty and republicanism. This discourse claimed that war was due to kings and aristocracies. Kant argued that replacing monarchies with republics would diminish war. If the people were sovereign, he thought, they would never vote to squander their blood and treasure in senseless wars of glory. But this hope (still indulged by many today) proved illusory. The French Revolution replaced the person of the king with the person of the French nation as sovereign. Soon all of Europe would be speaking in a republican or democratic idiom, and, by the end of the nineteenth century, the age of large-scale mass democracies would be established. But there would be no diminishing of war.

Indeed, war would now expand on a scale and intensity unthinkable to the kings who had been overthrown. The reason is that, bad as they were, monarchies were limited in the resources they could extract from society, due to the resistance that could be made by independent social authorities (such as the nobility, church, provincial governments, and an independent judiciary), all of which had titles as good as the king's. The state, in mass democracies, eliminated or weakened these independent buffers to centralization and, consequently, had a freer hand in extracting resources. In his book *Democracy: The God That Failed*, Hans Hoppe argues that in the period of monarchy that ended in the mid-nineteenth century, kings were never able to extract more than 5 percent to 8 percent of GNP; whereas modern democracies have been able to extract from 40 percent to 60 percent.

No eighteenth-century monarch, for example, could have imposed an income tax or ordered universal conscription. But mass democracies, beginning with the French Revolution in 1789, could and did. The result was a spectacular growth in centralized financial and military power. On the eve of the French Revolution the armies of European monarchs had grown to unprecedented size: France, 180,000; Prussia, 195,000; Austria, 240,000. But by ordering universal conscription, the new French republic could place in the field more than the total of all three kingdoms. The force of 600,000 that Napoleon brought into Russia was, at the time, the largest force ever assembled in a single theater in history. By the end of the Napoleonic wars, the French republic had raised some 3 million troops! A century later, as each turn of the ratchet of centralization grew progressively tighter, the modern state showed what it could really do. World War I resulted in around 11 million battle deaths, and millions more wounded and missing—a mortality rate greater than all the wars fought in Europe in the two preceding centuries.

And civilians were no longer safe. The code of civilized warfare, established by monarchs in the early eighteenth century, prohibited war against civilians. According to the distinguished British military historian B. H. Liddell-Hart, this code was broken by the Lincoln Administration—the first government in modern history to direct war against civilians. By 1945, the distinction between civilians and combatants had entirely collapsed. Some 60 million died in World War II, which amounts to 29,000 killed every day for six years!

But not even war has been the worst of it. R. J. Rummel has carried out extensive research to determine the number of people killed by their own governments. He estimates that nearly four times as many people have been killed by their own governments as have been killed in all the wars, domestic and foreign, fought around the globe in the twentieth century (See his *Death by Government*). It is as if nuclear war had occurred, Rummel concludes, and no one noticed.

Far from establishing peace and security within its borders, the vast-scale modern state, in its 350-year career, has been a greater threat to human life within those borders than wars from foreign invasion. Viewed in this light, can we continue to assert the Hobbesian postulate that large centralized modern states are necessary for peace and security without being ashamed of our credulity?

There is no escaping the conclusion that the modern state—defined as a territorial monopoly on coercion that can expand but can never be divided by secession because it is "one and indivisible—is and continues to be a baneful instrument. Indeed, the modern state itself can be viewed as a weapon of mass destruction that has to be managed and restrained with more care than nuclear weapons. Nuclear fission requires the concentration and acceleration of forces. Division makes fission impossible. Where it is possible and prudent to do so, we should support the territorial division of modern states through peaceful secession.

Thomas Jefferson imagined that as Americans moved westward, they would form new states that would secede and form new Unions of states. Had Jefferson's vision of three or more American Unions on the continent been realized, it is doubtful that all would have agreed to enter World War I, or that any one of them would have done so on its own. Americans were strongly opposed to fighting in a European war in 1914 and in 1940, but the dazzling prospect of imperial leadership—of reconstructing Europe according to an ideology of human rights—danced before Wilson's (and later Roosevelt's) eyes. A similar vision of reconstructing the Middle East—and indeed of leading a "global democratic revolution," backed by force if need be—has guided U.S. foreign policy whether in the hands of "liberals," or "neoconservatives." These hubristic visions are made possible by the sheer size and scale of the U.S. empire. A Jeffersonian division of the empire into three or more unions (each of which would surpass the larger European states) would considerably reduce the temptation to such fantasies.

To be sure, liberty and prosperity have been enjoyed in large modern states, but the enjoyment has been episodic. And it is arguable that it has been achieved in spite of monster-centralized states, not because of them. Little states such as Switzerland and Norway have refused to join the European superstate; yet they are regularly in the ten richest states in the world. Norway was the richest in 2006.

A thoughtful public debate on how to break up this ever-expanding latter-day Tower of Babel—first established by the egoism of monarchs and made worse by mass democracy—is long overdue. The natural place for this debate to begin is in the land of the Declaration of Independence, where the just-emerging modern state met its first successful resistance.

War and the Second Vermont Republic

Ben Scotch

Issue no. 7 • November 2005

Here's an easy question to invite you into my meanderings: How many times did the first Vermont Republic begin a war? None? Bingo. Okay, there are huge differences between the world of the late eighteenth century and the post-9/11 twenty-first-century world. But there are similarities as well, and it is time to reexamine the role of U.S. states and their National Guard units in questions of war and peace, with special emphasis on wars of choice—wars that have no credible relationship to national defense.

In the nation we joined as the fourteenth state in 1791, the focus of the military was the state militias, rather than a national army. Indeed, fear of a standing army was one of the issues that the colonies had with their British rulers. The decline in the independence of state militias and the simultaneous rise of the United States as the dominant world military power during the twentieth century are not coincidental. During the nineteenth century the states retained significant powers over their militias (renamed the National Guard in 1903), though they exercised no power under the War Clause and could not act independently when the president undertook military action without a declaration. However, Article 1, Section 8 gave the states significant authority with respect to appointing officers and training the militia. No, these were not war-making powers, and no state could maintain its own army. But even limited powers gave the states a sense of ownership of and a unique bond with their Guards.

Federal call-up for a foreign war was solemn business. If the nation was threatened, the Guard was there, in a flash. But Guard members were never considered the core of a U.S. military force in a war that was not defensive. In sum, state militias retained their dual status—they were available primarily to support their home states during emergencies and to defend the nation if a foreign attacker dared to come near. The dual role of the National Guard may have faded in the public mind in the conflagrations of the twentieth century, but, in a modest way, the roles of local wisdom and greater state independence are being reborn in the twenty-first. It is not at all odd that Vermont, a demographic speck on the world map, should be the midwife to this rebirth. Nor is it surprising that profound differences in prevailing attitudes about war and peace are central to what I will call paradigm secession—departure by Vermont from the apparently dominant national sense that our greatness as a nation must be projected through military force, rather than by passing on our customs of constitutional rule, due process, equal protection, freedom of conscience, gender equity, national and ethnic diversity, generosity of spirit, and—perhaps the greatest gift—the enduring example of the peaceful transfer of power.

A modern, robust, and equitably populated military serving in defense of our homeland would be consistent with the projection of national greatness. But the definition of defense, though complex in the post-9/11 world, should never become a euphemism for military conquest. America, the hegemon, is not the America that can credibly export humanism and a history of successful constitutional struggle. On Town Meeting Day, March 1, 2005, some fifty-two towns and cities adopted resolutions about the war in Iraq and the Vermont National Guard. Most towns requested that the legislature set up a committee to study the impact of Guard deployment. Less noted but of equal importance was the call by nearly every town to "request the members of Vermont's Congressional Delegation to urge Congress to restore the balance between the federal government and the states, limiting the nearly complete federal control over state National Guard units to cases where there is reasonable evidence that war powers are requested in order to protect against a threat to the territory of the United States, where there is an insurrection or a plausible threat of insurrection; or where there is a declaration of war under the United States Constitution."

This was a powerful call to restore and indeed to extend some state powers—the establishment or restoration of any state power would be an amazing step—where war and peace was the issue at the threshold. War would remain a purely federal matter where the United States was threatened. But states would be able to withhold their National Guard units in wars of choice. The practical impact of such a change would be less important than the symbolic impact. It is unlikely that many state chief executives would withhold Guard troops where a president had been persuasive in the call for a war, even a war of choice. And in any case, by instituting the draft, Congress would be able to populate the military ranks, with or without contributions by recalcitrant governors. But the debate over the draft would be a healthy one and would be a sensible hurdle for a chief executive to have to vault in order to begin a war of choice. In turn, the debate over greater state powers where wars of choice are at issue would be a debate worth having, whatever the political odds of succeeding in the near term.

However modest the step, reinvigorating state, and inevitably local, influence on questions of war and peace would have a profound impact in how we think about the inevitability of war. It could also inform the wider discussion of what political independence means in twenty-first-century Vermont. The point is that the goal of returning even modest powers to the states where wars of choice are at issue is a window looking out at a landscape of much wider change, though the time line for that change is substantial and the dream, like the dream of a more peaceable kingdom, may lie over the far horizon.

It will be a very independent Vermont's task to convince other states that taking back some powers where wars of choice are before us will strengthen us militarily by creating greater consensus about when military force is needed and by restraining a zealous and fallible leader who wants to drag us into a fruitless military venture. In the wake of that restraint, there will be space to remind the world of the true reasons this is a great nation.

Origins of the New England Secession Tradition

Donald W. Livingston

Issue no. 18 • Spring 2007

The Vermont independence effort is guided by a peaceful group of thoughtful citizens who believe that Vermont would be better off as a small independent country like Iceland, Lichtenstein, Monaco, Luxembourg, or Switzerland than to remain under the domination of an overly centralized and increasingly out-of-control central federal government. To some, the idea of an independent Vermont is preposterous but harmless, more theater than serious policy. To others it smacks of treason. Did not the Civil War settle forever the question of whether a state within the United States can secede? It did not. Timeless moral and constitutional questions cannot be settled by the contingencies of war. That secession is a policy option available to any state within the United States today is admittedly unfashionable, but it is neither silly nor treasonous. It is an option rooted in the origin and foundations of the U.S. political tradition.

The Declaration of Independence is a legal brief in international law justifying the secession of thirteen self-proclaimed states from the British Empire. Vermont was not one of these states but seceded from Britain on her own in 1777 and remained an independent republic before joining the Union in 1791. Vermont and Texas came into the Union as independent states from prior secessions. Secession is an ever present possibility in any large political union created out of formerly independent political societies such as the United Kingdom, the Soviet Union, the European Union, or the United States. Since each political society preexisted the union, the political society is primary (an end in itself), while the union is secondary (an instrument). When an instrument (like the union) no longer serves its purpose, it should be discarded for a better one.

The Second Vermont Republic is possible because we live in interesting times. George Kennan, one of the twentieth century's great geopolitical strategists and architect of the United States' Cold War containment policy, argued in his autobiography, *Around the Cragged*

Hill, that the public corporation known as the United States has become simply too large for the purposes of self-government. When any corporation becomes so large that it is on the verge of collapsing under its own unwieldy bulk, the only remedy, Kennan concluded, is to downsize it. And he suggested that we begin a public debate on how to divide the U.S. empire into a number of independent unions of states associated under a commonwealth model. Kennan endorsed the idea of a Second Vermont Republic a few years before his death as a worthy effort to begin a debate about how such division should proceed.

Yet for many, secession still appears alien—outside the boundaries of the U.S. political tradition. But this view springs from attending to only one part of our political tradition. From the formation of the United States, with the Articles of Confederation, on down to 1860, secession proved a policy option considered in every section of the federation by major political leaders. It was only after the so-called Civil War that Americans began to adopt the language of the French Revolution, language that absolutely prohibits secession. The French Republic was the first to declare itself a republic—one and indivisible—creating the paradigm of all modern states. But this language of indivisibility was entirely alien to the republican principles of the American Revolution under which the United States created a voluntary federation of states, not an aggregate of individuals ruled from the center.

It was not until the 1920s (at the high noon of the Western obsession with centralization) that the U.S. Congress approved the Pledge of Allegiance, verbally transforming a federation of states into the French Revolutionary slogan: "one nation indivisible." The result is that Americans have inherited a deeply fractured political tradition. On one side of the fracture is what we may call a Jeffersonian Americanism, beginning with the Declaration of Independence (a secession document) and running down to 1860. On the other side is a post-Lincolnian Americanism. The former is rooted in state sovereignty, favors small polities, and is open to secession. The latter is rooted in national sovereignty, views the individual states (like Vermont) mainly as administrative units of the center, and absolutely prohibits secession.

At a time when the 350-year adventure of the large unitary state has turned sour and the resources of post-Lincolnian centralization seem to be exhausted, it is perhaps time to recover and explore the Jeffersonian inheritance. The first thing to appreciate is that it was not until the post-Lincolnian era that the U.S. Constitution began to be seen as the sacred document of an organic American civil religion. In the Jeffersonian era, the Constitution was thought of as a secular compact between sovereign states. It was also a compromise that few were happy with. The region of the United States that first tested the Union for its viability was New England. Its leaders seriously considered secession in 1804 over President Jefferson's Louisiana Purchase; in 1808 over Jefferson's Embargo of their trade; and most seriously in 1814, over issues surrounding "Mr. Madison's War of 1812." Secession was advocated by New England abolitionists from the 1830s on to 1860; and by John Quincy Adams and other New England leaders over the Mexican war and the annexation of Texas.

The Union created by the Constitution of 1789 was hotly debated and passed only by a small margin. As early as 1794, Senators Rufus King of New York (formerly from Massachusetts) and Oliver Ellsworth of Connecticut told Senator John Taylor of Virginia that "it was utterly impossible for the union to continue," that North and South would never agree on public policy, and that it would be better to renegotiate the Union than to have a forced separation later. Both King and Ellsworth were Founding Fathers who had helped draft the U.S. Constitution, and both were political allies of Federalist leaders who would later lead serious secession movements in New England.

Nothing came of this move. But ten years later a more serious effort at secession arose in response to the 1803 Louisiana Purchase, which more than doubled the size of the United States. Since the Constitution had no provision for acquiring new territory, Jefferson's acquisition was thought to be unconstitutional. Moreover, New England had a commercial and maritime economy; consequently, its face was set to the East. The agricultural South meanwhile, looked to cultivate land in the West. Acquiring the Louisiana Territory meant more states in the West, greatly expanding the power of the Southern agrarian interest at the expense of New England's commercial interests. New England Federalists in Congress such as Timothy Pickering, Uriah Tracy, and Roger Griswold envisioned "a new confederacy, exempt from the corrupt and corrupting influence and oppression of the aristocratic Democrats of the South." Its nucleus would be New England, "to which New York would be added later," and with a hand of friendship extended to the British provinces in Canada.

This first secession movement, which counted among its leaders Founding Fathers who had drafted the U.S. Constitution, may seem surprising only because of the dominance of post-Lincolnian historiography that views U.S. history as the story of the inevitable unfolding of a unitary American State, one and indivisible. But in the Jeffersonian era, the Union was not considered organic and indivisible but an experiment, as Washington famously called it in his 1796 Farewell Address. An experiment that fails should be called off. And in the case of a federal union of states, each of which could be a viable country in the world, that can only mean secession. A distinguished historian of this period writes: "secession, even in 1804 was no new and unheard-of remedy for oppressed sectional minorities . . . most political thinkers of the first half-century of constitutional government had very little faith in the duration of the Union, and the statement that such-and-such a measure would 'inevitably produce a dissolution of the Union' was a familiar figure of speech in politics." It is not familiar now.

What faith can we rationally have in an overcentralized, post-Lincolnian empire that no longer knows how to stop growing? Would it really have been so bad if the New England states had formed a Northeastern federation with special ties to Canadian Britain? For more than a century, questions of this sort have not been asked. But given the great changes in the world today, they can no longer be suppressed and, indeed, appear to us now in a fresh light.

Beyond Our Independence Daze

Secession, Common Sense, and "the Spirit of 1777"

ROB WILLIAMS

Issue no. 24 • Summer 2008

A long habit of not thinking a thing wrong, gives it a superficial appearance of being right, and raises at first a formidable outcry in defense of custom. But the tumult soon subsides. Time makes more converts than reason.

— Thomas Paine, *Common Sense*, 1776

This month—July—marks a moment every year when citizens all over this country celebrate the writing of the "Declaration of Independence." Penned by Thomas Jefferson in 1776 at the behest of Philadelphia's first Continental Congress, the Declaration made a series of bold statements about the nature of the human condition, and the relationship between citizens and governments. We know these radical words well, and there is power and meaning in them.

> We hold these truths to be self-evident, that all men are created equal, that they are endowed by their Creator with certain unalienable rights, that among these are life, liberty and the pursuit of happiness. That to secure these rights, governments are instituted among men, deriving their just powers from the consent of the governed.
>
> That whenever any form of government becomes destructive to these ends, it is the right of the people to alter or to abolish it, and to institute new government, laying its foundation on such principles and organizing its powers in such form, as to them shall seem most likely to effect their safety and happiness.

In the midst of our twenty-first-century independence daze—the brouhaha and barbecues, the bunting and the beer—most of us imagine these famed and oft-quoted words marked "a new birth of freedom" (to quote

Abraham Lincoln in his 1863 Gettysburg Address) and the creation of the United States as a nation. Not so. The United States would not be born until 1783, with the official signing of the Treaty of Paris—and only then as a loosely allied group of thirteen sovereign states under the Articles of Confederation. Make no mistake—the Declaration of Independence was about secession.

The document marked the official declaration of independence from Great Britain by a small group of committed English colonists tired of being governed from afar by King George, London's Parliament, and large multinational monopolies like the East India Tea Company. Corruption, cronyism, and government by fiat drove these colonists—rebels all—to question their attachments to the richest and most powerful empire on earth (the British Empire, over which, it was said, the sun never set), and to begin to imagine new possibilities for their lives and those of their children.

We too easily forget that all of our founding fathers and mothers—George Washington, Abigail Adams, James Madison, Molly Pitcher, Ben Franklin, and the rest of the cast and crew—were, in fact, secessionists, and that the very first active verb in Jefferson's famous 1776 "shout heard 'round the world" is: "dissolve." Remember?

> When, in the course of human events, it becomes necessary for one people to dissolve the political bands which have connected them with another, and to assume among the powers of the earth, the separate and equal station to which the laws of nature and of nature's God entitle them, a decent respect to the opinions of mankind requires that they should declare the causes which impel them to the separation.

Almost one year to the day after the signing of the Declaration of Independence, citizens here in the Green Mountains created the first Vermont republic—independent of any control by the British, the Yorkers, and, for a time, the new United States government—with the July 8, 1777, signing of Vermont's first constitution in the town of Windsor. For the next fourteen years, the independent republic of Vermont convened an elected assembly, coined its own money (upon which was inscribed "Vermont res publica"), operated a postal service, conducted military operations and diplomatic relations and trade, recruited and commanded its own militia, and wrote its own laws in a legislature elected at town meeting, where the people also elected the governor and his twelve-member council. This fourteen-year period—the "Spirit of 1777"—marks a decisive historic moment for the citizens of this sovereign state, a time when Vermonters governed themselves and ran their own affairs, in concert with the rest of the world, rather than being governed by a distant government as a very small cog in a much larger machine.

We urge Vermonters to once again consider choosing this path. For the richest and most powerful nation of the twenty-first-century world is no longer Great Britain, but the United States.

And, as we have argued in these pages for three years now, the United States is no longer a constitutional republic responsive to the will of its citizens, but an aggressive empire acting at the behest of the few at the expense of the many. We face a twenty-first-century world very different from the twentieth.

"Let facts," as Jefferson said, "be submitted to a candid world."

- The twin twenty-first-century challenges of climate change and peak oil, which will compel us toward relocalization and "power down" living much more quickly than we may realize.
- The U.S. government's global (and profitable) pursuit of a policy of "full-spectrum dominance" by building an "empire of bases" (as many as 1,000) to engage in a multisequential energy war whose ultimate goal is to control oil-rich parts of the planet (a war that "will not end in our lifetimes").
- Federal implementation of a whole host of mandates that undermine our most basic rights and cherished freedoms: the USA PATRIOT Act, a proposed National Animal ID System, and the ever-increasing use of radio frequency ID, biometrics, and other "total information" surveillance technologies.
- Stupendous electoral fraud committed by collusion between political party hacks and corporately owned proprietary electronic voting codes and machines.
- Massive corporate corruption and a globalized "tapeworm economy" sanctioned by both major political parties.

All of this demands that we in Vermont reconsider our relationship with this "Leviathan" called the United States. Both Thomas Jefferson and Thomas Paine were right in 1776. "'Tis time to part." Secession is simple common sense, and Vermont's "Spirit of 1777" offers us a way forward. As Paine's *Common Sense* words remind us, time is on our side.

Free Vermont. Long live the *Untied* States.

The Second Vermont Republic

Frequently Asked Questions

Thomas Naylor

Issue no. 1 • April 2005

What is the Second Vermont Republic?

The Second Vermont Republic (SVR) is a peaceful, democratic, grassroots, libertarian populist movement opposed to the tyranny of the U.S. Government, corporate America, and globalization and committed to the return of Vermont to its rightful status as an independent republic, as it was between 1777 and 1791.

What is the primary objective of the movement?

Independence. To extricate Vermont peacefully, legally, and democratically from the United States as soon as possible and create an independent nation-state based on the Swiss model.

Does that mean secession?

Yes.

Why does Vermont want to secede?

First, the United States suffers from imperial overstretch and has become unsustainable politically, economically, agriculturally, socially, culturally, and environmentally. Second, Vermont finds it increasingly difficult to protect itself from the debilitating effects of big business, big agriculture, big markets, and big government, who want all of us to be the same— just like they are. Third, the U.S. Government has lost its moral authority because it is owned, operated, and controlled by corporate America. Fourth, American foreign policy, which is based on the doctrine of full-spectrum dominance, is immoral, illegal, unconstitutional, and in violation of the United Nations charter. Fifth, as long as Vermont remains in the Union, its citizens face curtailed civil liberties, the risk of terrorist attack, and the risk of military conscription of its youth.

But isn't secession unconstitutional?
No. "Whenever any form of government becomes destructive, it is the right of the people to alter or abolish it, and to institute a new government," said Thomas Jefferson in the Declaration of Independence. Just as a group has a right to form, so, too, does it have a right to disband, to subdivide itself, or withdraw from a larger unit. The U.S. Constitution does not forbid secession. According to the tenth amendment, that which is not expressly prohibited by the Constitution is allowed. All states have a Constitutional right to secede.

To which other principles does the Second Vermont Republic subscribe?
Direct democracy, Swiss federalism, sustainability, economic solidarity, quality education, humane healthcare, nonviolence, political neutrality, and international solidarity with its neighbors New Hampshire, Maine, Quebec, and the Atlantic provinces of Canada. Notwithstanding its policy of neutrality, the Second Vermont Republic does not rule out some form of political alliance with the aforementioned states and provinces.

Does the Second Vermont Republic want to take over the government of Vermont?
Absolutely not. The people of the independent Republic of Vermont will decide how it is governed. Unlike the Free State Project in New Hampshire, our aim is not to take over the government. For that reason, the Second Vermont Republic takes no official position on such controversial issues as abortion, gay marriage, school prayer, and legalizing marijuana. These are issues for the citizens of the independent republic to decide.

Could Vermont survive economically as an independent nation-state?
Unquestionably. Of the 200 or so independent nation-states in the world, 50 of them have a smaller population than Vermont's 620,000. Five of the ten richest countries in the world as measured by per capita income are smaller than Vermont: Liechtenstein, Iceland, Luxembourg, Bermuda, and Cayman Islands. Independence does not mean economic or political isolation. Over 600 Vermont firms export nearly 24 percent of the state's gross product. We see no reason why this should change after independence.

A New Vision of the Future for SVR (2012)

Over the past seven years SVR has evolved beyond the stage of simply wanting to free Vermont from the clutches of an immoral, unsustainable, ungovernable, unfixable empire. It now views itself in a much broader context.

Vermont, like most small nations and most aspiring nations, finds it increasingly difficult to cope with the chaos of a meganation world under the cloud of empire. Fifty nine percent of the 7.035 billion people of the world live in one of eleven countries having a population in excess of 100 million people. These mega-countries bear the primary responsibility for a plethora of global megaproblems including the 2008 financial meltdown (ongoing), the euro crisis, the threat of terrorism, imperialism, excessive population growth, poverty, peak oil, and climate change.

In light of these developments SVR has broadened its mission to include a commitment to 1) the peaceful breakup of meganations such as the United States, China, and Russia; 2) the self-determination of breakaway states such as Quebec, Scotland, and Vermont; and 3) a strategic alliance with other small, democratic, nonviolent, socially responsible, egalitarian, sustainable nations such as Austria, Finland, and Switzerland, which share a high degree of environmental integrity and a strong sense of community.

Above all, SVR now sees itself as pursuing a path that will enable Vermont to join the community of small nations of the world.

Is Vermont independence politically feasible?

Yes. Ultimately whether or not Vermont achieves political independence is a question of political will. Is the will of the people of Vermont for independence strong enough to overcome the will of the U.S. government to prevent them from achieving their goal? In 1989 six Eastern European allies of the Soviet Union unseated their respective Communist governments and seceded from the Soviet sphere of influence. With the bloody exception of Romania, this all took place nonviolently. The Second

Vermont Republic has been particularly influenced by the solidarity movement in Poland, and Czech leader Vaclav Havel's concept of the "power of the powerless."

What are the necessary steps?

The Vermont legislature must be persuaded to authorize a convention of the people to vote on rescinding the petition for statehood approved by the Vermont Assembly in January 1791 and ratified on March 4, 1791. To be credible, the vote should pass by at least a two-thirds majority. Articles of Secession should then be submitted to the U.S. President, Secretary of State, President of the Senate, and Speaker of the House. Diplomatic recognition should be sought from Canada, Quebec, Mexico, England, France, and the United Nations. And then the moment of truth—Vermont would start behaving like an independent nation-state.

What if the Vermont independence movement fails?

Vermont still provides a communitarian alternative to the dehumanized mass production, mass consumption, narcissistic lifestyle that pervades most of the United States. Vermont is smaller, more rural, more democratic, less violent, less commercial, more egalitarian, and more independent than most states. It offers itself as a kinder, gentler metaphor for a nation obsessed with money, power, size, speed, greed, and fear of terrorism.

Fall of Empire
A Time for Renewal

Ben Hewitt

Issue no. 43 • Fall 2011

Early August and already I can feel it. I feel it mostly at the fringes of each day, like a photo with its edges slightly out-of-focus. The mornings are cool now, and darker, and in the evenings I look up from the task at hand to find the sun already dropping behind the Greens and everything disappearing into the wash of night. Fall. Not quite yet, but soon. And winter, inevitably to follow.

I am more energized now than at any other time of year, including spring. Paradoxically, as the nights get longer, I awake earlier and earlier, frequently soft-stepping down the stairs to find that it is only 3:00 or 3:30 and then soft-stepping back up to try and lull myself back to sleep for another hour or two. I lie there and listen to my family breathing, the dog softly snoring, the early, bedraggled crows of Brutus, our rooster. I lie there and watch the stars, and rather than wonder at how big the universe is, I find myself amazed by how small it seems. Because doesn't it look like if you really tried, you could reach up and grab one of those suckers?

I used to find it strange that it feels like I am opening at the precise time of year when nature is closing. It is as if I am absorbing the energy being shed by the trees in our forest, the grasses in our fields, and the animals we slaughter, their blood soaking into the dun-colored soil of our barnyard, their entrails buried deep in the compost pile, where they'll succumb to the same process that will eventually take us all. Only to be spread across our fields or atop the raised beds of our crops, bringing all those little shoots to life. Our animals are generous; they don't know how to stop giving.

It is only when I allow myself to see the larger picture that it all makes sense. We tend to categorize these things—*this season is for that, that season is for this*—but of course it is all part of the same balled up, interconnected, cyclical nature of things. We think of spring as the season of renewal, but forget that nothing can be renewed without something having been taken. And so the taking, the dying, and the shedding are all parts of the renewal, no less crucial than the early tender buds emerging from the trees or the first tentative suckles of a newborn calf.

There is so much talk lately of collapse, of the vulnerability inherent to the complex and convoluted systems that, like it or not, we are all dependent on. But I sometimes wonder if we're thinking about it all wrong. For what is it we're afraid of collapsing? A financial system that funnels profits to the top single percent? An energy supply that enables such false prosperity and wreaks such widespread havoc? Perhaps the true collapse was in the creation of and our subsequent dependence on these systems. Perhaps what we bear witness to, in the early years of the twenty-first century, is nothing less than the early stage societal composting necessary to feed the cycle. We have all fed well (though obviously, some better than others) off the meat of these arrangements, and now it is time to bury them with all the guts and shit and detritus of our nation.

Now it is time for renewal.

Afterword

Ron Miller

Adapted for this volume from an article published in
Issue no. 32 • Stick Season 2009

In October 2007, the Declaration of the Second North American Secessionist Convention began by asserting "The deepest questions of human liberty and government facing our time go beyond right and left, and in fact have made the old left-right split meaningless and dead." I would argue that the first part of this claim is undoubtedly true. The massive consolidation and expansion of power by the U.S. government during the past 150 years, which would have troubled most of the founders of the republic, has served the purposes of both ends of the political spectrum. Both the mainstream right and mainstream left seek to manipulate the political system to achieve their goals—economic expansion and globalization on the one hand, or greater social equality and economic opportunity on the other. Aside from wherever we might stand on the goals themselves, it is the extent of national power, and the enormous distance between the governing and the governed, that the critics of this system abhor, no matter whose agendas are being served.

We decentralists also come from both the right and the left; we share some basic principles, such as community, democracy, and sense of place, that "go beyond" more specific partisan agendas. Both serious conservatives and radical democrats (with a lowercase *d*) now agree that the "liberty" promised by the American Revolution and Constitution is deeply threatened today by the massive expansion of the powers of transnational corporations and the federal government. All of us, regardless of our specific political and cultural preferences, have much reason to worry about the enormous control that the national government now exerts over so many aspects of society, and the enormous influence that elite institutions and cliques (corporations, lobbyists, Wall Street, think tanks, the media, and so on) wield on policymaking. Our culture, community, and liberty are being overwhelmed by this political juggernaut that controls the economy for the benefit of corporate elites, tells us what our children must learn, oversees hundreds of military bases around the globe, and alienates millions of citizens by its heavy-handed actions.

However, the second half of the secessionist Declaration, claiming that distinctions between left and right are "meaningless and dead," is not really accurate because genuine philosophical and cultural differences do exist among us. Were we to actually free ourselves from imperial domination and policies imposed from above, it is clear that there would be much diversity among the communities and regions that currently comprise the United States. Our specific grievances are considerably, sometimes radically, different. Those on the right are bothered by different manifestations of national governance than those on the left.

On one hand, the Vermont secession movement gained traction during the Bush years because most of us were horrified and outraged by the naked imperialism of the Iraq war and every other facet of U.S. foreign policy, by the trashing of due process and other Constitutional rights embodied by the USA PATRIOT Act, by the encouragement given to war profiteers, private security forces, corporate raiders and gamblers, and other results of neoconservative rule. There is a definite libertarian streak in the Vermont approach, but, philosophically and culturally, we tend to be "progressive" on issues of civil rights, social justice, and economic fairness, and for us the Bush administration represented a disaster.

On the other hand, many other state sovereignty and secession movements that have arisen in the United States are motivated by a quite different worldview, by moral and political concerns associated with the "right." Free marketeers and cultural conservatives, who were relatively comfortable with the Bush presidency, view the Obama Administration as a mortal enemy of American liberty and identity. The tea party movement and radicalization of the Republican party do not simply reflect a decentralist critique of federal power, but a deep-seated antipathy to cultural change represented by an African American president, who (at least rhetorically) calls for greater public responsibility for healthcare and economic justice, constructive international engagement, and a truly multicultural society. Aspects of Obama's presidency that seemed most encouraging to liberals are the very causes of right-wing rebellion.

A very real cultural and political gulf separates decentralism of the left and right. For instance, the Second Southern National Congress, which met in 2009, proclaimed allegiance to a "Southern culture" that is "founded on the enduring and permanent: trust in God, family, tradition, manners, property, community, loyalty, courage, and honor." It is not that progressives reject all these qualities out of hand, but this emphasis on the "permanent" reflects a different set of priorities from an agenda of social progress and equality, of expanding human and civil rights, of nonviolence and multiculturalism, that motivates liberal decentralists. And then there is the question of racial justice. The Congress did not explicitly mention race, but in the context of the South's history, liberals are surely justified in wondering which "tradition" they mean.

Some progressives in Vermont have denounced the independence movement here because some of us have discussed secession with these southern—as well as equally conservative western—activists. Our critics label the southern decentralists "neoconfederates"—implying that they are inherently racist and might even bring back slavery if they could. Employing guilt by association, they suggested that we in the Vermont movement must therefore condone racism ourselves. The charge is completely erroneous. No one among the Vermont secessionists is sympathetic to racist views or policies, and their willingness to dialogue with more conservative decentralists does not blind them to such morally repugnant attitudes. The fact is that the southerners themselves have disavowed racist intentions in conversations with Vermonters as well as with journalist Bill Kauffman, who documented the emerging move-ment in *Bye Bye Miss American Empire*. Secession is admittedly a radical and controversial strategy, but not because it endorses any regression to Jim Crow or antebelleum racial norms.

It is true, however, that liberal decentralists, unlike conservatives, have to wrestle with the paradox that social progress has often been achieved in the United States through the expansion of federal power. Slavery and legal racial discrimination were abolished by the overwhelming force of the national government, not voluntarily by the southern states. Other achievements that the left believes improved life in this country, such as workers' rights and child-labor legislation, food and drug safety laws, social security, banking regulations, the jurisprudence of the Warren Court, policies promoting equality and opportunity for women, and environ-mental legislation, to name a few, owe their success to federal authority. It is understandable that progressives would be alarmed by a movement that wants to curtail this authority, but the charge of "racism" is an unfortunate and misleading substitute for a serious, genuine dialogue about the benefits and costs of decentralizing governance in the United States. We urgently need to engage in that dialogue in these times; we need to work through the paradox of liberal decentralism.

I am myself a green/civil libertarian/progressive as well as a decentralist, and it troubles me to think of the Bill of Rights, environmental protection, civil rights protections, and other social and political advances now enforced by the federal government seriously compromised if that authority is dissolved. However, it troubles me even more to see the national government itself compromise those advances! Between the post-9/11 regime of surveillance, covert operations, and military intervention, and the relentless consolidation of corporate power (*Citizens United* and the "bailout" of Wall Street being recent manifestations), the U.S. government is evermore committed to an imperialist path that seriously jeopardizes progressive values. We are not only losing the gains made in the last century but (as the battle over our aging nuclear power plant, Vermont Yankee, so clearly demonstrates) closing off political options for challenging the corporate state as federal authority overwhelms state and local decision-making.

Decentralists—and secessionists in particular—have come to the conclusion that the costs of granting authority to distant and coercive governing bodies are now too high to tolerate or ignore. Progressives may be pleased when a New Deal or Great Society is inaugurated, but the same government, in other hands, pursues policies that are militaristic, tilted toward corporate interests, and threatening to civil liberties. Even a "progressive" leader obeys the logic of empire: For all his accomplishments in the realm of social justice, Lyndon Johnson saddled the nation with the imperialist war in Vietnam. Barack Obama, the erstwhile community organizer, is hardly the "socialist" the right portrays him to be and has proved to be a good friend of the corporate and Wall Street interests that underwrite his campaigns. So we ask: Are the benefits of expansive federal authority worth the sacrifice of participatory democracy? The spread of military power and secret intelligence operations around the planet? The irrepressible influence of well-funded lobbyists and corporate interest groups? Do we entrust an empire to promulgate liberal values?

Furthermore, is the triumph of a progressive agenda worth the divisive pitting of region against region, one set of values against another? When one central government in Washington, D.C., amasses so much authority over the lives of so many people, communities, and cultures, the stakes around its policy decisions are extremely high: Large segments of the population come to believe that they cannot afford to lose. Thus we have political gridlock. The fact is that large swatches of America prefer their traditionalist culture and bitterly resent the imposition of progressive values by "elites" from the east and west coasts. (For a provocative treatment of this cultural divide, see Chuck Thompson's *Better Off Without 'Em: A Northern Manifesto for Southern Secession*.) The progressive legislation that has managed to take hold in the United States since 1900 has failed to convert southern culture or conservative populism to the version of social democracy that some of us favor. Why not let the "red" regions of America live by the values they prefer, instead of driving them into a frenzied hatred of liberalism imposed from above? The federal civil rights laws, Warren Court decisions, and other achievements of the 1960s proved to be monumental, but they provoked bitter resistance, a major political realignment that produced today's uncompromising and solidly entrenched Republican party. The result is that progressive legislation is forestalled throughout the nation, even in places where it might be welcomed. It is not certain that the gains of earlier generations can be preserved in an increasingly hostile and conservative political climate. Ask organized labor.

The proliferation of sovereignty and secession movements can be seen as a signal that neither the left nor the right can tolerate the imposition of the other's agenda by a distant government controlled by inaccessible and unaccountable elites. What is the cost to democracy when the ascendance of one side so deeply disturbs and threatens the other that civil dialogue is no longer possible? Perhaps, we suggest, it makes sense to trust local people more than the technocrats and war profiteers who run the empire. Decentralism is based on the belief that people will act more rationally, more compassionately, more democratically, when they feel that their voices matter, that the system is responsive to their concerns. True, some regions and communities will use this democratic process to choose values, practices, and policies that other communities disdain. As decentralists, we hold that in the long term this diversity is far more beneficial than the imposition of one subgroup's ideological preferences—even if we happen to belong to that group. Decentralists do not claim to have all the answers to deeply rooted social pathologies, like racism. But surely imperialism, even if it is able to force communities to change some of their behavior, does not provide the answers either.

The decentralist position advanced in *Vermont Commons* goes beyond, and deeper than, conventional "left" and "right" ideologies. We acknowledge regional and cultural differences, even as we represent and describe what most would consider a "progressive" culture rooted in Vermont's distinctive history and political climate. Our state motto is "Freedom and Unity"—a pairing that cogently blends the often competing values of diversity and common values. Extreme individualism is tempered by responsible participation in community. Coercive authority is tempered by trust in human-scale democracy. We believe that the freedom to fashion community and culture at their roots nourishes a democratic society.

V For Vermont: A Concluding Call To Action

Juliet Buck and Rob Williams

"Ideas are bulletproof."
—*V For Vendetta*

"There is no idea like an idea whose time has come."
— Victor Hugo

First.

Turn off the TeeVee. Stop reading the newspaper and the mainstream media (MSM) outlets on your computer and tracking device (a.k.a. "smart phone") for a while. Give yourself a break from being constantly marketed to, cajoled, lied to, and manipulated.

Then.

Read a nice long book about this stuff, something from Matt Taibbi or Chris Hedges that digs deliciously deep or some classic like *1984*. Give yourself the mental space to stop rationalizing your role in perpetuating an imperial system that is crooked and unjust.

Next.

Come out of the closet. Write a letter to the editor calling bullshit on some aspect of this ruinous empire, use the word *Empire* in it, and sign your real name. Keep doing this. Then speak the truth whenever the lies come up. Yes, this means you can't make polite political small talk at parties anymore. You'll be "that person." Embrace it. Most important, stop saying "I can't do anything!"

Once you've been doing this a while and are comfortable being a contrarian tempest of awesomeness, why not try to BE THE MEDIA? This is what we do at *Vermont Commons*. If the MSM won't tell us the vital stories that need to be told to understand twenty-first-century life in the empire (and they most assuredly do not, because they are owned by the very transnational corporate commercial interests that profit from the dissonance and manufactured conflict of ignorance and misinformation), then it's our job to find these stories and put them in front of eyeballs. Our job is to inoculate people with unburnished reality, steeling them to become immune to imperial propaganda.

Hands. Head. Heart.

Do something with them, other than clacking away at a computer keyboard. We all need to prepare ourselves for "the Great Re-Skilling" ahead—grow a plant, raise an animal, rediscover hand tools, and get outside as early and as often as you can, both alone (solitude is in increasingly precious supply in our wired age) and in the company of people whom you care about, and who care about you.

Last.

Please support Vermont independence by supporting the folks doing the work of independent media and civic journalism every day. Here at *Vermont Commons* and among all our allied organizations, we labor sincerely in the service of the best interests of our neighbors; laying the groundwork for a successful, maybe even joyous, transition from empire to independence. A little money goes a long way in an organization like ours, filled with smart, motivated people doing their heart's work to advance ideas that can work.

Visit us online—www.vtcommons.org—to learn more.

And let's raise a glass (because the beer here in the Green Mountains is UNREAL), and drink to a free and independent Vermont, in loose and mutually beneficial voluntary association with the rest of the *Untied* States.

JULIET BUCK, Editor

ROB WILLIAMS, Publisher

Vermont Commons: Voices of Independence

The Middlebury Declaration

Issue no. 2 • May 2005

The following declaration—a team effort originally conceived for a 2004 secession conference in Middlebury, Vermont—sets the Vermont independence movement in a national and international context.

We gather here to explore the possibilities of a new politics that might provide a realistic and enactable alternative to the familiar sorry political scene around us. We are convinced that the American empire, now imposing its military might on 153 countries around the world, is as fragile as empires historically tend to be, and that it might well implode upon itself in the near future. Before that happens, no matter what shape the United States may take, we believe there is at this moment an opportunity to push through new political ideas and projects that will offer true popular participation and genuine democracy. The time to prepare for that is now.

In our deliberations we considered many kinds of strategies for a new politics and eventually decided upon the inauguration of a campaign to monitor, study, promote, and develop agencies of separatism. By separatism we mean all the forms by which small political bodies, dedicated to the precept of human scale, distance themselves from larger ones, as in decentralization, dissolution, disunion, division, devolution, or secession, creating small and independent bodies that rule themselves. Of course we favor such polities that operate with participatory democracy and egalitarian justice, which are attainable only at a small scale, but the primary principle is that these states should enact their separation and self-government as they see fit.

It is important to realize that the separatist/independence movement is the most important and widespread political force in the world today and has been for the last half-century, during which time the United Nations, for example, has grown from 51 nations in 1945 to 193 nations in 2004. The breakups of the Soviet Union and the former Yugoslavia are recent manifestations of this fundamental trend, and there are separatist movements in more than two dozen countries at this time, including such well-known ones as in Catalonia, Scotland, Lapland, Sardinia, Sicily, Sudan, Congo, Kashmir, Chechnya, Kurdistan, Quebec, British Columbia, Mexico, and the Indian nations of North America. There is no reason that we cannot begin to examine the processes of secession in the United States. There are already at least 28 separatist organizations in this country—the most active in Alaska, Texas, Hawaii, Vermont, Puerto Rico, and the South—and there seems to be a growing sentiment that, because the national government has shown itself to be clumsy, unresponsive, and unaccountable in so many ways, power should be concentrated at lower levels. Whether these levels should be the states or coherent regions within the states or something smaller still is a matter best left to the people active in devolution, but the principle of secession must be established as valid and legitimate.

To this end, therefore, we are pledged to create a movement that will place secession on the national agenda, encourage nonviolent secessionist organizations throughout the country, develop communication among existing and future secessionist groups, and create a body of scholarship to examine and promote the ideas and principles of secessionism. It does seem that we have set ourselves a daunting task. And yet almost every week the papers bring news of the continuing action of the world's powerful centrifugal force, and that should stand as steady encouragement in this work. For example, the Basque Parliament recently approved a measure proclaiming the region to have the right to secede from Spain and proposing a plan for a new political relationship.

Of course the Basques have been asking for greater autonomy for 30 years or more, and the ETA terrorist group has killed a good many people in this cause. But what is significant about the proposed plan is that it is attempting a peaceful breakaway from Spain that would be authorized by a popular referendum. As the principal author of the measure has put it: "The Basque country is not a subordinate part of the Spanish state. The only way there will be a shared relationship with the state is if we decide there will be one." It is not fanciful to imagine Vermonters coming to the point of declaring just such an arrangement. And on the other side of Spain, in Catalonia, where the Catalan Republican Party cheered the Basque plan, the pressure is growing for something similar to enhance the region's autonomy. Catalans—whose first language is not Spanish—have pushed for greater independence for several decades now. Regionalism is so strong in Spain these days that almost all the seventeen regions that make up the country are asking for greater autonomy from Madrid.

"Things fall apart, the center cannot hold," is the way Yeats put it. He was enunciating an eternal truth that the violence of the nation state and global empire cannot negate. Power and coercion, bribery, and bread and circuses may keep large entities intact for a while, but eventually, because they are overlarge and out of scale, they collapse and divide into the real regions by which people live and identify themselves. The center cannot hold.

CONTRIBUTOR BIOGRAPHIES

ERIK ANDRUS writes and farms with draft horses in Ferrisburgh, Vermont, with his wife Erica and two young boys. Since the writing of this piece, the farm's work has shifted toward ecologically modeled wet rice cultivation.

IAN BALDWIN moved to Vermont from New York City in 1982. In 1984 Ian and his wife Margo founded Chelsea Green Publishing Company. In 2005 he cofounded the bimonthly journal *Vermont Commons: Voices of Independence.* He was one of the founders, with Kirkpatrick Sale and others, of the E.F. Schumacher Society in 1980, now the New Economics Institute. Ian is an artist and writer. He lives in South Strafford, Vermont.

PETER BARNES is an entrepreneur and writer who has founded and led several successful companies, including Working Assets/Credo. His latest book is *Capitalism 3.0: A Guide to Reclaiming the Commons.*

GAELAN BROWN has a background in journalism, Internet business development, consulting, and values-based marketing along with leadership experience in sustainability-focused nonprofit organizations. He currently works as Director of Visibility and Communication for 1% for the Planet, a global network of businesses committed to investing in environmental causes. Gaelan writes a regular column and blog for *Vermont Commons* as "An Energy Optimist," and he is cofounder/ Board Chair of www.CompostPower.org, which is focused on generating energy as a by-product of compost systems.

FRANK BRYAN is the John G. McCullough Professor of Political Science at the University of Vermont. A Vermonter since conception, he has published extensively on Vermont politics and town-meeting democracy including his major work *Real Democracy: The New England Town Meeting and How It Works* (University of Chicago Press). He maintains an active public-speaking agenda and is currently a trustee of the Vermont Historical Society.

JULIET BUCK is a bioregional decentralist, a writer/satirist, and delicate flower of Yankee womanhood with a profound lack of respect for authority. She is the Web editor of *Vermont Commons*, where she labors to liberate the public from the flagrantly false notion that they live in a functional democracy that serves any purpose other than to siphon off the surplus value of their labors to the elites who write our laws and dictate our policies via congressional proxies to serve that end.

ROBERT COSTANZA is Distinguished University Professor of Sustainability at Portland State University. His transdisciplinary research integrates the study of humans and the rest of nature to address research, policy, and management issues at multiple time and space scales, from small watersheds to the global system. He is cofounder and past-president of the International Society for Ecological Economics and was chief editor of the society's journal, *Ecological Economics,* from its inception in 1989 until 2002. He is founding editor in chief of *Solutions* (www.thesolutionsjournal.org) a new hybrid academic/popular journal.

CHARLES EISENSTEIN is the author of *The Ascent of Humanity* and *Sacred Economics*. Links to his essays, films, and other work can be found at www.charleseisenstein.net.

CARL ETNIER has worked with sustainability issues since the 1980s, with much of that time in sustainable water and wastewater treatment. In 2006, he turned his attention full time to educating people to prepare for peak oil. A founding member of Washington County's Post-Carbon Sustainability Network and Transition Town Montpelier, Carl hosts radio shows and blogs about the transition to a low-energy future.

BEN FALK developed Whole Systems Design, LLC, as a land-based response to biological and cultural extinction and the increasing separation between people and elemental things. He is a designer, builder, ecologist, tree-tender, and backcountry traveler, has studied architecture and landscape architecture, and holds a master's degree in land-use planning. Ben has taught at the University of Vermont, Harvard's Arnold Arboretum, and the Yestermorrow Design-Build School, as well as classes on permaculture and microclimate design.

GARY FLOMENHOFT is a research fellow for the Gund Institute at the University of Vermont, managing the Green Tax and Common Assets Project. He helped devise the Vermont Common Assets Trust Fund bill. Previously, he worked for eight years on the foundation and ballot status of the Green Party in California and the United States. When he realized that the political system is entirely immune to reform from third parties, he turned his attention to alternative economic systems and studied, then worked in ecological economics. Gary came to the conclusion that the United States has become a militaristic, corporatist global empire, destined to collapse like all empires before. He joined the Vermont secession movement when he determined that Vermont could implement a commons-based economy, but never as part of the U.S. global empire.

RICHARD FOLEY has served on the faculty at Keene State College in New Hampshire for thirty-four years, working in the interdisciplinary fields of sustainability, media literacy, and science, technology, and policy. As a longtime resident of Brattleboro, Vermont, he has been active in numerous grassroots groups promoting local media, peace and justice, the 9/11 truth movement, climate protection, and renewable energy.

BEN HEWITT was born and raised in northern Vermont, where he still lives with his wife and two sons. He operates a small scale diversified farm and writes just enough to pay for his farming habit. To read more of his work, go to www.benhewitt.net.

JAMES HOGUE is an actor and radio host who operates a small farm. He is currently working on monetary reform, including plans for a state bank and state/public currency.

ROWAN JACOBSEN is the author of numerous books, including *Fruitless Fall, American Terroir,* and *Shadows on the Gulf.* He lives in Calais, Vermont.

AMY KIRSCHNER is the founder of Vermont Resilience Lab, an open source innovation center, which created the Vermont Businesses for Social Responsibility (VBSR) Marketplace, a peer-to-peer mutual credit system. Amy grew up in Vermont and returned shortly after earning a B.S. in Business Management from Purdue University and then completed an M.S. in Natural Resources from the University of Vermont. She was a recipient of a 2010 Rising Star Award from *Vermont Business* magazine.

JAMES HOWARD KUNSTLER is the author of over fifteen books, including many novels. His recent work, including *World Made by Hand* and *Too Much Magic*, focuses on the destiny of industrial civilization. He lives 15 miles from the Vermont border in Washington County, New York.

ADRIAN KUZMINSKI is research scholar in philosophy at Hartwick College, the author of *Fixing the System: A History of Populism, Ancient and Modern*, and of the forthcoming work, *The Ecology of Money: Debt, Growth and Sustainability*. He is moderator of Sustainable Otsego, a social network with several hundred subscribers in central New York State.

DONALD W. LIVINGSTON is professor of philosophy, emeritus, Emory University. He is also a National Endowment for the Humanities Fellow, and a Fellow of the Institute for Advanced Study in the Humanities at the University of Edinburgh.

JOHN McCLAUGHRY served in the Vermont House and Senate, was a Senior Policy Advisor in the early Reagan White House, and with Frank Bryan coauthored *The Vermont Papers: Re-creating Democracy on a Human Scale* (1989). For eighteen years he was president of the Ethan Allen Institute, and he has been Kirby Town Moderator since 1966.

ROBIN MCDERMOTT is the cofounder of the Mad River Valley Localvore Project and a local food enthusiast. She and her husband Ray grow much of their own food in their Waitsfield home garden and preserve the food for eating throughout the winter. When not canning, freezing, or making jam, Robin does programming and marketing for their Web-based training business, QualityTrainingPortal.com.

RON MILLER spent nearly thirty years as an educational scholar and activist, known internationally as a founder of the holistic education movement. He authored or edited nine books, established two journals, cofounded an alternative school, and was on the faculty of the progressive Education program at Goddard College. His work is archived at www.pathsoflearning.net. In 2011 he retired to run an independent bookstore in Woodstock, Vermont. He has served on the *Vermont Commons* editorial board since 2007.

THOMAS NAYLOR passed away in December 2012. He was a retired economics professor at Duke University, and wrote about the problems of imperial America in books such as *Downsizing the U.S.A.* (1997), *Affluenza* (2005), and *Secession* (2008). He was the primary founder of the Second Vermont Republic (http://vermontrepublic.org/).

KIRKPATRICK SALE is the author of twelve books, including *Human Scale*, and is the director of the Middlebury Institute for the study of separation, secession, and self-determination (MiddleburyInstitute .org).

BEN SCOTCH is a retired lawyer living in Montpelier. He served with Senator Patrick Leahy as a Senate Judiciary Committee aide from 1981 to 1985, after leading environmental enforcement duties in the Vermont Attorney General's Office during the 1970s. In 1985 Ben began a fifteen-year term as chief staff attorney of the Vermont Supreme Court and then served for three years as executive director of the ACLU of Vermont. Since retiring, Scotch has worked as a citizen on issues of how we decide to go to war, money in politics, and law and policy concerning genetically modified foods.

HERVEY SCUDDER has directed the efforts of the NorthEast Center for Social Issues Studies (NECSIS) since 1996, promoting a sustainable energy future for Southern Vermont, most notably the successful 2001–4 lobbying campaign that resulted in the attempt by the state of Vermont to purchase the dams on the Connecticut and Deerfield rivers. More recently, he has focused on initiating biomass co-generation district heating systems projects in southeastern Vermont.

AMY SHOLLENBERGER has more than thirteen years of grassroots organizing, policy, and political issue campaign experience, including work as a press secretary for a member of the U.S. House of Representatives, senior policy analyst for Public Citizen's Critical Mass Energy and Environment Program, and executive director of Rural Vermont. In 2010, she was the campaign manager for a gubernatorial primary candidate in Vermont. Her consulting firm, Action Circles, helps clients with political strategy, organizational capacity building, and meeting facilitation. Amy is a member of Vermont Businesses for Social Responsibility, Women's Business Owners Network, and other networks. Her organization's website is at www.action-circles.com.

TAYLOR M. SILVESTRI is a part-time Vermonter, hailing originally from Scranton, Pennsylvania, who studies Creative Media at Champlain College, impulse-buys used books five at a time, wants to see the world from the belly of a whale, cries at books, movies, songs, blogs, weddings, and news headlines. She spends spare time experimenting in the kitchen.

WOODY TASCH is founder and chairman of Slow Money, a non-profit formed in 2008 to catalyze the flow of investment capital to small food enterprises and sustainable agriculture. Woody is chairman emeritus of Investors' Circle, a nonprofit network of investors that has facilitated the flow of $150 million to 230 sustainability-minded, early stage companies and venture funds. He was previously treasurer of the Jessie Smith Noyes Foundation, where he pioneered mission-related investing, and has served on numerous for-profit and nonprofit boards. In 2010, *Utne Reader* named Woody one of "25 Visionaries Who Are Changing Your World." He is the author of *Inquiries into the Nature of Slow Money*.

ANNIE DUNN WATSON has been a counselor, educator, and conscientious planetary resident for many years. A reluctant activist, she nevertheless assisted in networking Vermont's peak-oil activists, developing a public website and newsletter as well as opportunities for regional meetings during the activists' pioneering years. Today, she focuses her attention on her beloved college students in hopes that their time together will bring about more good than mischief on Planet Earth.

JUDY WICKS is founder, in 1983, of Philadelphia's landmark White Dog Cafe, a pioneer in the local food movement. She is a leader in the localist movement nationally and in Philadelphia as cofounder of the Business Alliance for Local Living Economies (BALLE), a network of some 30,000 independent, locally owned businesses in the United States and Canada, and founder of Fair Food Philly and the Sustainable Business Network of Greater Philadelphia.

ROB WILLIAMS is the publisher of *Vermont Commons*. He is a Vermont-based professor, farmer, musician, historian, and journalist who teaches F2F and online courses at a wide variety of colleges, plays pholk phunk music with the Phineas Gage Project (www.phineas gage.com), and raises grass-fed yaks in the Mad River Valley (www.vermontyak.com). Also see his website at www.robwil liamsmedia.com.

ENID WONNACOTT has been the executive director of the Northeast Organic Farming Association of Vermont since 1987. NOFA-VT works to increase consumer access to local and organic foods, provides educational opportunities for farmers, gardeners, and homesteaders, and offers technical assistance to commercial farmers. Wonnacott grew up in Weybridge, Vermont, and holds a master's degree in Natural Resource Planning from the University of Vermont. She lives in Huntington on a small homestead with her family.

MICHAEL WOOD-LEWIS and his wife Valerie founded Front Porch Forum in 2006 from their home in Burlington's Five Sisters neighborhood. In the pre-Internet era, Michael worked for the Institute for Local Self-Reliance in Washington, D.C.

RESOURCES FOR FURTHER READING

EMPIRE AND OVERSHOOT

Overshoot: The Ecological Basis of Revolutionary Change, by William R. Catton, Jr. Urbana: University of Illinois Press, 1982

Collapse: How Societies Choose to Fail or Succeed, by Jared Diamond, New York: Penguin Books, 2005.

The Long Descent: A User's Guide to the End of the Industrial Age, by John Michael Greer, Gabriola Island, B.C.: New Society Publishers, 2008

The Sorrows of Empire: Militarism, Secrecy, and the End of the Republic, by Chalmers Johnson, New York: Henry Holt, 2004

Crossing the Rubicon: The Decline of the American Empire at the End of the Age, by Michael Ruppert, Gabriola Island, B.C.: New Society Publishers, 2004

Reinventing Collapse: The Soviet Example and American Prospects, by Dmitry Orlov, Gabriola Island, B.C.: New Society Publishers, 2011 (revised edition)

Too Much Magic: Wishful Thinking, Technology, and the Fate of the Nation, by James Howard Kunstler, New York: Atlantic Monthly Press, 2012

The Long Emergency: Surviving the End of Oil, Climate Change, and Other Converging Catastrophes of the Twenty-First Century, by James Howard Kunstler, New York: Grove Press, 2006

The Crash Course: The Unsustainable Future Of Our Economy, Energy, And Environment, by Chris Martensen, New York: Wiley, 2011

Why America Failed: The Roots of Imperial Decline, by Morris Berman, New York: Wiley, 2011

Hamilton's Curse: How Jefferson's Archenemy Betrayed the American Revolution—and What It Means for America Today, by Thomas J. DiLorenzo, New York: Crown, 2008

ECONOMY

The Real Wealth of Nations: Creating a Caring Economics, by Riane Eisler, San Francisco: Berrett-Koehler, 2007

The Wealth of Nature: Economics as if Survival Mattered, by John Michael Greer, Gabriola Island, B.C., Canada: New Society Publishers, 2011

Small is Beautiful: Economics as if People Mattered, by E. F. Schumacher, Point Roberts, WA: Hartley & Marks, 1999

Agenda for a New Economy: From Phantom Wealth to Real Wealth, by David Korten, San Francisco: Berrett-Koehler, 2010 (revised edition)

Beyond Growth: The Economics of Sustainable Development, by Herman Daly, Boston: Beacon Press, 1997

What Matters? Economics for a Renewed Commonwealth, by Wendell Berry, Berkeley: Counterpoint, 2010

The Small-Mart Revolution: How Local Businesses Are Beating the Local Competition, by Michael Shuman, San Francisco: Berrett-Koehler, 2007

Good Morning, Beautiful Business: The Unexpected Journey of an Activist Entrepreneur and Local Economy, by Judy Wicks, White River Junction, VT: Chelsea Green, 2013

Owning Our Future: The Emerging Ownership Revolution, by Marjorie Kelly, San Francisco: Berrett-Koehler, 2012

Business Alliance for Local Living Economies: www.livingeconomies.org

Report to the United Nations for the 2012 Rio + 20 Conference, by Robert Costanza, et. al.: http://www.un.org/esa/dsd/dsd_sd21st/21_pdf/Building_a_Sustainable_and _Desirable_Economy-in-Society-in-Nature.pdf

MONEY

"Exponential Money in a Finite World," by Chris Martenson, *Vermont Commons* 25, Fall 2008

The End of Money and the Future of Civilization, by Thomas Greco, White River Junction, VT: Chelsea Green, 2009

Sacred Economics: Money, Gift & Society in the Age of Transition, by Charles Eisenstein, Berkeley: Evolver Editions, 2011

The Web of Debt: The Shocking Truth about Our Money System, by Ellen H. Brown, Baton Rouge, LA: Third Millennium Press, 2010

Debt: The First 5,000 Years, by David Graeber, Brooklyn: Melville House, 2011

Inquiries into the Nature of Slow Money: Investing as if Food, Farms, and Fertility Mattered, by Woody Tasch, White River Junction, VT: Chelsea Green, 2010

Out-of-print classics:

A New Monetary System, by Edward Kellogg (1861)

Wealth, Virtual Wealth, and Debt: The Solution of the Economic Paradox, by Frederick Soddy (1926)

ENERGY

Hubbert's Peak: The Impending World Oil Shortage, by Kenneth Deffeyes, Princeton, NJ: Princeton University Press, 2008

Confronting Collapse: The Crisis of Energy and Money in a Post Peak Oil World, by Michael Ruppert, White River Junction, VT: Chelsea Green, 2009

The Party's Over: Oil, War and the Fate of Industrial Societies, by Richard Heinberg, Gabriolia Island, B.C.: New Society, 2005

Blackout: Coal, Climate and the Last Energy Crisis, by Richard Heiberg, Gabriola Island, B.C.: New Society, 2009

The End of Oil: On the Edge of a Perilous New World, by Paul Roberts, New York: Mariner Books, 2005

Power Plays: Energy Options in the Age of Peak Oil, by Robert Rapier, New York: Apress, 2012

Energy Switch: Proven Solutions for a Renewable Future, by Craig Morris, Gabriola Island, B.C.: New Society, 2006

Power from the People: How to Organize, Finance, and Launch Local Energy Projects—A Community Resilience Guide, by Greg Pahl, White River Junction, Vermont: Chelsea Green, 2012

The Citizen-Powered Energy Handbook, by Greg Pahl, White River Junction,Vermont: Chelsea Green, 2007

Post-Carbon Institute: www.postcarbon.org

Transition U.S. www.transitionus.org

FOOD

Food Politics: How the Food Industry Influences Nutrition, and Health, by Marion Nestle, Berkeley: University of California Press, 2007 (revised edition)

Bringing it to the Table: On Farm and Food, by Wendell Berry, Berkeley: Counterpoint, 2009

In Defense of Food: The Myth of Nutrition and the Pleasures of Eating, by Michael Pollan, New York: Penguin, 2009

The Town that Food Saved: How One Town Found Vitality in Local Food, by Ben Hewitt, Emmaus, PA: Rodale, 2011

Making Supper Safe: One Man's Quest to Learn the Truth about Food Safety, by Ben Hewitt, Emmaus, PA: Rodale, 2011

Folks, This Ain't Normal: A Farmer's Advice for Happier Hens, Healthier People, and a Better World, by Joel Salatin, New York: Center Street/Hachette, 2011

The Good Food Revolution: Growing Healthy Food, People and Communities, by Will Allen, New York: Gotham, 2012

Stuffed and Starved: The Hidden Battle for the World Food System, by Raj Patel, Brooklyn: Melville House, 2012 (revised edition)

Rural Vermont: www.ruralvermont.org

INFORMATION

A Room for Learning: The Making of a School in Vermont, by Tal Birdsey, New York: St. Martins Press, 2009

The Self-Organizing Revolution: Common Principles of the Educational Alternatives Movement, by Ron Miller, Brandon, VT: Holistic Education Press, 2008

Free Schools, Free People: Education and Democracy After the 1960s, by Ron Miller, Albany: SUNY press, 2001

One Size Fits Few: The Folly of Educational Standards, by Susan Ohanian, Portsmouth, NH: Heinemann, 1999

Susan Ohanian's writings on educational standards: www.susanohanian.org

John Green's speech at the 2012 Freedom to Read Foundation's Banned Author Event: http://www.youtube.com/watch?v=rqzNxerwuGw&feature=player_embedded

COMMUNITY

Capitalism 3.0: A Guide to Reclaiming the Commons, by Peter Barnes, San Francisco: Berrett-Koehler, 2006

All That We Share: How to Save the Economy, the Environment, the Internet, Democracy, Our Communities and Everything Else that Belongs to All of Us, by Jay Walljasper, New York: The New Press, 2010

Silent Theft: The Private Plunder of Our Common Wealth, by David Bollier, Oxford, UK: Routledge, 2003

The Great Transformation: The Political and Economic Origins of Our Time, by Karl Polanyi, Boston: Beacon Press, 2001

Bowling Alone: The Collapse and Revival of American Community, by Robert Putnam, New York: Simon and Schuster, 2001

"Whose Common Future? Reclaiming the Commons", http://www.thecornerhouse.org.uk/resource/reclaiming-commons

Community Environmental Legal Defense Fund - http://www.celdf.org/

La Via Campesina, http://viacampesina.org/en/
Commons Magazine, www.onthecommons.org

RESILIENCE

The Transition Handbook: From Oil Dependency to Local Resilience, by Rob Hopkins, White River Junction, VT: Chelsea Green, 2008

The Transition Companion: Making Your Community More Resilient in Uncertain Times, by Rob Hopkins, White River Junction, VT: Chelsea Green, 2011

The Ecotechnic Future: Envisioning a Post-Peak World, by John Michael Greer, Gabriola Island, B.C., Canada: New Society Publishers, 2009

DECENTRALISM

Human Scale, by Kirkpatrick Sale, New Society Publishers (reissued) Gabriola Island, B.C., 2007

America Beyond Capitalism: Reclaiming Our Wealth, Our Liberty, and Our Democracy, by Gar Alperovitz, New York: John Wiley, 2004

The Breakdown of Nations, by Leopold Kohr, Chelsea Green (reissued) White River Junction, VT, 2001

The Vermont Papers: Recreating Democracy on a Human Scale, by Frank Bryan and John McClaughry, White River Junction, VT: Chelsea Green, 2008

The Local Politics of Global Sustainability, by Thomas Prugh, Robert Costanza, and Herman E. Daly, Washington, D.C.: Island Press, 1999

SECESSION

Is Secession Treason?, by Albert Bledsoe, New York: Anza Publishing, 2005.

Out! The Vermont Secession Book, by Frank Bryan and Bill Mares, Shelburne, Vermont: The New England Press, 1987.

The Untied States of America: Polarization, Fracturing, and Our Future, by Juan Enriquez, New York: Crown Publishers, 2005

The Political Economy of Secession: A Source Book, edited by Jurgen G. Backhaus and Detmar Doering, Neue Zurcher Zeitung Publishing, 2004

A Constitutional History of Secession, by John Remington Graham, Gretna, Louisiana: Pelican Publishing, 2002.

One Nation, Indivisible? A Study of Secession and the Constitution, by Robert F. Hawes, Jr., Fultus Books, 2006.

Bye Bye Miss American Empire, by Bill Kauffman, White River Junction, VT: Chelsea Green, 2010

Rethinking the American Union for the Twenty-First Century, edited by Donald Livingston, Gretna, Louisiana: Pelican Publishing, 2012.

Secession: How Vermont and All the Other States Can Save Themselves from the Empire, by Thomas H. Naylor, Port Townsend, WA: Feral House, 2008

Secession: The Ashgate Research Companion, edited by Aleksansar Pavkovic and Peter Radan, Great Britain: MPG Books Group, 2001

Better Off without 'Em: A Northern Manifesto for Southern Secession, by Chuck Thompson, New York: Simon & Schuster, 2012

Reclaiming the American Revolution: The Kentucky and Virginia Resolutions and Their Legacy, by William J. Watkins Jr., Oakland, California: Palgrave/MacMillan, 2004

MEDIA/EDUCATION

Feed, by M.T. Anderson, Boston: Candlewick Press, 2002.

Manufacturing Consent: The Political Economy of the Mass Media, by Noam Chomsky and Edward Herman. New York: Pantheon Books, 2002.

Censored 2013: The Top Censored Stories and Media Analysis of 2011-2012, by Mickey Lee Huff and Andy Roth, editors. New York: Seven Stories Press, 2012.

The Death and Life of American Journalism: The Media Revolution that Will Begin the World Again, by Robert W. McChesney and John Nicols. New York: Nation Books, 2010.

Amusing Ourselves To Death: Public Discourse In The Age of Show Business, by Neil Postman. New York: Penguin, 1985.

INDEX